College NNU April 2018 - Spring-

Holy Fire Fell

Holy Fire Fell

A History of Worship, Revivals, and Feasts
in the Church of the Nazarene

Dirk R. Ellis

Foreword by Karen Westerfield Tucker

WIPF & STOCK · Eugene, Oregon

Wipf & Stock
An Imprint of Wipf and Stock Publishers
199 W. 8th Ave., Suite 3
Eugene, OR 97401
www.wipfandstock.com

PAPERBACK ISBN: 978-1-5326-0068-5
HARDCOVER ISBN: 978-1-5326-0070-8
EBOOK ISBN: 978-1-5326-0069-2

Manufactured in the U.S.A.   DECEMBER 6, 2016

The author expresses gratitude to the following publishers for granting permission
to include quotations from their works.

Nazarene Manifesto by Ross E. Price © 1968 by Nazarene Publishing House, Kansas City, MO. Used by permission. All rights reserved.

Outward Sign and Inward Grace by Rob L. Staples © 1991 by Beacon Hill Press,
Kansas City, MO. Used by permission. All rights reserved.

Phineas F. Bresee: A Prince in Israel by E. A. Girvin © 1982 by Nazarene Publishing House, Kansas City, MO. Used by permission. All rights reserved.

The Preacher's Magazine, copyright © 1977, 1989, 1992, 1993, 1994, and 1996 by Nazarene Publishing House, Kansas City, MO. Used by permission. All rights reserved.

Two Men of Destiny by Neil B. Wiseman © 1983 by Beacon Hill Press, Kansas
City, MO. Used by permission. All rights reserved.

Wesleyan Theological Journal, copyright © 1992 by the Wesleyan Theological
Society. Used by permission. All rights reserved.

From "The Works of John Wesley—The Bicentennial Edition," Copyright © 2005
Abingdon Press, an imprint of The United Methodist Publishing House. Used by
permission. All rights reserved.

To our twin granddaughters:
Brayleigh, who fills our hearts with great joy;
and Cambrie, who awaits our reunion with her in glory.

Contents

List of Tables | *viii*

Foreword by Karen Westerfield Tucker | *ix*

Preface | *xiii*

Acknowledgments | *xvii*

Abbreviations | *xx*

Introduction | *xxi*

Chapter 1	The Meaning of Worship for Formation	1
Chapter 2	Worship and Spirituality in John Wesley's Practical Theology	13
Chapter 3	The Development and Nature of Worship from American Methodism to the Church of the Nazarene	48
Chapter 4	The Structure and Characteristics of Sunday Worship in the Church of the Nazarene	83
Chapter 5	The Sacraments	144
Chapter 6	Occasional Services	187
Chapter 7	Conclusion: An Earnest Appeal for the Cultivation of Doxology in Worship	199

Bibliography | *213*

Index | *229*

List of Tables

Table 1. Suggested order of worship in the February 11, 1909, *Nazarene Messenger* | 85

Table 2. Suggested orders of worship in the June 1939 issue of *The Preacher's Magazine* | 90

Table 3. Rituals for the administration of the Lord's supper: First People's Church, Brooklyn, New York, and the 1908 *Manual* | 156

Foreword

STUDIES OF WESLEYAN/METHODIST WORSHIP have, until the past several decades, been extremely rare—certainly in comparison to the examinations of liturgical texts for the Roman Catholic, Lutheran, Anglican, and some Reformed traditions. Notable exceptions for the American Wesleyan/ Methodist traditions include the contributions of Thomas O. Summers (mid nineteenth century) and Nolan B. Harmon (early twentieth century), both ministerial leaders of the Methodist Episcopal Church, South. The principally recognized achievement of Summers and Harmon was their work with liturgical texts: the liturgical revisions that stood behind the *Book of Common Prayer* of 1662; John Wesley's adaptation of the 1662 Prayer Book under the title *The Sunday Service of the Methodists*, first issued in 1784; and the subsequent revisions of texts or instructions produced in America by the Methodist Episcopal Church and the Methodist Episcopal Church, South. While these are valuable studies in themselves, they did not paint the full picture of American Methodist/Wesleyan worship praxis where the authorized liturgical texts were never mandated for use.

Methodists/Wesleyans of all stripes have always had authorized, printed resources for the Lord's Day, for the sacraments, and for other occasional services (e.g., the solemnization of marriage, the burial of the dead, ordinations). But given that Methodists/Wesleyans routinely preferred to pray with their eyes closed rather than open to read a printed prayer, and were long familiar with (and preferred) an informal service of scripture, preaching, prayer, and song of various configurations (the practice of the earliest Methodists in Europe), an accurate study of worship praxis cannot be limited to what is found in the official books. Pastors and worship leaders always have had the liberty to organize worship according to what best enabled the praise and prayer of a particular community. Thus, to find out what Methodists/Wesleyans did in worship and what they understood to be the purpose(s) of worship requires an investigation of other materials in addition to official worship texts. Such materials include orders of worship in printed programs or other local church publications, descriptions of worship practices in personal diaries and journals, reflections upon worship praxis in published essays in denominational periodicals and journals, and legislation related to worship discussed and approved at various levels of denominational decision-making. Examination of these materials is labor-intensive and at times frustrating since full descriptions are often hard to find; in diaries and journals, preachers typically commented upon sermon texts or themes and often little else relative to worship. Mining all these sources may not yield a mother-load of information that would give the most complete accounting of worship praxis for a particular denomination—or even a geographical region within a particular denomination. Yet this is necessary work if a full study of worship in the Methodist/Wesleyan tradition is to be made.

To date, research has largely followed Summers and Harmon in analyzing the liturgical texts and practices of the largest bodies within the American Methodist/Wesleyan tradition: the Methodist Episcopal Church; the Methodist Episcopal Church, South; the Methodist Church; the United Methodist Church. Even so, the particular practices and traditions of the Methodist Protestant Church, which united with the Methodist Episcopal Church and the Methodist Episcopal Church, South, in 1939, to form the Methodist Church, have largely been neglected. Less attention has been paid to the historic African-American Methodist denominations and to the churches in the Holiness tradition. Thus, the valuable study offered here by Dirk Ellis fills a significant lacuna in liturgical research related to the American Methodist/Wesleyan liturgical traditions.

Providing a liturgical study of the Church of the Nazarene is no easy task given the complexity of the denomination's origins. Yet Ellis is careful to tease out the Church's historic background and notes that it, in fact, influenced the diversity of worship practices within the Church today. He carefully does his homework, looking beyond print worship texts to examine the writings of key church leaders in addition to a range of other relevant sources. In so doing, he brings together in one volume important documents that constitute components of a previously untold Nazarene liturgical history.

But this book also looks to the future at the same time as it reflects upon the Church's past. For example, Ellis reads discussions by Nazarenes today regarding baptismal issues (i.e., believer and infant baptism) with an eye to Wesley and Nazarene history as well as to the creation of a renewed

Nazarene baptismal theology. In this way, Ellis supplies a constructive work toward the creation of what he terms a Nazarene "liturgical theology" that takes seriously a doxological approach to worship and with it a sacramental theology more deeply grounded in the writings of the Wesleys. With this appeal to serious liturgical reflection, Ellis speaks not only to Nazarene pastors and congregations, but beyond to other Methodist/Wesleyan denominations that may have lost their Wesleyan and liturgical moorings, particularly in regard to understanding the intimate relationships between worship, the spiritual life, and the moral/ethical life.

Karen Westerfield Tucker
Boston University School of Theology

Preface

ONE OF THE MOST colorful depictions of early Nazarene worship practice, is found in a 1905 *Beulah Christian article. Tom Dalton writes, "Holy fire fell and melted the saints and sinners."*[1] Dalton was describing the extraordinary presence of God he witnessed in a worship service at Lowell, Massachusetts where A. B. Riggs was pastor. I find Dalton's words endearing because they are reminiscent of my own experience and appreciation for vibrant encounters with God in Nazarene worship, revival services, and camp meetings during the formative years of my youth. Those events were pivotal not only in my spiritual formation but also in my call to ordained ministry.

It was, in part, the impact of those God imbued transformative experiences exacted on my own life which motivated the writing of this text. *Holy Fire Fell* consists of the historical segment of my doctoral thesis, which examines the relationship between Nazarene liturgical practice and spirituality. My ultimate concern is in the way worship shapes and forms us; even without our awareness. Specifically, my intent is in discovering the role worship plays in forming Christian identity; especially as it relates to Wesley's doctrine of Christian perfection. This is important in an age when denominational leaders and scholars recognize that we are in danger of losing our distinctive identity as Wesleyans.[2]

Due to the influence revivalism placed on my life I spent my college and seminary years gathering resources and tools that could equip me in the task of facilitating transformation, spiritual renewal, and growth to the congregations and communities in which I would serve. During that period I was convinced the key to this approach was focusing on the tools that would enable me to deliver sermons that were exegetically sound, compelling, and

1. Dalton, "From Correspondents," 15; italics mine.
2. See, Dunning, "Christian Perfection," 151, Bond, "This We Believe."

xiii

applicable to life. When in the summer of 1989 I arrived at my first church in Western Pennsylvania, fresh out of seminary, I was certain that preaching was the primary means through which transformation and discipleship occurs. At the very least I was confident that the domineering focus of worship was the sermon.

Even though I was quite fortunate in my first pastoral assignment to serve in a wonderful, tolerant, supportive, and loving congregation, it wasn't long before I realized that change was not happening as quickly as I imagined it should. I began to question our habitual gathering for worship on Sunday morning, Sunday night, and prayer meeting on Wednesday when the spiritual and numerical growth everyone desired did not ensue. I began to wonder if there was something I was missing. It was then that a friend suggested I read Robert Webber's classic text *Worship Is a Verb*. Webber's simple book was profoundly enlightening and launched me on a journey into liturgical and Wesleyan studies from which I never returned.

One of the unforeseen discoveries I stumbled across on this journey centered upon Wesley's liturgical theology and praxis. I was somewhat aware of Wesley's revivalism and doctrinal concerns but had no clue of his love for the Anglican prayer book, sacramental passion, and his expectation that the British Methodists attend worship and receive the sacraments in the Church of England. I had never experienced worship outside of the free church tradition into which I was born. Therefore, I was unaware of what exactly transpired in higher forms of worship whether they be Catholic, Episcopal, Orthodox, Lutheran, or another prayer book congregation. Even now, I find my own former ignorance of this critical sacramental and liturgical piece of our Wesleyan heritage astounding.

I firmly believe it is beneficial for both clergy and laity to know our own liturgical roots as Nazarenes. Roots that extend backwards to Wesley's era and far beyond. On occasion I have had conversations with well-meaning people in the church who are confused as to why as Nazarenes we would refer back to the teaching of John Wesley, Augustine, Chrysostom, or another important voice from the past. I remind them that we are not isolated in history but are part of a larger church that not only spans the globe, but also reaches back into history. An awareness of our ecclesial roots in both the Wesleyan tradition and Christian antiquity enables an informed evaluation and critique of current worship practice and provides insight into the ramifications of that practice. The intent of this book is to assist Nazarenes in learning from their own rich history by examining worship in Wesley's Methodism, the American Holiness Movement, and from our early Nazarene forbears to today.

Chapter 1 of this book describes the relationship between worship and belief. Drawing from the fields of liturgical theology and ritual studies it briefly lays out arguments pointing toward the formative potential residing within the practices of Christian worship. Chapter 2 provides a succinct review of John Wesley's praxis and theology of worship and the sacraments. Chapter 3 traces the events which led John Wesley's spiritual heirs, in the American holiness movement and Church of the Nazarene, to separate Wesleyan doctrine from the sacramental and liturgical theology and praxis central to Wesley's method. Chapter 4 examines the practices and beliefs surrounding the preaching service in the Church of the Nazarene. The preaching service provided the central structure of Nazarene worship. Chapter 5 focuses on the beliefs and practices surrounding baptism and the Lord's supper and the transitions that occurred in both theology and practice during the mergers and in later years. Chapter 6 is concerned with the occasional services most often occurring outside of Sunday morning worship. This includes many of the services found within early Methodism including the watchnight, covenant renewal service, and the love feast. Finally, chapter 7 summarizes the ramifications of Christian worship for Christian identity and formation. It reiterates the argument that scholars, denominational leaders, clergy, and congregations should think critically and theologically about the worship practices in which Nazarenes engage weekly.

My aim in this historical exploration of worship in the Church of the Nazarene is twofold. First, I desire to help persons both within and without our denomination to appreciate the rich history and tradition handed down from generations of men and women who faithfully, passionately, and sacrificially lived out their faith for the glory of God. Second, my intent is to provide a resource to help scholars, denominational leaders, pastors, and congregations critically reflect upon the practices in which Nazarenes currently engage every week. It is my hope that this history serves as a corrective lens empowering the church to offer worship that is authentic, glorifies God, and leads to the sanctification of her people.

Acknowledgments

I SUPPOSE, THAT IN some measure, the writing of this book was a project I backed into quite unexpectedly. Writing a book on worship is not something I originally planned to do so many years ago during my formative years at home, or during college and seminary, or even when I first launched into pastoral ministry. Although, nearly since the day I was born I have attended weekly worship—worship was an experience I never gave much thought.

Yet, my interest in liturgy and the pursuit of meaningful worship did not happen by accident. It was cultivated, by the Spirit's leading, out of my own baptism into the life of the church as an infant, the influence of the academy, and my experience as a pastor. Therefore, this book was not created in isolation, but rather is the product of the many persons who have served as my mentors and friends offering guidance and support. It is through their care and selfless giving that a seed was planted so long ago, nourished through the years, and has now come to fruition.

I am grateful for the influence of Asbury Theological Seminary and Don Boyd, who first introduced me to the rich liturgical heritage shared by Wesleyans and Nazarenes. I am also thankful for parishioners in Sheakleyville, PA; Worth, IL; and Bradley, IL, who were tolerant of a pastor struggling to learn about more vibrant liturgical forms while simultaneously attempting to lead worship. However, it is doubtful I would have pursued the terminal degree, that lies behind this text, were it not for Robert Branson, who invited me to teach a general education class at Olivet Nazarene University during the late 1990s. My desire to further my education was the combined result of the joy I experienced in the classroom and my hunger for the deeper things found in prayer book worship.

I am grateful to the many faculty members at Andrews University sympathetic to my academic and ecclesial concerns who supported me in this work. I especially want to thank my dissertation committee members: Jane Thayer, Jimmy Kijai, and Russell Staples. They were always available to provide encouragement and direction through many years of research and writing. John Witlvliet of the Calvin Institute of Christian Worship encouraged me to publish my dissertation by offering his support and my dissertation committee recommended this work to the publisher. Russell Staples assisted me in editing and reformatting my original thesis into a more suitable format. He patiently read through various editions multiple times providing guidance. I am also grateful to the editorial staff at Wipf & Stock Publishers who guided me through the publishing process.

During this journey I have been amazed by the generosity of faculty from other academic institutions who selflessly showed interest in me and the research I was doing. Ed Phillips, whose course I was enrolled at Garrett Evangelical Theological Seminary, instilled a deep desire to learn more of the origins of Christian worship. Ron Anderson provided encouragement and guidance to this study. His wisdom in the earliest days of survey development was invaluable. Throughout the process he was always available to answer questions or offer advice. Karen Westerfield Tucker invited me to sit-in on a semester of classes she was teaching on American Methodist worship at Boston University. Her interest and insights concerning my work were beneficial and thought provoking. My former professor at Asbury Theological Seminary, Laurence Wood, graciously responded to my queries on matters concerning Wesleyan theology. Likewise, Brent Peterson not only responded to questions via email, but provided me with an early draft of his theology of worship written for Nazarenes. Keith Drury thoughtfully sent me a copy of his book *Counterpoint*. Also, the following scholars from the Wesleyan tradition gave of their time by providing crucial feedback to my research: Jay Akkerman, Ron Anderson, Dean Blevins, William Greathouse, Doug Hardy, Robert Mulholland, Ed Phillips, Rob Staples, Brook Thelander, Karen Westerfield Tucker, and Laurence Wood.

This book was not possible without the help provided by the people at the International Headquarters of the Church of the Nazarene including the General Secretary's Office, Ken Crow from the Nazarene Research Center, and Stan Ingersol and Meri Janssen from Nazarene Archives. I am grateful to Debbie Ward and Bonnie Proctor for their editorial guidance during the dissertation phase. The late General Superintendent, William Greathouse, who on various occasions voiced his concern about the state of Nazarene worship, encouraged this research and supported it by providing a letter urging pastors to participate in a study that underlies this text. I am thankful for the pastors and their parishioners who followed Dr. Greathouse's recommendation and were willing to participate.

Equally important is the unwavering support and encouragement I have received from those closest to me. The call of God on my life into pastoral ministry was first sensed, and then nurtured, within the warm and vibrant Nazarene congregation of my youth in Potomac, IL. I still value the relationships forged in that church many years ago. During the last nine years, I have sensed similar support and encouragement from my church family at Grace Chapel Church of the Nazarene in Hooksett, NH, where I serve as their pastor. Not only did they provide me with the time needed to complete this project, they were willing to take this liturgical journey with me in pursuit of worship that is truly doxological.

My friend and colleague, Brook Thelander, was both a sounding board and mentor, prodding me to keep moving forward as I wrestled through the various issues and stumbling blocks one faces in doctoral research. I am grateful to my mother, Wilma, who has unknowingly pushed me forward in this journey by reminding me on various occasions that my father would be pleased with the work I am doing. My daughter, Jenaé, also shouldered some of the burden of this project that encompassed ten long years during her formative years. She was patient with her father on those occasions when I missed a birthday or other important event because I was away from home attending class. Now as a young mother herself we reminisce of those days. Most importantly, I am indebted to my wife, Mardi. None of this was possible without her sharing this adventure with me. She is my closest friend, an example of unwavering faith in God, and my chief source of encouragement as we walk this road together.

Abbreviations

BCP	*The Book of Common Prayer* (1662)
Collection	*A Collection of Hymns for the Use of the People Called Methodists*. London: John Mason, 1780.
Manual	*Manual: Church of the Nazarene*
NCMA	National Camp Meeting Association for the Promotion of Holiness
Sunday Service	*John Wesley's Sunday Service of the Methodists in North America*
Works (BE)	*The Bicentennial Edition of the Works of John Wesley*. 35 vols (projected). Edited by Frank Baker and Richard Heitzenrater *et al.* Nashville, TN: Abingdon.
Works (Jackson)	*The Works of John Wesley*. 14 vols. Edited by Thomas Jackson. 1872. Reprint. Grand Rapids: Baker, 2007.

Introduction

PRIOR TO DISCUSSING THE history of worship thought and practice in the Church of the Nazarene it is beneficial to briefly address some of the terminology that appears in this text. The vocabulary we use can be confusing—even when it comes to the words we choose in describing and discussing Christian worship. It is my experience that people regularly categorize different types of worship with words such as high church or low church, liturgical or non-liturgical, formal or informal, traditional or contemporary—to name a few. Clarity is often lacking with the labels we attach.

Due to the influence of worship scholars such as Ron Anderson and Ed Phillips I have chosen to dispense with the above categories (e.g. high church, liturgical, formal, etc) and instead adopt the term prayer book to designate those worshiping congregations that use written forms in worship (e.g. Anglican, Orthodox, Roman Catholic, etc). Whereas, the term free-church is indicative of those congregations, like most worshipping congregations in the Church of the Nazarene and other evangelical groups, that do not use a prayer book or written texts but are drawn to spontaneous forms of worship.

My reason for this choice in terminology, which may differ from what many are accustom to, resides in the fact that the term liturgical, as a designation for a type of worship, is misleading. The truth is every worshipping community has a liturgy—whether that liturgy comes from the set forms found in a prayer book, is unwritten and spontaneous, or if it lies somewhere in-between those polarities. Liturgy simply means the work of the people. As James White reminds us, in ancient Greek culture, liturgy was "a work performed by the people for the benefit of others. . . . [In the church, the body of Christ, liturgy] is the quintessence of the priesthood of believers that the whole priestly community of Christians shares."[1] For White liturgical worship then, is not passive, rather it is worship that engages the active participation of every member of the Christian community in the glorification of God.[2] Therefore, in an effort towards language that is inherently more precise and lucid, the designations prayer book and free-church are used throughout this text. Furthermore, when the words liturgy or liturgical appear they are employed as equivalents to the term worship, rather than serving as designations for a specific type or style of worship.

1. White, *Introduction to Christian Worship*, 26.
2. Ibid.

Chapter 1

The Meaning of Worship for Formation

THE CHURCH OF THE Nazarene was born out of the holiness movement of the late nineteenth century. Although the founders of the church came from a variety of denominations (i.e., Reformed, Anabaptist, Wesleyan, etc.), they were drawn together by a mutual passion for recovering, experiencing, and promoting the Wesleyan doctrine of Christian perfection. More specifically they understood entire sanctification to be an instantaneous experience of heart cleansing occurring simultaneously with the baptism with the Holy Spirit. Although these early pioneers were interested in retaining Wesley's central doctrine, albeit with modifications, their worship practices differed radically from his. Many of the elements central to the Anglican worship of John Wesley were left behind in favor of a spontaneous form of worship that revolved around the sermon.[1] The Nazarene liturgy was evangelistic in nature, since *the winning of souls* became the focus of the worship experience; however, the distinctive nature of Wesley's liturgical and sacramental praxis was lost.

The circumstances and historical setting surrounding the formation of the Church of the Nazarene led to an emphasis on Wesley's doctrine of Christian perfection, but the practices enveloping Wesley's theology were largely abandoned. Many factors contributed to this outcome, including the temporal distance between Wesley and the formation of the Church of the Nazarene; the influences of American Methodism; the American revivalistic movement; and the theological diversity of the holiness groups that merged to form the Church of the Nazarene.

1. Staples, *Outward Sign*, 24.

The Rule of Prayer: Worship, Belief, and Ethics

Some may wonder exactly why a departure from Wesley's liturgical practice matters to Nazarene spirituality and identity. The study of liturgy for Nazarenes, like many evangelicals, is off the radar. I clearly remember my thoughts during seminary upon learning I was required to take a class on worship. "What possibly could I learn about worship that I did not already know?" I was working from a deeply ingrained paradigm instilled by the worship experience I knew since my developmental years. The content of worship was simple—the preliminaries (i.e. announcements, music, prayer, and offering) followed by the sermon and altar call. If your roots are similar to my own, you also may wonder why the study of liturgy is necessary or why reading about the history of liturgical practice in the Church of the Nazarene matters.

Through the Latin expression *lex orandi, lex credendi* liturgical theology has long expressed the firm conviction that the practices of Christian worship have a profound effect on what one believes. This Latin label is the truncated version of a statement attributed to the fifth-century monk Prosper of Aquitaine, who was a "literary disciple and defender of St. Augustine."[2] E. Byron Anderson indicates that the phrase *lex orandi statuat legem credendi*, "the law of prayer establishes the law of belief,"[3] is significant because it summarizes a key issue within liturgical theology: the interdependent relationship between worship, belief, and ethics.

No doubt there are those who interpret *lex orandi, lex credendi* in a manner which gives the liturgy predominance over doctrine. Aidan Kavanagh asserts this position by stating "the law of worship transcends and subordinates the law of belief."[4] Protestants tend to emphasize the opposite extreme. A more balanced understanding of *lex orandi, lex credendi* is set forth by Anderson, Saliers, Wainwright, and others who perceive a reciprocal relationship between worship and doctrine. That is to say, "liturgy 'norms' doctrine"[5] and doctrine influences the liturgy. This assertion raises important questions regarding authority; namely, what makes a church's worship authoritative in matters of doctrine?

Wainwright provides three criteria to determine the validity of the church's liturgy to inform doctrine. The first of these finds its source in God incarnate. "Most weight will be given to ideas and practices which go back

---

2. Wace and Piercy, *Dictionary Early Christian*, 224–5.

3. Anderson, "Worship and Belief," 432.

4. Kavanagh, *On Liturgical Theology*, 46.

5. Schaefer, "*Lex Orandi, Lex Credendi*," 472.

to Jesus. Prayers which treat God as 'Abba' and seek the coming of his king-dom *as Jesus preached it* will score heavily. . . . The post-Easter Church, as the first to feel the impact of the total event of Jesus, must be credited with an authority of historical origination second only to Jesus himself."[6]

The second test is that of time and space. It is based upon the argument that God works amid human error and sets forth to correct it. Therefore, those practices within the church, enduring the test of time and experienc-ing near-universal acceptance are reliable sources for doctrine.[7]

The final criterion for assessing the reliability of a liturgical practice to inform doctrine is found in the "ethical component."[8] Wainwright states that Augustine and Prosper believed that "the holiness of the Church indwelt and led by the Holy Spirit gave authority to its liturgical practice as a source of doctrine."[9] He qualifies this test with the following statement: "A liturgical practice which is matched with *some directness* by holiness of life makes a weighty claim to be treated as a source of doctrine; and any link that could be traced between a liturgical practice and moral turpitude would to that extent disqualify the liturgical practice as a source of doctrine."[10]

As mentioned previously, the usage of *lex orandi, lex credendi,* is not only concerned with the authority of the liturgy in substantiating or affect-ing the church's doctrinal claims. It also explores the way that the liturgy shapes the beliefs of its members and their resulting ethical behavior. Saliers indicates that the critical reciprocity existing between liturgy and belief is realized in the action of the church.[11] In other words, not only is there an interdependent relationship between prayer and belief, but one also exists between prayer, belief, and "living the moral, spiritual life."[12] Kevin Irwin refers to this as: *lex orandi, lex credendi, lex vivendi.*[13] This understanding re-connects the doxology of God with how persons live in the world. One's true worship and love for God manifest themselves in one's relationship with others. Neither a person's worship nor love of God can simply be internal-ized in a private relationship with him.[14]

6. Wainwright, *Doxology*, 243.

7. Ibid.

8. Ibid.

9. Ibid., 245.

10. Ibid., italics mine.

11. Saliers, *Worship As Theology*, 187.

12. Irwin, *Context and Text*, 55–56.

13. Ibid.

14. Anderson, *Worship and Christian Identity*, 27–28.

This understanding is essential when it comes to issues of identity. Emphasizing doctrinal standards while overlooking the implications of unchecked liturgical patterns creates a paradox. This is because the weekly practices of corporate worship affect the beliefs and actions of its members. Therefore, it is essential for those who design and lead worship to be aware of the philosophical and theological implications of those practices upon identity. Worship is formative. A deficient liturgy that is more reflective of secular philosophies and beliefs (e.g., individualism, consumerism, nationalism, etc.) than it is representative of the values of the Kingdom of God eventually leads to decay in belief and ethics. The written doctrine of the Church, as recorded in the church discipline, is the last to experience the effects of this erosion.[15]

Identifying Patterns of Worship

So how does one determine the liturgical pattern or patterns of the Church of the Nazarene? One of the obvious distinctions among congregations of the free-church tradition is the absence of any prayer book. However, this does not mean there is a total absence of written texts even for free-church congregations.[16] Written texts for the Church of the Nazarene can be found in the rituals contained in the church discipline as well as the music located in the hymnal. Even the spontaneous pastoral prayer can follow a repetitious, even jaded, pattern. The revivalism in which the church was born gave consistency to the liturgy for many years. The focus and structure of worship were designed to yield seekers at the altar. The music, the prayers, the sermon, and altar call were structured for this purpose. However, the worship order has undergone transition in the last several years as congregations have experimented with a variety of marketing strategies to increase the attractiveness of their worship to both the church and unchurched *markets*. This phenomenon is most readily exemplified in the music.[17]

Today the fluidity of music forms within any given congregation is greater than ever before with the availability of music through chorus books and online resources. To a large extent the hymn book has gone into disuse with the advent of resources that make contemporary music readily available.[18] Even the overall picture of the Nazarene liturgy has changed over the

---

15. Drury et al., *Counterpoint*, 28–29.

16. Hohenstein, "*Lex Orandi, Lex Credendi*," 142–7.

17. Ibid.

18. It is also worth noting that the last denominational hymnal (*Sing to the Lord*) was published in 1993 and there doesn't appear to be a new one on the horizon.

past forty-five years. There is no guarantee that the rituals found within the *Manual* are followed. Instead pastors often opt to celebrate the sacraments of the eucharist and baptism spontaneously. Although a less common occurrence, some clergy borrow materials from other resources such as the *Book of Common Prayer (BCP)* or the *United Methodist Book of Worship*. Both the content and purpose of preaching have changed as well. All of this serves to remind us that the current liturgical structure of Nazarene congregations is not rigid but both pluralistic and changing. Due to the diversity and fluidity of Nazarene worship the *lex orandi* of Nazarene worship becomes exceedingly difficult to pin down.

Worship as Doxology

Recent research in the social sciences supports the claim made by liturgical theologians who suggest that worship is formative. Paul Bradshaw charges that one of the essential tasks of anyone attempting to do liturgical theology is not only to invest oneself in sound historical research, but also "to utilise fully the tools provided by anthropologists, psychologists, and sociologists in order to explore more deeply the essentially multivalent character of worship."[19] Although Bradshaw's advice was a caution addressed to those already steeped in the discipline of liturgical theology, it should also serve as a wakeup call to those who have approached worship on more pragmatic grounds and have avoided thinking methodically about the liturgy.

What occurs in worship is frequently seen simply as something we do to express our corporate and personal faith. Often the primary focus is on the latter. Leander Keck believes that the worship of the church is often secularized. A movement has occurred away from God. Although God is still "talked about"[20] in evangelical congregations, its worship has shifted from "the theocentric praise of God"[21] to a human centered and utilitarian liturgy. No longer is the focus and purpose of worship doxological; rather "what matters most is that everyone gets something out of the service."[22] Those designing and implementing worship in evangelical groups have tended to be overly focused upon a concern for subjective experience and the feelings it generates. Influenced by the church-growth movement, many have searched for ways to increase church membership and have envisioned the liturgy as a place to implement marketing strategies. However, due to

19. Bradshaw, "Difficulties," 194.
20. Keck, *Church Confident*, 34.
21. Ibid.
22. Ibid.

the formative character of worship, there is an inherit danger in engaging in such methods. Anderson warns that making liturgical changes for pragmatic reasons, such as church growth, without an awareness of the implications of those changes can be a dangerous thing. Often "the theological content of the liturgy"[23] is sacrificed and "the historical voice of the church as found in Scripture and tradition"[24] is lost. "What good is a church that can neither critique nor console the world?"[25]

The words, actions, rhythms, and patterns found within a church's worship are not inconsequential. Not only do healthy practices have the capacity to assist in shaping us in the image of Christ, but allowing unhealthy practices to seep into the liturgy yields malformation. Therefore, it is of vital importance that denominations and local churches thoughtfully consider and, in many cases, rethink the practices with which their pastors and congregations engage during the Sunday morning liturgy.

Word Versus Symbol

Traditionally Nazarenes have envisioned the transformative moment of worship as occurring in the sermon and the altar call which followed. The main purpose of all aspects of the liturgy was directed toward the sermon. The prayers, the music, and the testimonies were intended to prepare one to hear the message and to place the candidate in such a receptive state to receive the sermon positively and thus assist the work of the Holy Spirit toward the intended goal of conversion or entire sanctification. Practically speaking, the sermon was the primary means of God's grace, while the other aspects of the worship service were secondary and thus referred to as *the preliminaries*. This perspective was birthed in Enlightenment thought where transformation was viewed primarily as a rational decision to follow Christ. Concern was focused upon *orthodoxy*, rather than *orthopraxy*. The purpose of the Nazarene liturgy was evangelism.

When revivalism began to wane in the 1960s, it was this liturgical pragmatism that opened the door to various strategies and practices that would serve to increase attendance and gather more people to hear the

23. Anderson, *Worship and Christian Identity*, 39.

24. Ibid.

25. Ibid. Anderson's comments are directed towards the liturgical reform that has taken place in Roman Catholicism and other prayer book denominations because of Vatican II, but in my estimation, it is applicable to the Church of the Nazarene and other free-church denominations who either have failed to engage in liturgical theology or neglected to think intentionally about the liturgy.

sermon without much thought given to the consequences of those practices. Conversely Anderson argues for a transformation in individuals that exceeds mere rational assent when he contends "that even as we perform the liturgy, liturgy is also 'performing us.' It is inscribing a form of the Christian faith in body, bone, and marrow as well as in mind and spirit."[26]

Mark Searle suggests that this bodily dimension of worship has even been overlooked by those who study the liturgy. The influence of the enlightenment and rationalism has focused primary attention upon rational thought at the expense of corporeal knowing. Even liturgical theologians have, for the most part, concentrated their efforts upon written texts. In contrast, Searle claims the liturgy is foremost about a way of knowing that occurs through bodily engagement, both as individuals and as corporate body. "Ritual best makes sense . . . in an anthropology that sees the community as prior to the individual, and sees the mind coming to self-consciousness only in interaction with the external world . . . It is where we lead with the body and the mind follows . . ."[27]

Being formed into Christlikeness through the liturgy is not typically instantaneous, as has been traditionally expected of the sermon, with a crisis moment and instant decision at the altar. Rather it develops over time and reinforces the idea that becoming Christian is more than merely an individual decision. Certainly, there is the personal dimension, but the journey towards Christlikeness occurs and is lived out in community. This is not to deny or downplay the need of a crisis experience or the importance of the cognitive dimension in being shaped into the image of Christ, but rather to emphasize that the Holy Spirit works both gradually as well as instantaneously in the process of transformation. Process anticipates and follows the crisis moments as the Holy Spirit works dynamically to bring authentic transformation in a person's life.

The notion that the Holy Spirit works primarily through a cognitive decision in response to the sermon limits the way God has chosen to work through the means of grace incorporated within the liturgy. Such an emphasis is not based in antiquity or even classical Wesleyanism, but rather the result of rationalism that has influenced much of Protestant thought.[28] The sermon is not alone in providing a means of transformation, but rather the

26. Ibid., 58.

27. Searle, "Ritual," in Bradshaw and Melloh, *Foundations in Ritual Studies*, 13–14.

28. "Classical Wesleyanism" is a term employed by Rob Staples, which is used to distinguish the thought and practice of John and Charles Wesley from their Wesleyan descendants. Classical Wesleyanism refers to the "vitality and viewpoint" that was a part of the eighteenth-century Wesleyan revival in the era in which John and Charles Wesley lived. Staples, *Outward Sign*, 15.

other aspects of worship that we engage in bodily, emotionally, and spiritually also serve to shape us. This shaping that occurs in worship can either be a negative or positive force. This is even more reason for the church to be intentional about what occurs in the various dimensions of the liturgy, of which the sermon is but only one part.

Ritual Knowing

The claim that liturgy is formative leads to an important question. What exactly takes place in worship to make transformation possible? Anthropologist Mary Douglas advises that ritual serves primarily to communicate. Like language, it transmits thoughts and thus makes possible the revelation of knowledge that could not be known otherwise.[29] Those who despise ritual do so because external symbolic expressions and the use of rehearsed and routine verbal expressions are held to be suspect; for the *anti-ritualist*, the only authentic piety is those beliefs that are internalized and expressed through the spontaneous words that emanate from the heart.[30] However, what the anti-ritualist fails to realize is that ritual, and the symbols found there within, transmit culture and meaning; without such forms of communication cultures are at best a fragment of their original selves and at worst completely lose their connection with the past. Douglas explains, "Symbols are the only means of communication. They are the only means of expressing value; the main instruments of thought, the only regulators of experience. For any communication to take place, the symbols must be structured. For communication about religion to take place, the structure of the symbols must be able to express something relevant to the social order."[31]

29. Douglas, *Purity and Danger*, 79.

30. Douglas noted that within the Roman Catholicism of her day the anti-ritualist sentiments resulted in "the adoption of one set of natural symbols in place of another." When the early Nazarenes followed the pattern of the holiness movement in abandoning the ritualism they noticed in the more formal worship of various Protestant denominations, they retained some symbolic forms and also incorporated other symbolic expressions, which they felt were acceptable to experiential worship. These would include the ritual actions surrounding the altar call, shouting, marching, public testimonies, the waving of handkerchiefs, etc. However, today even those outward expressions of inward piety have been generally lost; religion is further internalized, absent of most outward expressions. The sacraments when implemented are minimalized with nominal symbolic action and are often accompanied with spontaneous verbal utterances by the pastor rather than written ritual forms from the *Manual* or a prayer book. Douglas, *Natural Symbols*, 54, 178.

31. Ibid., 40.

Those organizations or societies who reject ritual do so at their own peril. Since ritual serves to communicate, the society that has rejected ritual has severed itself from the primary means of connecting historically to its roots, the source of its identity. Douglas states that the movement away from ritualism follows three phases, "First, there is the *contempt* of external ritual forms; second, there is the private *internalizing* of religious experience; third, there is the move to humanist *philanthropy*. When the third stage is under way, the symbolic life of the spirit is finished."[32] Christian denominations that have abandoned ritual, discarding the primary means of transmitting their connectedness to the past, eventually lose the distinctive characteristics of their identity thus making it difficult to distinguish one from another.[33] Douglas alleges that this evinces itself in Christendom with denominations that by outward appearances are very similar. All demonstrate concern over ethical issues, and launch social programs, but are "less willing"[34] (or perhaps incapable) to distinguish themselves doctrinally from other denominations.

Societies cannot reject ritual and continue to exist. The form of communication found in ritual expression is essential to their long-term and continued existence. Douglas reminds us that ritual expression is essential to every person.

> It is an illusion to suppose that there can be organization without symbolic expression. It is the old prophetic dream of instant, unmediated communication. Telepathic understanding is good for brief flashes of insight. But to create an order in which young and old, human and animal, lion and lamb can understand each other direct, is a millennial vision. Those who despise ritual, even at its most magical, are cherishing in the name of reason a very irrational concept of communication.[35]

Anti-ritualist attitudes are only viable "in the early, unorganized stages of a new movement,"[36] and eventually ritualism will reappear; albeit in a form different from the rituals the organization originally rejected. As Douglas indicates, "Fundamentalists, who are not magical in their attitude to the eucharist, [do] become magical in their attitude to the Bible."[37] However, whenever a society abandons ritual and then returns to it out of

32. Ibid., 7., italics mine.
33. Ibid., 22.
34. Ibid.
35. Ibid., 52–53.
36. Douglas, *Purity and Danger*, 77.
37. Douglas, *Natural Symbols*, 21–22.

No rituals ! ↘

necessity, something irretrievable is lost: "We arise from the purging of old rituals, simpler and poorer, as was intended, ritually beggared, but with other losses. There is a loss of articulation in the depth of past time. The new sect goes back as far as the primitive church, as far as the first Pentecost, or as far as the Flood, but the historical continuity is traced by a thin line."[38]

Knowing Through the Body

Ritual serves not merely as a tool for communicating beliefs or thoughts; rather the church's sacramental and liturgical practices serve to shape the "faith, character, and consciousness of its members."[39] The knowledge acquired through the various actions of worship is primarily received corporeally rather than cognitively. Theodore Jennings asserts that ritual "performs noetic functions in ways peculiar to itself. . . . Ritual is not a senseless activity but is rather one way of many ways in which human beings construe and construct their world."[40] It is through active engagement in the rites and rituals of Christian worship that one learns what it means to live and act as a Christian in the world. During the rhythms of the yearly cycle one hears and recites the Christian story through various words, gestures, rites, and actions. Over time an immersion in those stories enables a person to grasp "how to be a Christian . . . [through] the ritual actions of the Christian community, in the dying and rising experienced in baptism, in the grateful reception of bread and wine, in kneeling, bowing or standing for prayer."[41]

It is important to remember that the primary purpose of knowledge gained through the liturgy is not to obtain a different point of view about the world, but rather to cause one to act differently in the world by providing a different pattern on which to model one's life.[42] This transformation occurs bodily through habituation. Paul Connerton argues that "habit is a knowledge and a remembering in the hands and in the body; and in the cultivation of habit it is our body which 'understands.'"[43] When ritual actions become habituated, they serve as means to assist in the transformation of an individual. The celebration of commemorative rites, like the eucharist, is eventually embodied when it becomes habituated. It is this embodied

---

38. Ibid., 22.

39. Anderson, *Worship and Christian Identity*, 4. Also, see Anderson, "Liturgical Catechesis," 349–62.

40. Jennings, "On Ritual Knowledge," 112.

41. Anderson, *Worship and Christian Identity*, 80.

42. Ibid., 81; Jennings, "On Ritual Knowledge," 117.

43. Connerton, *How Societies Remember*, 93–95.

memory that helps one to know how to live and act in the world. Nathan Mitchell suggests that habituation inscribes knowledge upon our bodies; it is "'thinking' with our skin."[44] The actions found within worship "teach the body how to develop spiritual virtues by material means."[45]

Therefore, to understand what is taking place in any given liturgy, that is, to know what the worshippers believe, it is not enough to simply ask what is being said within the context of worship through the prayers, music, sermon, etc. Rather, one must examine "what is being done"[46] bodily, since "what we know in our bodies is more powerful than what we know in words."[47] The temptation to design worship that encourages "passivity and non-commitment"[48] should be avoided at all costs. This occurs when distinctions are made between those leading worship, which makes them the performers, and the congregation is relegated to an audience. Such a practice employs worship in a utilitarian fashion, as a tool to attract the unchurched as well as a mechanism to excite the bored from within the church. Means are implemented to excite, arouse, and stimulate the congregation—anything that will avoid monotony and boredom.[49] In contrast, *meaningful* worship practices that become habituated get beneath our skin and into our bones, providing opportunities for the Holy Spirit to work in transforming ways through both words and bodily actions. It is for these reasons that both the words and actions of Christian worship should be approached with careful thought and preparation.

Conclusion

What some may find interesting is that even though the early Nazarenes were not guided by a liturgical theology to assist them, they were concerned about worship becoming audience driven and degrading to entertainment. Although their perspective was biased against the prayer book and limited

44. Mitchell, "New Directions Ritual Research," in Bradshaw and Melloh, *Foundations in Ritual Studies*, 112.

45. Ibid.

46. Searle, "Ritual," in Bradshaw and Melloh, *Foundations in Ritual Studies*, 14.

47. Anderson, "Liturgical Catechesis," 355.

48. Ibid., 356.

49. Ronald Grimes argues that monotony is perfectly fitting to the liturgy. "Like any work, a liturgy needs monotony. Only when monotony, a quality we do not know how to appreciate, degenerates into boredom, does the liturgical vehicle break down. . . . What many students of ritual consistently fail to recognize is that a ritual does not have to be exciting to exercise power." Grimes, "Modes of Ritual Sensibility," in Bradshaw and Melloh, *Foundations in Ritual Studies*, 141.

to a worship pattern handed down to them from American revivalism, they were aware of certain dangers posed by misguided and haphazard worship. Their primary concern was that degraded forms of worship would impinge on the ability of the church to evangelize humanity. Through denomination-al correspondence and other avenues, they worked tirelessly to correct per-ceived problems occurring in Nazarene liturgical and sacramental practice.

In contrast, John Wesley who was a voracious student of the early church, had a more profound and wholistic understanding of liturgical the-ology and practice. He was quite cognizant of the importance the Anglican liturgy held in his paradigm for the formation of the Methodists. What he deemed as lacking in Anglican worship, he addressed in Methodist society meetings, but he never discharged the importance of the church's liturgy found within the *Book of Common Prayer* (*BCP*). Wesley envisioned an in-dispensable connectedness between what occurs in worship and the way individuals are spiritually formed. The liturgy of the church, both its ritu-alization and sacramental life, were not inconsequential but had immense implications for Christian piety. Since the headwaters of Nazarene doctrine begin within classical Wesleyanism the next chapter appropriately examines John Wesley's sacramental and liturgical theology and praxis.

Chapter 2

Worship and Spirituality in John Wesley's Practical Theology

Religious and Political Climate in Seventeenth and Eighteenth-Century England

CHURCH HISTORIANS TYPICALLY PAINT a very grave picture of the moral and spiritual condition of both the church and society in eighteenth-century England.[1] Stephen Neill summarizes the century as a "spiritually depressing period."[2] The internal war between the various religious groups (e.g., Catholics, Anglicans, Presbyterians, and Independents) overshadowed both the religious and political landscape of the seventeenth century. Stephen Sykes and associates offer the following summary of the period: "[This] struggle between militant reformers and supporters of the establishment dominated English religious history from the middle of the reign of James I until the 1689 Toleration Act."[3]

Although the immense trouble which loomed over England began at the time of the reign of James I, it was during the kingship of his son, Charles I, that the internal fighting reached its crescendo. The result was a civil war, driven predominately by hostile disagreements over religion, which raged

1. One who questions the general consensus that the condition of the eighteenth-century Anglican Church was a rather dismal one is John Dray. His analysis, however, is directed specifically at one segment of the Anglican Church—Cornish Christianity. Dray suggests that although there were structural weaknesses in the Cornish Established Church, in actuality the church was more vibrant than the image often portrayed. Dray, "Church Chapel Mining Parish," 48–61.

2. Neill, *Anglicanism*, 201.

3. Sykes, Booty, and Knight, *Study of Anglicanism*, 19.

Spiritually depressing Period!

between the King and Parliament. The ensuing conflict eventually resulted in the King's capture and execution. Following the beheading of Charles I, the various religious groups, once united by their opposition to the King, now turned upon each other. Due to this sequence of events, "chaos [now] threatened the land."[4] It was at this point that the staunch Puritan, Oliver Cromwell, assumed the reins of power and stamped out the rebellion. Although Cromwell brought a temporary peace to England, the infighting resumed after his death.

Justo González points out that following Cromwell's death and "the failure of the Protectorate,"[5] there was no alternative which remained except to restore the monarchy. However, the battle between religious groups reappeared under Charles II. During Charles's reign the *Test Act* was introduced which stated that no one could hold office, either civil or military, without having first received the holy communion in accordance with the rubrics instituted by the Church of England.[6] This piece of legislation was directed primarily against Roman Catholics, since the oath renounced the doctrine of transubstantiation. However, the Test Act also "bore hard"[7] on other religious groups that refused to conform to the Anglican rubrics for the celebration of the eucharist (i.e., Nonconformists). The Puritans, Presbyterians, Congregationalists, and Quakers were among those religious groups that refused to conform. It also served only to aggravate the religious and political hatred characteristic of eighteenth-century England.

Following Charles II's death, his brother, James II, took the throne. During the reign of James II the English revolted because of his full embrace of Roman Catholicism. The deposed James escaped to France, and, in 1688, the throne was given to William of Orange, and his wife, Mary. Neill states that the Revolution of 1688, inaugurated by the arrival of William III, ended the medieval age and ushered in the modern world. A nation torn by political and religious strife was finally given the opportunity to heal:

> Under the circumstances of the Revolution of 1688, toleration could no longer be denied to Protestant Dissenters. By the Toleration Act of May 24, 1689, all who swore, or affirmed, the oaths of allegiance to William and Mary, rejected the jurisdiction of the Pope, transubstantiation, the mass, the invocation of the Virgin and saints, and also subscribed to the doctrinal positions of the Thirty-nine Articles, were granted freedom of

4. González, *Reformation to the Present*, 161.
5. Ibid., 162.
6. Neill, *Anglicanism*, 180.
7. Walker, *History of the Church*, 417.

worship. . . . Diverse forms of Protestant worship could now exist side by side.[8]

Even though the Toleration Act did not initially provide relief to Roman Catholics, it was the beginning of dramatic religious and political changes in England.[9] This Glorious Revolution brought much needed stability to English soil.[10]

Residual Effect of the Toleration Act Upon Wesley and the Methodists

There were eventual repercussions of the Toleration Act upon Wesley's life as a loyal churchman and his work with the Methodist societies. It was passed a little more than a decade prior to Wesley's birth but would directly impact both him and the Methodist movement for years to come. Wesley's commitment to the Church of England cannot be fully understood without considering the Act's political and ecclesial ramifications for Wesley years later. Pragmatically it would have been easier if Wesley registered the Methodists as dissenters under the protection of the Toleration Act. However, his refusal to do so resulted in both persecution and repeated accusations that the Methodist practice of "holding separate assemblies for worship"[11] was a violation of church order. The tension between Wesley's claims that he was not a dissenter and the demands of the Methodist societies, moving him towards separation, proved to be a thorn that would remain embedded in his flesh for his entire life.

Frank Baker indicates that the strain between John Wesley's loyalty to the church and the breach actuated by his work with the Methodist societies came to a head between 1754 and 1755. Against Charles Wesley's own wishes, John gave considerable thought to the possibility of seeking protection under the Toleration Act by allowing Methodists to register as dissenters:

> In 1745, in his Farther Appeal, Part I, Wesley had stated explicitly that because they were not dissenters from the church, Methodists could not make use of the Act of Toleration. Ten years later he was clearly prepared to make two compromises, first to accept the technical designation of 'dissenter' even

8. Ibid., 418.

9. Ibid. Religious toleration was fully realized in 1829 when it was extended to Roman Catholics.

10. Neill, *Anglicanism*, 168–9.

11. Baker, *John Wesley*, 91–105.

though disavowing its implications, and second to regard such dissenting preaching licences as authorizations to administer the sacraments. Charles Wesley was strongly opposed to both these steps.[12]

After considerable thought over the issue, John Wesley responded at the Leeds Conference in 1755 with his paper, *Ought We to Separate from the Church of England?* John concluded that the Methodists "separated neither from the people, the doctrine, nor the worship of the church, and submitted to its laws and governors 'in all things not contrary to Scripture.'"[13] Although his decision was decisive, it did not fully resolve the tension. This is further exemplified when, to the dismay of Charles, John finally acquiesced to the issue of ordaining preachers. Through the act of ordaining his own clergy, even though it was out of practical necessity, Wesley had in effect committed the cardinal act of dissension, an accusation the staunch churchman denied until his death.

to check or stop the flowing of
To stop the flow of blood.

Lingering Division in the Eighteenth Century

Although the Toleration Act of 1689 did ease the political and religious tension within England, the division between the various religious groups continued into the eighteenth century. One example of the seriousness of this problem involved political maneuvering, initiated by those with more high-church leanings. In an effort to circumvent the Test Act, established under Charles II years earlier, it was common for Nonconformists to accept the sacramental requirements of the Test Act so that they could still fulfill the law and hold public office. Therefore, they would receive the eucharist in the Church of England when necessary but continue to worship in their own Nonconformist church.

Rather than abolishing the Test Act, which would have eased tensions, the "high churchmen"[14] decided to put an end to those evading the Test Act by passing the Occasional Conformity Act of 1711. It stated that any office holder who "after receiving the Sacrament in the Church of England should knowingly or willingly resort to or be present at any conventicler, assembly or meeting . . . for the exercise of religion in other manner than according to the liturgy and practice of the Church of England"[15] would be penalized

12. Ibid., 163.
13. Ibid., 166.
14. Neill, *Anglicanism*, 180.
15. Ibid., 181.

and removed from office. The Act was repealed in less than a decade, but the damage was already inflicted. The most sacred ordinance of the church, the celebration of the eucharist, became an instrument that was "prostituted to political ends."[16] Neil proposes that "the real question of the times was not as to which group or party should have predominant influence in the [Anglican] Church; it was, whether there should within a few years be any Church for anyone to belong to at all."[17]

Anglican Spirituality and Worship in Eighteenth-Century England

The fierce battles that consumed England for the greater part of the seventeenth century and into the eighteenth century drained the spiritual resources of the church; this result was devastating to English spirituality. Neill suggests that one of the most serious threats to the Church of England as it moved into the eighteenth century was the problem of Deism and the effects of the Enlightenment. Matthew Tindal's *Christianity as Old Creation* exemplified some of the most thought-provoking deistic literature of the day. Tindal's work was disguised in language similar to that used by the most influential theologians and writers of the Anglican Church—the Caroline Divines. However, Deism's sole insistence on natural revelation made both special revelation unnecessary and arguments over the existence of miracles irrelevant. While asserting the importance of natural religion, the Deists denied the reality of supernatural religion.[18] Therefore, religion, rather than existing in the context of an intimate relationship with a living God, became "a system of ideas and a code of moral precepts."[19] The fact that the Church of England was for the most part ill prepared to respond to this assault upon orthodox Christianity, leveled against it by Deism and Enlightenment thought, served only to amplify the problem.

Methodist bishop and Wesley contemporary, Richard Watson's description of eighteenth-century English society and the church is rather bleak:

> At this period the religious and moral state of the nation was such as to give the most serious concern to the few remaining faithful. . . . The degree of ignorance on all scriptural subjects,

16. Ibid.
17. Ibid.
18. Plummer, *Church of England*, 89.
19. Neill, *Anglicanism*, 183.

and of dull, uninquiring irreligiousness . . . is well known to those
who have turned their attention to such inquiries. . . . Infidelity
began its ravages upon the principles of the higher and middle
classes; the mass of the people remained uneducated, and were
Christians but in name, and by virtue of their baptism; whilst
many of the great doctrines of the Reformation were banished
both from the universities and the pulpits. . . . An evangelical liturgy [was reduced] to a dead form, which was repeated without
thought, or so explained away as to take away its meaning. . . . A
great portion of the clergy, whatever other learning they might
possess, were grossly ignorant of theology.[20]

Illiteracy and poverty in the rapidly expanding lower classes were viewed
by many as being one of the chief causes of the ever-increasing immorality
and vice in English society.[21] Robert Shoemaker characterizes the streets
of eighteenth-century London as crowded and often ungovernable to the
point that social upheaval was a common occurrence.[22] Even Oxford University was not exempt from moral decay. Richard Heitzenrater suggests
that "many of the problems that characterized English society as a whole"[23]
existed at Oxford while John Wesley was enrolled as a student.

Henry Rack states that even though the bishops were political appoin-
tees they were for the most part "of good character and often men of learning and devotion."[24] The major problem related to the bishops was systemic.
Their Parliamentary duties prevented them from being more involved in
their dioceses, which made them "essentially a remote figure, seldom seen
by [the] clergy."[25]

Likewise, the greatest difficulty with the clergy concerned the organizational structure of the church. It created significant limitations for clergy
in performing their duties. The majority of parishes were either in rural
areas or they were poor, which meant that in the eighteenth century more
than half the parishes were without clergy in residence.[26] Additionally Rack
reminds us "that the clerical profession was a profession which many adopted as the best and most natural available without seeing the need for the

20. Watson and Summers, *Life of John Wesley*, 68–71.

21. Heitzenrater, *People Called Methodists*, 24.

22. Shoemaker, *London Mob*, xii.

23. Heitzenrater, *People Called Methodists*, 31.

24. Rack, *Reasonable Enthusiast*, 14.

25. Ibid., 15.

26. Jacob challenges the popular notion that the non-residence of clergy was a major problem in the eighteenth-century Anglican Church. Jacob, *Lay People*, 22.

divine call thought essential by later Evangelicals and Anglo-Catholics."[27] Regardless of these limitations most clergymen were faithful in both discharging their duties and in moral conduct. W. M. Jacob notes, "There is evidence of steady piety, of an awareness of the eternal dimension of life, of the mercy of God and of the duty of charity amongst apparently prosaic and conventional men. Devotion might be prosaic, yet genuine."[28]

Although it is difficult if not impossible to provide an exact picture of liturgical practice, especially since it differed from parish to parish, Rack furnishes the following generalization of clerical duties that give us some insight into the Anglican liturgy. "The dutiful parson ideally held two services on Sunday, preaching two sermons; and theoretically read morning and evening prayer daily or at least on Wednesdays, Fridays and feast days. He would catechize the young, apprentices and servants and visit the sick. Communion would be administered at least three times a year."[29] Historically it is assumed that eucharistic practice was infrequent and devalued in the eighteenth century; in reality the picture is more complex. Most cathedrals and even some of the town churches celebrated communion much more frequently. One example is the Collegiate Church in Manchester which celebrated weekly eucharist.[30]

No doubt this era was filled with significant problems for the established church. However, when reading historical accounts of the eighteenth century, it is prudent to remain aware of potential bias that serves to either exaggerate or understate the true nature of the period. Furthermore, some argue that despite the eighteenth-century church's dark reputation among church historians, the truth is that most of these issues precede that period. Problems, systemic in nature, dating back to the medieval period were only amplified by the Reformation and were beyond the ability of the clergy to repair them.[31] Sykes maintains that "as an institution the church remained antiquated and cumbrous, and this hindered its effectiveness."[32] Therefore it was unable to meet the demands resulting from the population growth, urbanization, and

---

27. Rack, *Reasonable Enthusiast*, 17.

28. Jacob, *Lay People*, 21.

29. Rack, *Reasonable Enthusiast*, 16.

30. Ibid., 19. Wesley indicates in *The Duty of Constant Communion* that cathedrals and collegiate churches were ordered by the church to communicate a minimum of weekly. Outler points out that the *BCP* allowed an exception to this rubric if "reasonable cause" existed not to proceed accordingly. Wesley, "Duty of Constant Communion," in *Works* (BE), 3:438.

31. Rack, *Reasonable Enthusiast*, 11.

32. Sykes, Booty, and Knight, *Study of Anglicanism*, 32.

the beginning of the Industrial Revolution characteristic of the century.[33] It was within this age and ecclesial atmosphere that John Wesley was born and served as both pastor and leader of the Methodist movement.

Wesley and Methodism

The methodical pattern that eventually characterized Wesley's life initially developed during his days at Oxford and was fueled by the writings of men like Jeremy Taylor, Thomas à Kempis, and William Law.[34] His spiritual journey focused upon the pursuit of an inward religion, whereby all thoughts, feelings, and actions where subject to the pattern set forth by Christ. Wesley referred to this inward religion as holiness or perfection.[35] Heitzenrater indicates that this quest launched Wesley on a

> spiritual and intellectual pilgrimage that led him through the pages of hundreds of books . . . across the paths of a multitude of new acquaintances. . . . [It] eventually led him to tie together the perfectionism of the pietists, the moralism of the Puritans, and the devotionalism of the mystics in a pragmatic approach that he felt could operate within the structure and doctrine of the Church of England.[36]

Wesley's growing conviction that the pursuit of inward holiness is necessary for the Christian life becomes evident by 1725.[37] His journal entry dated May 24, 1738, records personal reflections on the series of events that led to his experience at the society meeting on Aldersgate Street. It was here that Wesley felt his heart "strangely warmed."[38] However, as Wesley describes in his journal, the journey leading to the crisis at Aldersgate began years earlier:

> When I was about twenty-two (i.e., 1725) my father pressed me to enter into the holy orders. At the same time, the providence of God directing me to Kempis's *Christian Pattern*, I began to see that true religion was seated in the heart and that God's law

---

33. J. C. D. Clark argues that although urbanization and the industrial revolution existed in Wesley's era it was not as extensive as was once thought. See Clark, "Eighteenth-Century Context," in Abraham and Kirby, *Oxford Handbook*, 3–6.

34. Wesley, "Plain Account," in *Works* (BE), 13:136–7.

35. Rack, *Reasonable Enthusiast*, 73.

36. Heitzenrater, *People Called Methodists*, 31.

37. Ibid., 36.

38. Wesley, "Journal February 1737 to August 1738," in *Works* (BE), 18:249–50.

Inward Holiness

extended to all our thoughts as well as words and actions. . . . I
began to aim at and pray for inward holiness.[39]

Wesley's experience at Aldersgate was only part of an extended journey in pursuit of inward holiness, first manifesting itself during his Oxford
days. Although it is perhaps the most well-known crisis moment in his life,
Aldersgate was not the only one. During the remainder of his life, Wesley
experienced other significant events which continued to shape his spiritual
pilgrimage.[40]

The Circumcision of the Heart, which Wesley preached at St. Mary's on
January 1, 1733, is one of his most complete explanations of the doctrine of
holiness.[41] Although it was preached early in his ministry, Wesley attested to
its significance as late as 1778. "I know not that I can write a better [sermon]
on *The Circumcision of the Heart* than I did five and forty years ago. . . . I may
have read five or six hundred books more . . . and may know more history or
natural philosophy than I did. But I am not sensible that this has made any
essential addition to my knowledge in divinity."[42] This pursuit of holiness
became the core not only for Wesley's theology but also the basis for the
practices he considered essential to living out a holy life. His insistence on
the necessity of regular participation in the means of grace was driven by
his concern over the possibility of backsliding and the ever-present dangers
of antinomianism.[43] When confronted by a group of Methodist quietists
who were resisting water baptism and the eucharist, Wesley responded with
his sermon, *The Means of Grace*, in which he stresses both the "validity and
. . . the necessity, of the means of grace as taught and administered in the
Church of England."[44]

Attempting to maintain balance, he carefully stresses the exigent nature of the outward ordinances (i.e., means of grace), while at the same time
indicating that they have no value in and of themselves.[45] God detests the

---

39. Ibid., 243–4.

40. Outler, "Aldersgate Experience," in *John Wesley*, 51–53.

41. Ibid., 251.

42. Wesley, "Journal January 1776 to August 1779," in *Works* (BE), 23:105.

43. Heitzenrater, *People Called Methodists*, 36.

44. Outler, "Means: Introductory Comment," in *Works* (BE), 1:376.

45. Wesley, "Means of Grace," in *Works* (BE),1:381–4, 396–7. Those who opposed
the use of the sacraments and other outward observances often referred to them as
ordinances. Wesley uses the term *means of grace* to refer to both the Lord's supper and
other outward signs that God uses to communicate his grace. Wesley states that he
chose the expression *means of grace* because he did not know a better way to describe
them and because it has been used by the Christian church and specifically the Church
of England.

appropriation of the means of grace apart from a heart fully devoted to him. Wesley provides this warning, "before you use any means let it be deeply impressed on your soul: There is no power in this. It is in itself a poor, dead, empty thing: separate from God, it is a dry leaf, a shadow."[46] Therefore the means of grace or *outward signs, words, or actions* are valid only when they become channels which promote a religion of the heart and "convey . . . preventing, justifying, or sanctifying grace."[47]

For Wesley, participation in the means of grace is necessary because they are God ordained channels enabling one to experience God's transforming grace in the pursuit of true holiness. Wesley defined these means of God's grace as the "outward ordinances, whereby the inward grace of God is ordinarily conveyed to man, whereby the faith that brings salvation is conveyed to them who before had it not."[48] Wesley, in his sermon, *The Means of Grace,* discusses the following outward signs as the chief means that God uses to communicate his grace:

> The chief of these means are prayer, whether in secret or with the great congregation; searching the Scriptures (which implies reading, hearing, and meditating thereon) and receiving the Lord's Supper, eating bread and drinking wine in remembrance of him; and these we believe to be ordained of God as the ordinary channels of conveying grace to the souls of men.[49]

Faith is not passive; rather it is essential to act upon the grace received. Wesley understands the means as the appropriate human response to the actions of God's grace. It is God who has provided these channels. Defending the use of the means of grace against those who suggest that the ordinances lead one to place their trust in the ordinances, rather than Christ alone, Wesley writes: "Does not the Scripture direct us to *wait* on salvation? . . . Seeing it is the gift of God, we are undoubtedly to *wait* on him for salvation. But how shall we wait? . . . All who desire the grace of God are to wait for it in the means which he hath ordained."[50]

Ole Borgen indicates that in his journals Wesley recognizes five chief means of grace: "prayer, the Word, fasting, Christian conference, and the Lord's supper. . . . And [Wesley] contends, they are all ordained by God in the Scriptures."[51] However, the activities that Wesley considered to be

46. Ibid., 396.

47. Ibid., 381.

48. Wesley, "Journal November 1739 to September 1741," in *Works* (BE), 19:121.

49. Wesley, "Means of Grace," in *Works* (BE), 1:381.

50. Ibid., 391–3.

51. Borgen, *John Wesley on Sacraments,* 107.

means of grace are broader than the instituted means. They encompass a vast array of actions found within "public worship, personal devotion, and Christian community and discipleship."[52]

The means of grace fall into one of three categories: general means, instituted means, and prudential means.[53] The general means include such things as being actively on guard to one's spiritual condition, obeying the commandments, and self-denial. Ted Campbell points out that the main difference separating the instituted from the prudential means is that the "instituted means were practices instituted in Scripture from the beginning of the Christian community"[54] and are therefore "binding on the church at all times and in all places."[55] The instituted or particular means of grace, those means that transcend both time and culture, include the five chief means of grace: public and private prayer, searching the Scriptures, eucharist, fasting, and Christian conference.

The final category, the prudential means, is contrasted to the instituted means in that they are not carved in stone. The prudential means fluctuate depending on the era, culture, and individual.[56] They evince God's imaginative ability to extend grace through a variety of ways and means. The prudential means were important practices because they proved beneficial to the Methodist people but could change conforming to the time and cultural context. Knight includes the following activities among those that fall into the category of prudential means of grace: the class and band meetings, love feasts, visiting the sick, and reading devotional classics.[57]

Knight warns that any attempt to understand Wesley's perception of the Christian life in isolation would be a mistake. It is essential to examine the "liturgical, communal, and devotional contexts within which Wesley himself understood it."[58] Knight's analysis of the way Wesley understood the *via salutis* and specifically the pursuit of holiness suggests that a thorough evaluation of Wesley's soteriology must consider all the facets that were important to his method. While our focus here is limited to Wesley's liturgical thought and praxis, the importance of the communal and devotional contexts as it

52. Knight III, *Presence of God*, 2.

53. Borgen, *John Wesley on Sacraments*, 104.

54. Campbell, "Means of Grace," in Abraham and Kirby, *Oxford Handbook*, 282.

55. Ibid.

56. Knight III, *Presence of God*, 3.

57. Ibid., 5.

58. Ibid., 2.

relates to Nazarene spirituality is fully acknowledged and should be of utmost concern to pastors, church leadership, and congregations.[59]

Wesley's Liturgical Concerns

Prayer Book Revisions in the Sunday Service

Wesley notes his high regard for the Anglican Liturgy as manifested in the BCP. *John Wesley's Sunday Service of the Methodists in North America (Sunday Service)* contains the following letter from Wesley in the preface:

> I believe there is no liturgy in the World, either in ancient or modern language, which breathes more of a solid, scriptural, rational piety, than the Common Prayer of the Church of England. And though the main of it was compiled considerably more than two hundred years ago, yet is the language of it, not only pure, but strong and elegant in the highest degree.[60]

Although he found the Anglican prayer book of great value and important enough to be used in the colonies, Wesley also realized that some modification of the *BCP* liturgy for the American Methodists was needed. His love of the church's liturgy did not signify that the *BCP* was so sacred it was beyond the need for revision. Such convictions were reserved for Scripture alone. Therefore, Wesley modified the *Sunday Service* as he deemed appropriate to the American context.[61]

Wesley realized the shape of American Methodist worship differed significantly from the Church of England. Likewise, he understood the importance of granting them additional liturgical freedom. In a September 10, 1784, letter addressed to "Dr. Coke, Mr. Asbury, and our Brethren in North America,"[62] which was sent after the release of the *Sunday Service*, Wesley wrote the following:

> As our American brethren are now totally disentangled both from the State, and from the English Hierarchy, we dare not intangle [sic] them again, either with the one or the other. They are now at full liberty, simply to follow the Scriptures and the primitive

---

59. Wesley specifically mentions the liturgy as a means of grace. "The public worship of God" appears in the General Rules as one of the ordinances required of society members. Wesley, "Nature of Societies," in *Works* (BE), 9:73.

60. Wesley, *John Wesley's Sunday Service*, 2.

61. Tucker, *American Methodist Worship*, 5–8.

62. Wesley, "Letter of September 10," i.

church. And we judge it best that they should stand fast in that liberty, wherewith God has so strangely made them free.[63]

When Wesley granted liturgical liberty to the Methodists in America he places the authority of their liturgical theology in Scripture and the primitive church. He does so because he believes Scripture holds the most authoritative voice in all things and that the primitive church offered Christianity in its purest and most authentic form.[64] Tucker maintains that the measure for determining sound worship practice, "was to be located in Scripture, though Wesley did not expect that the biblical text should provide the precise *ordo* or rubrics for worship."[65]

Wesley's instructions to the North American church were consistent with his belief in the primacy of Scripture and his understanding that the early church (i.e., prior to Constantine), because of its chronological proximity to Christ and the Apostles, provides for us the most adequate model for living out one's Christian faith. Recent scholarship has argued that Eastern Christianity provided for Wesley a paradigm resonate of true Christianity in its purest form, since it reflected "faithfully the Gospel challenge to be conformed to the image of Christ."[66] It is this model Wesley intended when he gave the American Methodists liturgical freedom "to follow the Scriptures and the primitive church."[67]

Regardless of the necessity to grant such freedoms, it was still his hope that the North American church would employ the prayer book he had provided. Earlier in the same letter he advised the clergy and leadership in North America on the use of the *Sunday Service*:

> I have accordingly appointed Dr. Coke and Mr. Francis Asbury, to be joint Superintendents over our brethren in North America. . . . And I have prepared a liturgy little differing from that of the church of England . . . which I advise all the travelling-preachers to use, on the Lord's day, in all their congregations, reading the litany only on Wednesdays and Fridays, and praying extempore on all other days. I also advise the elders to administer the Supper of the Lord on every Lord's day.[68]

63. Ibid., iii.

64. Tucker, *American Methodist Worship*, 4.

65. Ibid.

66. Campbell, "Wesley and Asian Roots," 286. This would include Eastern Fathers such as Chrysostom, Basil, and Macarius.

67. Wesley, "Letter of September 10," iii.

68. Ibid., ii.

Taking such freedoms and making alternations to the liturgy were not new for Wesley. During the early days of his evangelical work he made modifications to the *BCP* liturgy when he believed they were necessary. Paul Sanders notes that even though Wesley held the written prayers of the Anglican liturgy in high regard and readily implemented them on a regular basis, he did not restrict his praying to form prayers alone. Wesley felt free to use extemporaneous prayers.[69]

It would be a mistake to assume that the sole purpose of Wesley's revision of the prayer book was "to please the Americans."[70] Some of the revisions were no doubt made due to the nature of rural life. For example, some of the resources readily available to British congregations were limited in North America, if available at all.[71] However, Wesley did not compromise those elements he deemed essential in the *BCP* liturgy.[72] Scholars have long debated the motivating influences that gave shape to the *Sunday Service*.[73] The exact reasons Wesley selected certain items for revision, eliminated some components entirely, and left other parts untouched are not completely clear. Sanders suggests that the revision of the Anglican prayer book reflects Wesley's own evangelical convictions as he sought to propagate a religion of the heart.[74]

White's thoughts are similar, "Wesley's intent . . . seems to be to insist only on central Christian doctrines and to avoid unnecessary controversy."[75] Despite making what he considered to be necessary changes, Wesley believed the essence of the Anglican liturgy was important in the journey toward inward holiness. However, the significance of Wesley's revising the *BCP* liturgy, rather than tossing it aside, is that it demonstrates "his high evaluation of the usefulness of a set liturgy."[76]

69. Sanders, "An Appraisal Wesley's Sacramentalism," 62–3.

70. Ibid., 246.

71. White, "Introduction," in *John Wesley's Sunday Service*, 10.

72. Sanders, "An Appraisal Wesley's Sacramentalism," 246.

73. A further discussion on Wesley's revision of the prayer book may be found in the following sources, see Sanders, "An Appraisal Wesley's Sacramentalism," 246; Tucker, *American Methodist Worship*; Wade, "History Public Worship," 1–86; White, "Introduction," in *John Wesley's Sunday Service*, 9–37.

74. Sanders, "An Appraisal Wesley's Sacramentalism," 246.

75. White, "Introduction," in *John Wesley's Sunday Service*, 35–36.

76. Sanders, "An Appraisal Wesley's Sacramentalism," 65.

Influences in Wesley's Liturgical Ordo

Insight into Wesley's liturgical theology is also evident in the society meetings in British Methodism. Although Wesley found great value in Methodist worship, he still expected Methodists to attend the worship services of their own church.[77] This was in part due to his loyalty to the church; however, the Methodist meetings were never intended to replace the Anglican liturgy. Rather they were a means to evangelize the church from within. During the 1766 Conference at Leeds, Wesley defends the Methodists against accusations that they are dissenters by pointing out the inadequacies of attending Methodist worship alone:

> But some may say, 'Our own service is public worship.' Yes, in a sense—but not such as supersedes the Church service. We never designed it should; we have a hundred times professed the contrary. It presupposes public prayer, like the sermons at the university. . . . If it were designed to be instead of Church service, it would be essentially defective. For it seldom has the four grand parts of public prayer: deprecation (i.e., penitence), petition, intercession, and thanksgiving. Neither is it, even on the Lord's day, concluded with the Lord's Supper.[78]

Wesley's argument is revealing of his expectations of the liturgy. Elements he deemed necessary in the worship *ordo* were by his design missing from Methodist worship. He not only looked to the Anglican Church in developing his liturgical praxis, but as Tucker points out, Wesley searched through early church documents in order to find examples of "liturgical ordines."[79] He did so because he was convinced that ante-Nicene Christianity was the age in which church doctrine and practice existed in its purest and most scriptural form representing the "normative pattern of catholic Christianity."[80] Scripture was always the primary authority for Wesley in all areas of life, including the liturgy. However, tradition, reason, and experience could also serve as guides to Scripture, in establishing praxis in worship.

Wesley was convinced that room existed for variance in worship, expressed through various styles. Still he was concerned that the liturgy both preserved and communicated those components that Scripture, tradition,

---

77. Ibid., 64; Taves, *Fits,* 64; Hildebrandt, Beckerlegge, and Dale, "Introduction," in *Works* (BE), 7:57.

78. Wesley, "Annual Minutes 1766," in *Works* (BE), 10:326.

79. Tucker, *American Methodist Worship,* 4.

80. Outler, "Introduction," in *John Wesley,* 9. Also see Tucker, *American Methodist Worship,* 4.

and reason deemed essential to Christian faith.[81] In addition to the Anglican triad there was a fourth, albeit subordinate, source of authority for the church—experience. Experience could justify deviations from traditional Anglican worship practices as long they withstood the scrutiny of Scripture and reason. As Tucker clarifies, "Though not equal in authority to the other three criteria . . . innovative practices in worship . . . could be evaluated not only in terms of their testimony to Scripture and tradition but also by the witness of the spirit in human life."[82]

Liturgy as a Means of Grace

The beginnings of Methodism had its earliest roots in Wesley's Oxford days when John, his brother Charles, William Morgan, and Bob Kirkham began meeting together for "study, prayer, and religious conversation."[83] Core to Wesley's motivation and purpose in these society meetings was his continual pursuit of holiness. Over time the small group began to take shape through the addition of new members, the inclusion of various disciplines, adherence to strict code of conduct, involvement in social concerns, and other activities that aided in the pursuit of a "distinctively Christian lifestyle."[84] However, as Wesley made clear, in all of these endeavors with the Methodist society meetings he was not a dissenter. The purpose of the societies, which eventually developed into the Wesleyan movement, was never to replace the Anglican Church, nor were the society meetings meant to be a substitute for worship at the local parish. Rather Methodism provided a means to evangelize the church from within. Even though Wesley was loyal to the established church, he did believe that deficiencies existed in the national church that required a response.

Dangers to Avoid

One of Wesley's chief complaints against the Anglican Church was directed toward the destructive influences of deism, rationalism, and the formalism that followed. Wesley, in his essay, *An Earnest Appeal to Men of Reason and*

---

81. Tucker, *American Methodist Worship*, 4.

82. Ibid., 5.

83. Heitzenrater, *People Called Methodists*, 38.

84. Ibid., 47.

Religion, addresses "the apathy of nominal Christianity and . . . the rising tides of rationalism and unbelief"[85] ingrained in the national church:

> Do you say in your heart: "I know all this already. I am not barely a man of reason. I am a religious man, for I not only avoid evil and do good, but use all the means of grace. I am constantly at church, and at the sacrament, too. I say my prayers every day. I read many good books. I fast." . . . Do you indeed? Do you do all this? This you may do, you may go thus far and yet have no religion at all, no such religion avails before God. . . .
>
> Tis plain you do not love God. If you did, you would be happy in him. But you know you are not happy. Your formal religion no more makes you happy than your neighbor's gay religion does him. . . . Can you now bear to hear the naked truth? You have the "form of godliness," but not "the power." [Cf. 2 Tim. 3:5] . . . You love "the creature more than the Creator." You are "a lover of pleasure more than a lover of God." A lover of God? You do not love God at all, no more than you love a stone. You love the world; therefore, the love of the Father is not in you [Cf. 1 John 2:15]. . . .
>
> See, at length, that outward religion without inward is nothing; is far worse than nothing, being, indeed, no other than a solemn mockery of God. And inward religion you have not.[86]

The structure of Methodist worship was in part directed toward the dangers of formalism. The incorporation of experience into the Wesleyan quadrilateral, as well as the means through which experience manifested itself in liturgical practice, was key to combating the peril of dead religion. Experience manifested itself in Methodist worship through a variety of ways. However, Wesley was also cautious lest experience be overemphasized. He believed that authentic faith "was explicitly situated in opposition to both enthusiasm and formalism."[87]

Characteristics of Wesley's Liturgical Design

Wesley was continually striving to maintain balance between the dangers of formalism and enthusiasm. Formalism occurs when persons go through the motions of religion apart from the power and presence of God, it was a disease that had infiltrated the national church. The temptation for the

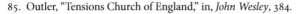

85. Outler, "Tensions Church of England," in, *John Wesley,* 384.

86. Wesley, "Tensions Church of England," 400–401.

87. Taves, *Fits,* 53.

Methodists was to drift into enthusiasm—a subjectively focused and imag-ined experience of God. Wesley "almost fell victim"[88] to enthusiasm and was well aware of its inherent dangers. Many of those society members who embraced enthusiasm were expelled from Methodism.[89] However, preven-tive methods were also implemented.

Attempts at reaching equilibrium were evinced in Wesley's structur-ing of the Methodist liturgy and the inclusion of the various components he felt essential to worship. Although Wesley held Anglican worship in high esteem, he did recognize its potential deficiencies and so he turned to other influences core to his own spiritual journey in order to reform the *BCP* liturgy. Lester Ruth makes the following observation, "Wesley's vision of Methodists living in two liturgical worlds was about drawing upon the riches of a longstanding liturgical tradition (Anglicanism) and infusing it with the power of Pietism that animated Methodist life. And the vision reflected a complexity in Wesley's liturgical thought in holding things to-gether in tension."[90] Structured into Methodist practices were channels used to promote inward religion. Knight underscores one of the benefits of the means of grace is found in their ability to provide balance between two extremes:

> The means of grace of the church—scripture, the Lord's supper, the prayer book—are the solution to this problem as they en-able us to remember who God is and what God has promised. God's presence through them is "objective," in that it evokes af-fections and invites imagination while it resists the projections of our imagination and desires onto it. Of course, the matter is more complex than this and the dangers more subtle, and this is the reason the means of grace form a mutually interacting pattern.[91]

Worship without a proper liturgical theology is not only haphazard but insufficient in countering the dangers of formalism or enthusiasm. The nature and design of worship are critically significant. Depending on its shape and content, worship serves either to counter the problems of formal-ism and enthusiasm or to reinforce them. This was evident in the formal-ism common to the Anglican Church as well as the enthusiasm affecting the Moravians, Methodists, Puritans, and other groups associated with the

---

88. Borgen, *John Wesley on Sacraments*, 99.

89. Taves, *Fits*, 65.

90. Ruth, "Liturgical Revolutions," in Abraham and Kirby, *Oxford Handbook*, 314.

91. Knight III, *Presence of God*, 47.

"transatlantic awakening."[92] Scripture, tradition, reason, and experience were the voices providing sound liturgical practice, with Scripture being the primary authority. Using these authorities as his guide Wesley both constructed and practiced the liturgy with careful thought and precision.[93]

Prayer

Borgen points out that Wesley believed Christians should be in a continual state of prayer whether it was through public or private prayer, spoken vocally or prayed silently in one's thoughts. He equated prayer as indispensable to the spiritual life in the same way that breathing is essential to our physical being and insisted that "God does nothing but in answer to prayer."[94] However the effectual prayer is not mechanical or prayed void of meaning but rather must come from the deepest yearnings of the heart:

> Beware not to speak what thou dost not mean. Prayer is the lifting up of the heart to God: all words of prayer without this are mere hypocrisy. Whenever therefore thou attemptest to pray, see that it be thy one design to commune with God, to lift up thy heart to him, to pour out thy soul before him. . . .
>
> The end of your praying is not to inform God, as though he knew not your wants already; but rather to inform yourselves, to fix the sense of your wants more deeply in your hearts, and the sense of your continual dependence on him who only is able to supply all your wants. It is not so much to move God—who is always more ready to give than you to ask—as to move yourselves, that you may be willing and ready to receive the good things he has prepared for you.[95]

Wesley determined there were four essential components of private, family, and public prayers. His list included "deprecation (i.e., penitence), petition, intercession, and thanksgiving."[96] These four aspects of prayer were

92. Taves, *Fits*, 20.

93. Knight reminds us that there must be a balanced approach to the means of grace. Those channels found within the context of the liturgy do not stand alone, but are dependent on the means existing in other contexts. This includes the general means of grace, the prudential means of grace, and other instituted means found outside of the liturgy. See Knight III, *Presence of God*; Borgen, *John Wesley on Sacraments*, 94–217; Wesley, "Means of Grace," in *Works* (BE), 1:376–97.

94. Borgen, *John Wesley on Sacraments*, 108–9.

95. Wesley, " Upon Sermon on the Mount (VI)," in *Works* (BE), 1:575–7.

96. Wesley, "Annual Minutes Late Conversations," in *Works* (BE), 10:326.

important enough to Wesley that he used them to defend himself against accusations of being a dissenter. Methodist worship by design did not contain these four parts, and, therefore, Wesley argued that it was "deficient"[97] by itself. Society members were expected to worship in the parish churches.

Wesley's use of spontaneous prayer in conjunction with the written prayers found in the *BCP* was one method within the liturgy of preserving balance. At various liturgical settings Wesley was known to combine both extemporaneous and written prayers.[98] Radically diverting from the *BCP*, he extended permission for the American Methodists to pray extempore. The rubric in the *Sunday Service* provided the option to use extemporary prayer at the conclusion of the order for the celebration of the Lord's supper.[99] Wesley's instructions to the North American church, as well as the advice of later Methodist leaders, indicated that the length of extemporary prayers should be modest (i.e., not to exceed ten minutes).[100]

Knight notes that in the *Sunday Service* it is significant that Wesley retains the collects from the *BCP*, since the true nature of God, as it is defined in Scripture, is laced throughout these "Cranmerian" prayers.[101] The discipline of praying written prayers, which are firmly established in Scripture (e.g. the collects) assists in the prevention of enthusiasm. The time-honored prayers of the church protect in this way by "offering concrete scriptural descriptions of God, and thus evoke and shape affections, inform Christian practice, and provide language and direction for extemporaneous prayer."[102] Wesley published several editions of prayers, written by himself and others, that were available for use in both public and private worship.

The Word of God

Wesley includes searching the Scriptures as one of the chief means of grace. Searching the Scriptures encompasses activities which are found in the context of the liturgy and in conjunction with those practiced in private.

97. Tyerman, *Life and Times of Wesley*, 321–2.

98. Wesley defends the use of extemporary prayer in his publication of *The Principles of a Methodist Farther Explained*. See Wesley, "Principles Farther Explained," in *Works* (BE), 9:187–8.

99. Tucker, *American Methodist Worship*, 32.

100. Ibid.

101. Knight III, *Presence of God*, 162.

102. Ibid.

Actions contained in searching the Scriptures include "hearing, reading, and meditating"[103] on the Word, as well as preaching.

Knight charges that it is important to encounter the entire scope of the Bible, with its vast spectrum of imagery, since reading Scripture is essential to our identity as the people of God.[104] Hearing, reading, and meditating upon Scripture is the means God employs to shape the affections as it instructs in doctrine, convicts of sin, and promotes spiritual healing in order that "the man of God may be perfect."[105] Borgen suggests that when Wesley includes searching the Scriptures as a means of grace, he is affirming that the same Holy Spirit who inspired the authors of Scripture to write also works inwardly in the lives of those who are the recipients of God's Word.[106] When faith is present, the Holy Spirit works to communicate God's grace. However, without faith and apart from the presence of the Holy Spirit, "it [the means] is in itself a poor, dead, empty thing."[107]

Furthermore, it is important to note that there exists a symbiotic relationship between prayer and Scripture. Knight adds the following observation, "If prayer is the 'breath' of the Christian life . . . then Scripture is . . . [its] heart; giving it a form and shape."[108] Prayer is preparatory by nature infiltrating each of the other means, including Scripture, and thereby enabling one to encounter the presence of God. Likewise, Scripture is also found within the context of prayer as well as in the other ordinances. Knight explains the relationship between prayer and Scripture in the following way. "Prayer opens us to the presence of God. . . . [Scripture] 'informs' our prayers through showing us to whom we pray, and for what we should offer our thanksgivings, confessions, intercessions, and petitions."[109]

Although Scripture is coalesced with reason, tradition, and experience in determining truth, it is Scripture that is the ultimate authority. Wesley gives us some insight into his estimation of Scripture and its purpose in the preface to his sermons:

> I want to know one thing, the way to heaven—how to land safe on that happy shore. God himself has condescended to teach the way: for this very end he came from heaven. He hath written it down in a book. O give me that book! At any price give me the

103. Wesley, "Means of Grace," in *Works* (BE), 1:387.

104. Knight III, *Presence of God*, 151.

105. Wesley, "Means of Grace," in *Works* (BE), 1:388.

106. Borgen, *John Wesley on Sacraments*, 115–6.

107. Wesley, "Means of Grace," in *Works* (BE), 1:396.

108. Knight III, *Presence of God*, 149.

109. Ibid.

Book of God! I have it. Here is knowledge enough for me. Let me be *homo unius libri* (i.e., a man of one book). . . . I sit down alone: only God is here. In his presence I open, I read his Book; for this end, to find the way to heaven. . . . I lift up my heart to the Father of lights: 'Lord, is it not thy Word,' . . . I then search after and consider parallel passages of Scripture, 'comparing spiritual things with spiritual' [1 Cor. 2:13]. I meditate thereon, with all the attention and earnestness of which my mind is capable.

I have accordingly set down in the following sermons what I find in the Bible concerning the way to heaven, with a view to distinguish this way of God from all those which are the inventions of men. I have endeavored to describe the true, the scriptural, experimental religion, so as to omit nothing which is a real part thereof, and to add nothing thereto which is not.[110]

Albert Outler clarifies that the expression *homo unius libri* is not to be taken literally. When Wesley indicates that he is *a man of one book*, it is in reference to the primacy of Scripture. He was an avid reader of literature beyond the Bible. *Homo unius libri* was a statement of "hermeneutical principle that Scripture would be his court of first and last resort in faith and morals."[111] Therefore, it is natural that Scripture stands among those channels, which for Wesley are the chief means of grace.

Borgen reminds us that preaching has from the beginning been one of the foremost methods within Methodism of hearing the Word.[112] It is therefore included within the means Wesley referred to as searching the Scriptures. Although initially Wesley's preaching focused predominately upon the conversion of unbelievers, this homiletical practice eventually shifted to encompass the entire *via salutis*. During a meeting in Bristol in 1745, he addressed his preaching practices:

At first we preached almost wholly to unbelievers. To these, therefore, we spake almost continually of remission of sins through the death of Christ and the nature of faith in his blood. And so we do still, among those who need to be taught the first elements of the gospel of Christ. But those in whom the foundation is already laid we exhort to go on to perfection; which we did not see so clearly at first; although we occasionally spoke of it from the beginning. Yet we now preach, and that continually,

---

110. Wesley, "Sermons Several Occasions Preface," in *Works* (BE), 1:105–6.

111. Outler, "Introduction," in *Works* (BE), 1:57.

112. Borgen, *John Wesley on Sacraments*, 116.

faith in Christ, as the Prophet, Priest, and King, at least, as clearly, as strongly, and as fully, as we did six years ago.[113]

Due to the dynamic nature of spiritual growth and since he was preaching to those who were walking in various stages of faith, Wesley found it important to preach the entire "*history of God,*"[114] found in both the Old and New Testaments.

Although preaching falls under searching the Scriptures as a means of grace, Knight warns that there exists a significant difference between the two. Intrinsically Scripture is always a sufficient channel of God's grace; however, sermons have the potential of misrepresenting biblical truth by failing to address thoroughly the *via salutis*.[115] If sermons are to function as a means of grace they must preach the whole gospel:

> I mean by 'preaching the gospel' preaching the love of God to sinners, preaching the life, death, resurrection, and the intercession of Christ, with all the blessings which in consequence thereof are freely given to true believers. . . .
>
> By 'preaching the law' I mean, explaining and enforcing the commands of Christ, briefly comprised in the Sermon on the Mount.
>
> Some think, preaching the law only; others, preaching the gospel only. I think, neither the one nor the other; but duly mixing both, in every place, if not in every sermon.[116]

Sermons have the capacity to either be an instrument of the Holy Spirit or destructive in nature. If the sermon misrepresents scriptural truth or if it presents only one part of the truth, then it can obstruct the work of God. The whole of Scripture must be preached.

Wesley reminds us that recipients of the sermon are in different stages in their relationship with Christ, and some are unbelievers. Therefore, they must hear both the law and the forgiveness offered through God's grace. Randy Maddox specifies if the sermon is to function as a means of grace then Christ must be represented in all his offices as prophet, priest, and king. The sermon should assure "us of God's pardoning love (Priest), while simultaneously revealing our remaining need (Prophet), and leading our further growth in Christ-likeness (King)."[117]

113. Wesley, "Bristol Conference," in *Works* (BE), 10:152.

114. Wesley, "On Divine Providence," in *Works* (BE), 2:536.

115. Knight III, *Presence of God*, 156.

116. Wesley, "To an Evangelical Layman," in *Works* (BE), 26:482–3.

117. Maddox, *Responsible Grace*, 209.

The whole of Scripture must be preached!

Campbell indicates that content was not the only concern Wesley had for his preachers. He admonished them to refrain from incorporating distracting gestures, facial expressions, bodily motions, or mannerisms that could infringe upon the message.[118] Likewise, they were to avoid irregularities in speaking. Among those issues Wesley admonished his preachers to consider were irregularities such as speaking too slow or too fast, speaking with an uneven voice, and using *unnatural tones*. "But the greatest and most common fault of all is speaking with a tone: Some have a womanish, squeaking tone; some a singing or canting one; some an high, swelling, theatrical tone, laying too much emphasis on every sentence, some have an awful, solemn tone; others an odd, whimsical, whining tone, not to be expressed in words."[119] The essence of Wesley's concern was the avoidance of anything that might obstruct the work of the Holy Spirit in moving the affections of those present.[120] The benchmark for finding the appropriate voice in preaching was simple: "Speak in public just as you do in common conversation. . . . Deliver it in the same manner as if you were talking to a friend."[121]

The Hymns

The hymnody characteristic of the revivals, small group meetings, and worship of the Wesleyan movement were experiential in nature but also served to provide doctrinal instruction to the Methodists. The most important of the Wesleyan hymnals was *A Collection of Hymns for the Use of the People Called Methodists (Collection).* Unlike other writers of the era, "every line [of the Wesley hymns] is a 'short hymn on select passages of the Holy Scripture.'"[122] Writing in the preface to the *Collection,* Wesley notes:

> It is large enough to contain all the important truths of our most holy religion, whether speculative or practical; yea, to illustrate them all, and to prove them both by Scripture and reason. . . . The hymns are not carelessly jumbled together, but carefully ranged under proper heads, according to the experience of real Christians. So that this book is in effect a little body of experimental and practical divinity.[123]

118. Campbell, *Religion of the Heart,* 123–4.

119. Wesley, "Directions Concerning Pronunciation," in *Works* (Jackson), 13:520.

120. Ibid., 525.

121. Ibid., 520.

122. Hildebrandt, Beckerlegge, and Dale, "Introduction," in *Works* (BE), 7:5.

123. Wesley, "Preface," in *Works* (BE), 7:74.

Wesley acknowledges that he did not compose most of the hymns found in the *Collection*;[124] rather most were the work of his brother Charles. However, John served as editor, and every hymn found in the *Collection* had to pass through the scrutiny of the editor's pen. It was John who not only selected the hymns for inclusion, but he examined each verse and deleted those not meeting with his approval. "It was John who took the liberty at times revising his brother's verses; it was John who arranged them so as to be a little body of divinity."[125]

Although the hymns are not listed by Wesley as one of the chief means, Knight indicates that they functioned as a means of grace.[126] There is no question that the hymns were of immense importance to the Methodists. Franz Hildebrandt contends that it is improbable that the Methodist revival would have occurred apart from the Wesleyan hymnody.[127]

The hymns were designed to address various themes within the entire scope of the *via salutis*, ranging from God's initial work of prevenient grace to the culminating goal of Christian perfection.[128] The religious experience described in the hymns is both imbued with Scripture and rooted in authentic human experience. Louis Benson indicates that the experiences in the *Collection* are a reflection of the whole range of affections encountered by the Wesleys in their spiritual journey.[129] However, Oliver Beckerlegge refutes the notion that Wesley used the hymns to "impose his own experience and his own preconceived theories of the nature of religious experience and growth on his people."[130] The Wesleyan hymns were not only a reflection of the Wesleys' own quest for a religion of the heart, but they were also the result of the religious experiences they had observed in others.

Wesley designed the *Collection* not simply as a hymnal. It facilitates spiritual nurture and provides catechesis by teaching an extensive range of doctrinal truths. Additional light has been shed upon this by Craig Gallaway's work on Methodist hymnody. He argues that the *Collection* is comprehensive in addressing the whole of Christian experience. The arrangement of the hymns is not random, but rather ordered in accord with the *via salutis*:

> If we examine the hymns of the Collection in the light of the
> elements already cited (repentance, justification, new birth,

124. Ibid.
125. Hildebrandt, Beckerlegge, and Dale, "Introduction," in *Works* (BE), 7:56.
126. Knight III, *Presence of God*, 166–7.
127. Hildebrandt, Beckerlegge, and Dale, "Introduction," in *Works* (BE), 7:1.
128. Knight III, *Presence of God*, 164.
129. Benson, *English Hymn*, 249.
130. Hildebrandt, Beckerlegge, and Dale, "Introduction," in *Works* (BE), 7:62.

sanctification, and perfection), we shall find that the hymn-
book follows just this pattern and sequence in the arrangement
of its five Parts. We shall also begin to discover, however, that
the exploration of these "themes" in the context of the hymns
intended for worship leads quite inevitably beyond the description of soteriology or experience per se. . . .

It will become apparent that the via salutis points beyond
itself, as a reflection on Christian experience, to the reality of
God's grace in Christ manifest in the ongoing formation of the
worshipping community.[131]

Their use of the hymns, the design of the hymnal pursuant to the *via
salutis*, and the way the Wesleys incorporated Scripture and biblical imagery
into their hymnody are not all that separated them from their contemporaries. Although Scripture was his primary text, Charles did not limit his
lyrics to Scripture alone but found sources in both classical and contemporary literature. Additionally, the hymns of Charles Wesley encompassed
"a body of divinity designed to illuminate not only Scripture, but also the
prayer book."[132]

It was the scriptural content and rich biblical imagery of the Wesleyan
hymns, their embodiment of authentic religious experience, their arrangement in the *Collection*, and their use in Methodist worship that worked
together to both counter formalism and prevent tendencies toward enthusiasm. When used in worship, the nature of the Wesleyan hymns enabled
them to bridge the tension between formalism and enthusiasm, rather than
launching the worshipper into an inordinate subjective experience leading
to ecstasy. This is due to the fact that the experience embodied in Wesleyan
hymnody is not egocentric; rather they are saturated with a calculated and
very precise use of "Christological imagery."[133] Knight points out that the
narrative and biblical imagery in the Wesleyan hymns serve as a means of
grace because they invite the worshipper into a more profound and dynamic encounter with God which can lead to growth and transformation
into Christlikeness.[134]

131. Craig B. Gallaway, "Presence of Christ," 42–45; italics mine.

132. Routley, *Musical Wesleys*, 31–32.

133. Gallaway, "Presence of Christ," 92.

134. Knight III, *Presence of God*, 166–7.

The Eucharist

J. Ernest Rattenbury provides insight into the significance of the eucharist for the Wesleyan movement. He states, "The early Methodists flocked to the celebration of Holy Communion in such numbers that the clergy were really embarrassed with the multitude of communicants with which they had to deal."[135] He also suggests that it was the Methodist emphasis placed upon the sacrament that, by the end of the eighteenth century, revealed a noticeable improvement in the frequency of Anglican eucharistic practice.[136]

Wesley's own eucharistic practice, as well as its central place in his writing, teaching, and preaching, established the Lord's supper at the forefront of the Wesleyan movement. The Methodist avidity towards the eucharist was the result of an inward religion that burned fervently within their hearts.[137] It was through the means of preaching and the implementation of all God's ordinances that an evangelical revival was ignited that swept across England. Due to the Wesleys' emphasis upon and the Methodist hunger for the Lord's supper, the evangelical revival proved to be a "*Sacramental revival.*"[138]

Wesley amplifies the preeminent place of the eucharist in his liturgical theology and praxis by his insistence that Methodists should participate in this sacrament as often as possible. Since he was not a dissenter, and because he didn't want to give cause for his people to separate from the Anglican Church, he expected the Methodists to receive communion in their parish churches. It was required that the eucharist be celebrated by ordained clergy. Maddox points out that over time obstacles emerged that prevented many Methodists from communicating with any great frequency.[139] In-

135. Rattenbury, *Eucharistic Hymns*, 2.

136. The national church's general neglect of the eucharist during the eighteenth-century is documented by various scholars; see Rattenbury, *Eucharistic Hymns*, 2; Sykes, Booty, and Knight, *Study of Anglicanism*, 23–24; Neill, *Anglicanism*, 192, 195.

137. Wesley records in his journal several instances of rather large numbers of participants celebrating the eucharist. On many occasions they numbered nearly one thousand or more. Although not exhaustive, the following references exemplify some of Wesley's remarks on the numbers that communicated. See Wesley, "Journal September 1782 to June 1786," in *Works* (BE), 23:269, 302, 325, 348, 387; Wesley, "Journal June 1786 to October 1790," in *Works* (BE), 23:404, 408; Wesley, "Journal January 1787 to October 1790," in *Works* (BE), 24:46, 59–60, 76, 102, 128, 146, 186, 193.

138. Rattenbury, *Eucharistic Hymns*, 1–5; italics mine.

139. Maddox, *Responsible Grace*, 202–5. According to Maddox one problem resulted from many Methodists being Nonconformists. These traditions did not celebrate the Lord's supper as frequently as Wesley urged his Methodists to practice the sacrament. Also, conflict between some Methodist societies and their local parishes caused some Methodists to be absent from Sunday worship.

creasingly Wesley accepted the necessity of "celebrating the Lord's Supper in society meetings"[140] on the condition that an ordained Methodist preacher officiated.

His sermon "The Duty of Constant Communion," not only sets forth his argument for the necessity of constant communion but also describes its purpose in the *via salutis*. Outler states that this sermon is "Wesley's fullest and most explicit statement of his eucharistic doctrine and practice."[141] For Wesley the benefits offered make the Lord's supper indispensable in the growth toward holiness:

> The grace of God given herein confirms to us the pardon of our sins by enabling us to leave them. As our bodies are strengthened by bread and wine, so are our souls by these tokens of the body and blood of Christ. This is the food of our souls: this gives strength to perform our duty, and leads us on to perfection. If therefore we have any regard for the plain command of Christ, if we desire the pardon of our sins, if we wish for strength to believe, to love and obey God, then we should neglect no opportunity of receiving the Lord's Supper. . . . Whoever therefore does not receive, but goes from the holy table when all things are prepared, either does not understand his duty or does not care for the dying command of his Saviour, the forgiveness of his sins, the strengthening of his soul, and the refreshing it with the hope of glory.[142]

Wesley envisions the benefits of the eucharist in a manner that transcends the Anglican tradition. His sermon "The Means of Grace" provides insight into Wesley's understanding of the essence of the grace communicated when the bread and cup are received:

> The cup of blessing which we bless, is it not the communion (or communication) of the blood of Christ? The bread which we break, is it not the communion of the body of Christ?" [1 Cor. 10:16] Is not the eating of the bread, and the drinking of that cup, the outward, visible means whereby God conveys into our souls all that spiritual grace, that righteousness, and peace, and joy in the Holy Ghost, which were purchased by the body of Christ once broken and the blood of Christ once shed for

---

140. Ibid., 202–3.

141. Outler, "Duty: Introductory Comment," in *Works* (BE), 3:427–8.

142. Wesley, "Duty of Constant Communion," in *Works* (BE), 3:429.

us? Let all, therefore, who truly desire the grace of God, eat that bread and drink of that cup.[143]

Although the eucharist was generally viewed as the chief confirming ordinance, Wesley "affirmed it to be a converting ordinance as well."[144] He believed it served to communicate preventing, justifying, or sanctifying grace. Still, as Sanders points out, Wesley was keenly "aware of the danger of *idolizing* the means of grace rather than *using them as means*."[145] He gives the same warning for the eucharist as he does all the ordinances; however, when it is received with a sincere faith, the Lord's supper is a real means of God's grace.[146] Wesley records in his journal the experience of a woman who received the new birth while participating in the sacrament:

> I think I did not meet with one woman of the society who had not been upon the point of casting away her confidence in God. I then indeed found one who, when many . . . laboured to persuade her she had no faith, replied, with a spirit they were not able to resist, 'I know that "the life I now live, I live by faith in the Son of God, who loved me, and gave himself for me." [Cf. Gal 2:20] And he has never left me one moment, since the hour he was made known to me in the breaking of the bread.'
>
> What is to be inferred from this undeniable matter of fact— one that had not faith received it in the Lord's Supper? Why, (1) that there are 'means of grace', i.e., outward ordinances, whereby the inward grace of God is ordinarily conveyed to man, whereby the faith that brings salvation is conveyed to them who before had it not; (2) that one of these means is the Lord's Supper; and (3) that he who has not this faith ought to wait for it in the use both of this and of the other means which God hath ordained.[147]

The testimony Wesley observed in others convinced him that the Lord's supper was far more than simply a memorial of Christ's death. When Wesley declared the Lord's supper a converting ordinance his argument is situated in God's freedom to communicate his grace through "whatever

143. Wesley, "Means of Grace," in *Works* (BE), 1:389–90.

144. Borgen, *John Wesley on Sacraments*, 119.

145. Sanders, "An Appraisal Wesley's Sacramentalism," 133.

146. Wesley, "Means of Grace," in *Works* (BE), 1:378–400. Although Wesley strongly affirmed that God transmits his grace through the various ordinances, he continually warns of the dangers of the means of grace becoming an end in themselves. He constantly asserts that there is no inherent power in God's ordinances. Those who participate in the means of grace without hearts that are earnestly seeking God are to be most pitied because such actions are done in vain.

147. Wesley, "Journal November 1739 to September 1741," in *Works* (BE), 19:120–1.

means he chooses, or without any means at all."[148] Wesley had personally witnessed several persons who experienced conversion while partaking of the Lord's supper.

While Maddox points out that Wesley establishes "no consistent hierarchy"[149] with the means of grace, since all are therapeutically essential, scholars have properly argued that he held the eucharist in very high regard. It was "the means of grace *par excellence*."[150] Wesley referred to it as the "grand channel"[151] whereby God communicates his grace to those who are seeking him.

When Wesley speaks of experiencing the *real presence* of Christ in the sacrament, it is crucial to understand that his is a drastic departure from Lutheran or Roman Catholic perspectives. Contrary to those traditions, Wesley rejects both consubstantiation and transubstantiation, which state that a change occurs in the substance of the elements. Even his personal view on the real presence changed as he matured. The *benefit*, for Wesley, transitioned from *a thing to possess* into a relationship which was more dynamic in nature. Maddox explains this transition in Wesley's eucharistic theology:

> [An] important contribution that Wesley's mother may have made was to suggest an emphasis on the agency of the Holy Spirit as the means by which Christ is present to faithful communicants. At the time the early Wesley was content simply to affirm that Christ's divinity is united with believers in communion. As his equation of grace with the Presence of the Holy Spirit (and correlated support of the epiclesis) matured, he more frequently specified that it was through the Spirit that Christ's benefits are present to faithful participants in the communion service. . . . What we encounter in communion is not the static presence of a "benefit" but the pardoning and empowering Presence of a "Person."[152]

Maddox also insists that it is because the benefits are dynamic, rather than static, that Wesley urges *constant communion*. The eucharist, as in all the means of grace, is therapeutic; therefore, participation over time contributes to the healing of the soul from the disease of sin. The more one receives the

148. Borgen, *John Wesley on Sacraments*, 197–8.

149. Maddox, *Responsible Grace*, 202.

150. Borgen, *John Wesley on Sacraments*, 120.

151. Wesley, "Upon Sermon on the Mount (VI)," in *Works* (BE), 1:585.

152. Maddox, *Responsible Grace*, 204.

eucharist in faith, the deeper that individual grows in his or her "encounter with God's empowering love."[153]

Innovations in Methodist worship

Baker indicates Wesley's exposure and experimentation with several un-usual religious practices originated in Georgia. This would include such things as his use of hymns "as opposed to metrical psalms"[154] in worship, as well as including laity in the work of parish ministry. His time in Georgia and return home by ship introduced him to "extempore prayer, extempore preaching, [and] preaching in the open air."[155] Baker believes the reason John experimented with these atypical methods was twofold. He reasoned that the frontier conditions of Georgia required innovation, but also, at that point in his life, he was "prepared to respond to realized need by any allow-able method"[156] so far as it did not violate Scripture.

The affective innovations in Methodist practice were not limited to extempore prayer or open air preaching, but they also encompassed the special services such as "the *love-feast* borrowed from the Moravians, the *watchnight*, a prudential adaption of the vigils of the early church, and the *covenant service*, which owed its origin to English Puritanism."[157] It was in Georgia where John initially encountered the love feast. The *agape* meal had its roots in the primitive church and in that context typically preceded the eucharist. Normally the love feast involved the sharing of bread and water. Moravians at times used bread and wine but then resorted to water only to avoid confusion with the eucharist. The love feast was reserved for so-ciety members only and required a ticket for admittance. Rack states that initially this practice among Methodists was used exclusively in the bands, but eventually it was extended to the whole society. The sharing of bread and water was accompanied with "testimonies, . . . prayers, hymns, and conversation."[158]

Traditionally the watch night service was reserved for the last night of the year and focused upon preparedness for Christ's second coming.[159] Wes-ley often observed the watch night on the Friday evening nearest the full

153. Ibid.

154. Baker, *John Wesley*, 51.

155. Ibid.

156. Ibid.

157. Ibid., 87; italics mine.

158. Rack, *Reasonable Enthusiast*, 410–11.

159. Tucker, *American Methodist Worship*, 67.

moon, typically lasting from mid-evening until a few minutes after midnight. It was a solemn service consisting of prayer, praise, and thanksgiving.[160]

Wesley's covenant service, like the love feast, was a private gathering of Methodist society members. Its purpose was to ritually express one's covenant commitment to God and "as a means of engaging his people together in the pursuit of more serious religion."[161] Typically eucharistic observance concluded the service.

The love feast, watch night service, and Wesley's covenant service found their way to North America and were important festivals in the spiritual life of American Methodists, but were services distinct from the prayer book tradition.[162] The love feast was one of the great festivals of Methodism and was practiced with zeal. It was celebrated in local congregations, at quarterly meetings, and during annual and quadrennial Methodist gatherings.[163] Gradually the love feast experienced decline within Methodism, and towards the end of the nineteenth century it started disappearing from Methodist practice, although it was never completely lost. While the love feast, watch night, and covenant services were to some extent implemented by the various holiness streams that eventually comprised the Church of the Nazarene, it was the love feast that would prove to be a beloved and important celebration for Phineas F. Bresee and many of the early Nazarenes.

Concluding Remarks on Wesley's Liturgical Thought

Each means of grace intrinsic to the liturgy has its own unique function. Borgen elaborates further, "Fasting is a great aid to prayer . . . prayer accompanies all of the other means, and serves the function of preparing him who prays, leading him into a frame of mind where he is both willing and able to receive God's grace . . . God uses [Scripture] to bestow spiritual life as well as sustaining and increasing life. . . . The Lord's Supper was usually considered the chief and superior confirming ordinance. But experience taught Wesley differently, and he affirmed it to be a converting ordinance as well."[164]

However, even though each of God's ordinances possesses a different function, it would be incorrect to assume they operate in isolation. Wesley believed that God uses the means in concert with each other to communicate

---

160. Ibid., 65–67.

161. Heitzenrater, *People Called Methodists*, 165.

162. Tucker, *American Methodist Worship*, 60.

163. Ibid., 63; Ruth, *Little Heaven Below*, 20.

164. Borgen, *John Wesley on Sacraments*, 118–9.

his grace. He explains God's redemptive activity through the means in the following analogy:

> We may observe there is a kind of order wherein God himself is generally pleased to use these means in bringing a sinner to salvation. A stupid, senseless wretch is going on in his own way, not having God in all his thoughts, when God comes upon him unawares, perhaps by an awakening sermon or conversation . . . or it may be an immediate stroke of his convincing Spirit, without any outward means at all. . . . If he finds a preacher who speaks to the heart, he is amazed, and begins 'searching the Scriptures.' . . . The more he hears and reads, the more convinced he is; and the more he meditates thereon day and night. . . . He begins also to talk of the things of God, to pray to him. . . . He wants to pray with those who know God, with the faithful 'in the great congregation.' But here he observes others go up to 'the table of the Lord.' He considers, Christ has said, 'Do this.' How is that I do not? I am too great a sinner. I am not fit. I am not worthy. After struggling with these scruples a while, he breaks through. And thus he continues in God's way—in hearing, reading, meditating, praying, and partaking of the Lord's Supper—til God, in the manner that pleases him, speaks to his heart, 'Thy faith hath saved thee; go in peace.'[165]

Wesley's example reveals to us the correlation that exists between the various means of grace found within the liturgy. However, this is not to suggest that God cannot use the means independently, but rather to highlight Wesley's belief that if the liturgy failed to incorporate all the instituted means (i.e., prayer, searching the Scriptures, and the eucharist) it was deficient.[166] Therefore, since God has chosen to use the means collectively, it is essential to thoughtfully incorporate these means into the liturgical design. Each ordinance has its own purpose, but they work corporately, within the liturgy to therapeutically address the problem of sin.

---

165. Wesley, "Means of Grace," in *Works* (BE), 1:393–4.

166. Wesley, "Annual Minutes 1766," in *Works* (BE), 10:325–6. Although the hymns were extremely important in Wesley's liturgy, they were not one of the instituted means, but rather they were a prudential means effectively used by the Methodists. This also suggests that it is possible for other items to be integrated into the liturgy, which could potentially function as prudential means of grace. However, any attempts at introducing new elements into the liturgy with such intentions should be approached with caution. It is important to note that the Wesleyan hymns functioned as a means of grace precisely because they were imbued with Scripture and thoughtfully incorporated into the liturgy.

Previously it was noted that Wesley expected the Methodists to attend worship in their parish churches. The society meetings were not designed to be a substitute for public worship. Maddox maintains that Wesley's fervent desire for his people to attend parish worship was driven more by "soteriological [rather] than ecclesiastical concerns."[167] The *BCP* liturgy was of prime importance as a means of grace in nurturing people in the ongoing pursuit of holiness. The failure of any individual to include the Church's liturgy in their discipline would have significant spiritual consequences.[168]

As the absence of many Methodists from worship in the Anglican Church proved increasingly problematic, Wesley eventually started assimilating more elements of the *BCP* liturgy into society meetings. However, he was selective of those elements he incorporated into Methodist worship. Maddox indicates that Wesley was concerned to integrate only those components that were "'edifying' in practice, *and* for which he believed he could find scriptural and 'primitive' warrant."[169] Obviously, this assimilation and the result of Methodists practicing the liturgy in the societies and outside of the State Church were not Wesley's ideal but rather were incorporated out of necessity.

The evolution of much of Wesley's liturgical thought eventually appears in the *Sunday Service*, which was a modified version of the *BCP* designed with the American context in mind with its demographic and cultural idiosyncrasies. White reminds us of the importance of the *Sunday Service* for Wesleyan theology and praxis. Not only is it a "prime source for liturgical theology . . . [but also] the distinctive elements of the whole Wesleyan movement are shown in the way Wesley orders worship."[170]

It is well documented that the American Methodists quickly abandoned the *Sunday Service* not long after Wesley's death.[171] This was primarily because of their increasing desire for spontaneity and the pursuit of freedom in worship. Most American Methodists even considered Wesley's modified prayer book far too binding, and with the patriarch of Method-

---

167. Maddox, *Responsible Grace*, 206.

168. Wesley continually warned against schism with the Church of England and encouraged his people to attend the Anglican liturgy even though they may experience difficulty from other Anglicans not sympathetic to the Methodist movement. For Wesley, a sound and complete liturgy, like that found in the *BCP*, was essential to spiritual growth; see Wesley, "The Important Question," in *Works* (BE), 3:189; Wesley, "Reasons Against Separation," in *Works* (BE), 9:339; Wesley, "Farther Appeal Part I," in *Works* (BE), 11:122; Wesley, "Annual Minutes 1766," in *Works* (BE), 10:325–6.

169. Maddox, *Responsible Grace*, 206.

170. White, "Introduction," in *John Wesley's Sunday Service*, 16.

171. For further discussion on the Methodist departure from the *Sunday Service*, see Wade, "History Public Worship," 87–206; Tucker, *American Methodist Worship*, 8–12; White, "Introduction," in *John Wesley's Sunday Service*, 12.

ism gone, the *Sunday Service* quickly fell into disuse. The following chapter will examine the liturgical developments in North America occurring after Wesley's departure; and preceding the American holiness movement and the birth of the Church of the Nazarene a century later. This will set the stage for an exploration of Nazarene liturgical development and the forces that influenced it from its beginning to the present day.

Chapter 3

The Development and Nature of Worship from American Methodism to the Church of the Nazarene

UNDERSTANDING CURRENT WORSHIP TRENDS and practices in the Church of the Nazarene requires an investigation of the complex dynamics surrounding the evolution of worship within American Methodism during the eighteenth and nineteenth centuries. As previously discussed, for Wesley liturgical practice and theology was a central component in pursuing inward holiness. However, the connection between Wesley's worship theology and practice within his Anglican context and the pursuit of Christian perfection was lost upon our Nazarene forebears. With few exceptions, they viewed the forms of worship found in the *BCP* and other prayer books as a hindrance to spiritual growth and not as a means to cultivate it. Instead they sought out forms of worship that were spontaneous and free. Understanding the dissociation between the pursuit of inward holiness and Wesley's liturgical theology and praxis requires a review of the circumstances that precipitated this separation. The rift between praxis and belief was, for the most part, realized prior to the American holiness movement and the origins of the Church of the Nazarene. It began in the early days of American Methodism following the Revolutionary War.

The Nature of Methodist Worship in the American Colonies

The war of the American colonies over political freedom and independence from England had significant consequences for ecclesial relationships. Regardless of the respect the North American Methodists had reserved for

Wesley, their desire for freedom from British interference was absolute. Wesley had, in a sense, aggravated the situation with his "ill-considered tract against the rebellion."[1] It resulted in accusations from American patriots that the Methodists were Tories. The repercussions of this series of events meant suffering for both "individuals and congregations."[2] Wesley's support of the crown had served to increase the strain in his relations with American Methodists. Wesley notes the seriousness of this contention, and his growing angst toward the American leadership, in a letter to Charles in October 1775:

> I find a danger of a new kind—a danger of losing my love for the Americans: I mean for their miserable leaders; for the poor sheep are "more sinned against than sinning," especially since the amazing informations [sic] which I have received from John Ireland. Yet it is certain the bulk of the people both in England and America mean no harm; they only follow their leaders, and do as they are bid without knowing why or wherefore.[3]

Rack points out that publicly Wesley instructed his preachers to be neutral in the conflict; however, the reality was that "most of them sympathized with the King's party."[4] Eventually the ensuing conflict resulted in the departure of nearly all of Wesley's clergy; by 1778, only Francis Asbury was left to tend the American flock.

Transitions from English Methodism in the Late Eighteenth Century

During the 1784 Christmas Conference in Baltimore, several months after the war concluded, the Methodist Episcopal Church was born. The new church exhibited its freshly acquired freedom by electing Asbury and Coke as its first Superintendents.[5] Although the American Methodists were willing to adopt Wesley's discipline, liturgy, and articles, they had chosen their

---

1. Smith, "John Wesley's Religion," in Dieter, *19th Century Holiness Movement*, 33.

2. Ibid.

3. Wesley, *Letters of Wesley*, 179.

4. Rack, *Reasonable Enthusiast*, 487.

5. Ibid., 516–7. Rack points out that it was Wesley's desire for Asbury and Coke to be Superintendents; however, Asbury insisted on being elected by the Americans, which they promptly did at the 1784 Christmas Conference. The name Methodist Episcopal Church was adopted a few years after the conference, and in 1787 the term superintendent was eventually changed to bishop.

own leadership and were in effect distancing themselves from his oversight. Asbury affirmed such sentiments of liberty when in an August 1788 letter he confided to Jasper Winscom his thoughts on the matter:

> I write to you as my confidential friend: my real sentiments are union but no subordination, connexion but no subjection. I am sure that no man or number of men in England can direct either the head or the body here unless he or they should possess divine powers, be omnipotent, omniscient, and omnipresent. That one thousand preachers traveling and local; and thirty thousand people would submit to a man they never have nor can see, his advice they will follow as far as they judge it right. For our old, old Daddy to appoint conferences when and where he was pleased, to appoint a joint superintendent with me, were strokes of power we did not understand.[6]

Heitzenrater states that the newly established church "relied heavily upon the precedents of the British Wesleyans and acknowledged a polite respect for Wesley. Nevertheless, American Methodism already bore the indelible marks of American liberty on its foundation, some of which Wesley could never understand."[7]

Clearly the desire for freedom, which was characteristic of American culture, affected the use and acceptance of Wesley's *Sunday Service* and the implementation of his liturgical *ordo*. Still there were other factors that posed problems for the Methodist liturgy as well. Earlier it was noted that Wesley expected the Methodists to partake of the Lord's supper as often as possible. Even the British Wesleyans found that it was not always possible to comply with his desire for "constant communion."[8] Often this problem resulted from the infrequent celebration of the sacrament in some Anglican churches or due to tensions between the societies and local parishes. Wesley eventually countered these obstacles by adding the Lord's supper to society worship. This remedy was infeasible in the American context. Even though Wesley expected the eucharist to be celebrated every Lord's Day, there were not enough ordained clergy to administer the sacrament.[9] Therefore Wesley's expectation of weekly communion for the American Methodists was unrealistic. Not only did the American Methodists lack enough elders to

6. Asbury, *Letters*, 63.

7. Heitzenrater, *People Called Methodists*, 292.

8. Wesley, "Duty of Constant Communion," in *Works* (BE), 3:427–39.

9. Wesley, "Letter of September 10, 1784," in *John Wesley's Sunday Service*, ii.

preside over the feast, but they "were as unaccustomed as [the] Anglicans of the time to weekly eucharist."[10]

Despite the official acceptance of the *Sunday Service* at the 1784 Baltimore Conference, its actual use by the American church is in question. Tucker indicates that while some congregations accepted and used the *Sunday Service*, especially those churches located in more urban areas, most Methodists preferred a simpler preaching service void of written forms.[11] Many congregations and clergy found the *Sunday Service* both foreign to their custom of worship and far too confining for the freedom and spontaneity they so greatly valued in worship. There were additional obstacles to Wesley's liturgy. The cost of acquiring it may have proved too great for the poor. Those who were illiterate were most likely drawn to the "energetic preaching, extempore prayer, and . . . [the] hymn singing"[12] of Methodist worship and not the more objective forms of the liturgy.

Many Methodists had in practice abandoned the prayer book not long after its arrival; however, officially radical changes to the *Sunday Service* did not occur until after Wesley's death in 1791. Tucker summarizes the fate of the Methodist liturgy following the General Conference of 1792:

> References to the Methodist "liturgy" or "prayer book" in the official Discipline . . . were completely struck from the Discipline in 1792. Morning and evening prayer services, the Litany, the psalter, the lectionary, and the propers disappeared and were replaced by a set of rubrics. . . . The rites of baptism, Lord's Supper, marriage, burial, and ordination from the Sunday Service were abbreviated, altered, and placed into a thirty-seven page section of the Discipline . . . "[13]

Clearly, significant alterations in the approved pattern of Methodist worship were made at the 1792 General Conference in Baltimore. However, what is not so evident is the motivation behind the basic repudiation of the *Sunday Service*. Although various theories regarding changes to the Methodist liturgy exist, for the most part mystery shrouds the reasons for the conference's action, since the minutes are no longer available.[14]

Even the measures adopted in 1792 allowing for more freedom in worship were not adhered to completely. The Methodist liturgy was to include a Scripture reading of one chapter from the Old and New Testaments, the

10. Tucker, *American Methodist Worship*, 7.

11. Ibid., 8.

12. Ibid.

13. Ibid., 9.

14. Wade, "History Methodist Worship," 94.

Lord's Prayer, and a benediction. Evidently there were churches omitting one or more of these elements. Similarly, license was taken with the sacraments. Some Methodists were either improvising on the ritual provided in the *Discipline* or neglecting it altogether.[15]

Tucker points out that during the early part of the nineteenth century attempts were made to bring uniformity to the structure of Methodist worship; however, such efforts were generally unsuccessful. Although many churches followed the approved worship order, there were others who desired greater liturgical freedom and felt at liberty to deviate from the order prescribed in the *Discipline*. Revivalism also had a significant impact on the liturgical *ordo*. Often practices were adopted that would lead to the evangelistic purposes of justification or entire sanctification. Following the lead of pioneers in American revivalism, like Charles Grandison Finney, Methodists opted for pragmatic methods to achieve these goals. Worship's structure was "determined by the worship leader's assessment of the spiritual needs of the community, not by some prescribed order, though the general pattern was to progress from the 'preliminaries' (e.g., singing, prayers, testimonies), to a 'message,' followed by an invitation to commitment."[16] Wade also supports the claim that Methodist worship was influenced by the Reformed and Presbyterian traditions. He observes that it was the emphasis on revivalism flowing out of these traditions which affected the shape of Methodist liturgy at the end of the eighteenth century.[17] The reasons for the radical changes to the *Sunday Service* are quite complex and beyond the scope of our discussion. However, it is significant to note the direct impact the decision of the 1792 General Conference had upon the shape of Methodist worship, and the residual effect it levied against the liturgy of those holiness groups with significant ties to the Methodist liturgical tradition.

The immediate result upon Methodist liturgical practice has been debated. Some have argued that the structure of the Methodist liturgy following the conference was a "non-sacramental pattern of public worship, consisting primarily of preaching with prayer, singing, and the public reading of Scripture."[18] Others suggest that some of the earlier appraisals of early American Methodist worship are not completely accurate. Ruth is among those who provide a richer portrait of early Methodist worship.

> When the writings of Methodist people themselves are explored in detail . . . a very different image emerges. Instead of liturgical

15. Ibid., 218.
16. Tucker, *American Methodist Worship*, 11–12.
17. Wade, "History Methodist Worship," 167–71.
18. Ibid., 88.

shallowness, early American Methodists practiced an amazing complexity of services and rituals. Instead of mere pragmatism and rabid individualism, they exulted in the communal dimension of their worship to the point where they struggled to find words adequate to describe their liturgical assembly. Instead of a sacramental depreciation, they exhibited a deep piety toward the Lord's Supper, a spirituality in continuity with Wesley in thought and practice. And instead of squandering their inheritance of hymnody and the Christian calendar, they supplemented and adapted what they received. In sum, early Methodists participated in what is now understood positively as inculturation.[19]

Ruth's examination of the quarterly meeting indicates that these gatherings, which were held every three months and lasted two days, were far more than a business meeting. Rather they provided a rich liturgical context for the Methodists. The quarterly meetings allowed for forms of worship that were difficult, if not impossible, in local congregations due to the nature of the itinerant ministry.[20]

During the latter part of the eighteenth century, the quarterly meeting found its way to the American Methodists via Wesley's itinerant preachers. Quarterly meetings initially only included a business session but became a focal point for multiple preaching services, the celebration of the Lord's supper, prayer meetings, and, on occasions, incorporated "distinctive Methodist services like love feasts and watch nights."[21] Although it did not always occur, often contained within these gatherings was the expectation of revival. Ruth points out that during the beginning days of the second Great Awakening, the quarterly meeting played an important part in contributing

19. Ruth, *Little Heaven Below*, 13–14. Ruth examines early Methodist worship through the lens of the Methodist Quarterly Meeting. He critiques previous scholarship for its heavy reliance upon liturgical texts, rather than considering people as the primary liturgical text. Ruth's investigation of early Methodist worship focuses upon the "voices" of Methodist people that appear in journals, diaries, letters, liturgical fragments, hymns, circuit records, histories, and autobiographies. These documents describe and provide insight into Methodist experiences of worship during the Quarterly Meetings. Ruth notes that the advantage of the Quarterly Meeting is that it provides a window into the "liturgical rhythms and practices" that were firmly established in early Methodist worship.

20. Ordained clergy were not always available to provide the sacraments, love feasts, and other pastoral rites. Even a weekly Sunday service was not available in all locations, especially those that were more rural. It was not uncommon in some circuits for an itinerant preacher to hold services once every two or three weeks in a local congregation. Generally, most communities *did not* have the benefit of worship occurring on Sunday. Tucker, *American Methodist Worship*, 6.

21. Ruth, *Little Heaven Below*, 20.

to the climate of revivalism.[22] The evangelistic atmosphere of the quarterly meeting was the predecessor to the great camp meetings, and it encompassed the complete sphere of Methodist liturgical practices.[23]

Further Developments in the Nineteenth Century

Changes in the nature of Methodism during the nineteenth century affected the structure of the quarterly meeting. Over time several contributing factors shifted the liturgical setting once found in the quarterly meeting to other Methodist gatherings. This would include the "two days' meetings"[24] (i.e., essentially the same format as the quarterly meetings but without the business conference), camp meetings, and various other forms of protracted meetings often unique to Methodism. During the early years of the nineteenth century, the revivals previously associated with the quarterly meeting were soon found in the camp meeting.[25]

Although not invented by the Methodists, the camp meeting had qualities similar to the quarterly meeting and therefore provided a form they quickly "adapted and transformed"[26] to meet their liturgical concerns. It became a medium "for large scale evangelical worship . . . throughout the nineteenth century by all the different branches of Methodism."[27] Worship emphasized not only the conversion of the lost but social change. Camp meetings frequently included celebration of the eucharist, love feasts, baptism, marriage rites, and the reception of members. Success was determined on a pragmatic basis by counting the number of those "who experienced tangibly and dramatically the power of God and claimed it for themselves."[28] Tucker notes that the influence of the camp meetings eventually impacted Sunday worship in local congregations and assisted in fueling the abandonment of Wesley's *Sunday Service*. Longing for the affectuous climate found in camp meetings some Methodist congregations adopted worship patterns modeled after revivalism. Elements included evangelistic-style preaching, testimonies, drawn-out extemporaneous prayers, the use of the communion rail for extended periods of prayer, and "camp meeting hymns."[29]

22. Ruth, "Reconsidering Second Great Awakening," 340–41.

23. Ruth, *Little Heaven Below*, 22.

24. Ibid., 185.

25. Tucker, *American Methodist Worship*, 74.

26. Ibid.

27. Ibid., 75.

28. Ibid., 77–81.

29. Ibid., 81.

Tucker indicates that along with the positive aspects of utilizing worship to emphasize evangelism, there was also a negative side to the camp meetings and other forms of revival. The influence of revivalism created an overemphasis on personal experience, while undermining the importance of community in the church body. This threatened the purpose of worship, which should focus upon the glorification of God, rather than following a direction that is overly subjective and centered upon the individual. Eventually this stress upon individualism and personal experience "contributed to the privatization of religion in America."[30]

It is evident that even after the abandonment of the *Sunday Service*, the early Methodists' liturgical tradition remained rich with their exuberant worship, sacramental emphasis, innovations in worship, and the variety of "liturgical outlets"[31] that they utilized to promote an inward religion. However, the rejection of a set liturgy made it difficult to bring uniformity in worship. Over time some congregations succumbed to the temptation to adopt a revivalistic liturgical model, inherent to camp meetings and other forms of protracted meetings, in their weekly Lord's Day worship. When a specified *ordo* was established in subsequent years, the Methodist liturgy favored that of the "revival structure."[32] The liturgical pragmatism that became evident in Methodism not only enabled them to devise creative means for evangelism, but it also provided the agency for further deviation from those liturgical principles that Wesley felt essential in maintaining the balance between formalism and enthusiasm.[33] This is especially true of the holiness groups that either branched off of Methodism or were heavily influenced by it in the mid to late nineteenth century. Likewise, the desire for spontaneity and liturgical freedom characteristic of American Methodist worship continued, not only in Methodism, but also in many of the groups, like the Church of the Nazarene, that descended from it.

Although Wesley granted the American Methodists liturgical freedom in his letter of September 10, 1784, by indicating that they were at "full liberty to follow the Scriptures and the primitive church,"[34] it was a qualified freedom. He had provided them with his version of the prayer book in the *Sunday Service* and set forth Scripture and the early church as the guiding

30. Ibid.

31. Ruth, "Reconcidering Second Great Awakening," 345.

32. Tucker, *American Methodist Worship*, 81.

33. The success of worship in the various liturgical outlets was often calculated by the number of individuals exhibiting a personal experience of the power of God in some measure. Methodists were creative in finding ways to both evangelize those seeking God and to encourage Christians in their daily commitment to Christ.

34. Tucker, *American Methodist Worship*, 272.

rule. Along with Wesley's letter and the *Sunday Service*, Tucker explains that the early Methodists were also provided with a book of discipline that addressed various worship-related topics. Therefore, they had at their disposal three authoritative sources for the liturgy, which "established that Methodist worship should not be haphazard, but rather organized according to certain principles."[35]

The Church of the Nazarene did not have the same standards that Wesley provided to the Methodists to guide their liturgical development. The denomination's formation is unique in that its genesis resulted from the union of several holiness streams emerging out of the American holiness movement during the latter part of the nineteenth century. The American holiness movement was rooted in the revivalism and camp meeting atmosphere of the early to mid-nineteenth century. The creation of the National Camp Meeting Association for the Promotion of Holiness (*NCMA*) in 1867 by a group of Methodist ministers ignited the revival fires temporarily dampened by the American Civil War.[36] Although John Inskip and NCMA leadership intentionally implemented strategies to prevent being accused of creating schisms or encouraging fanaticism, these strategies did not prevent the "creation of an ever-widening gulf between . . . the religion of the church and the religion of the camp meeting."[37] Ann Taves points out that despite the intention of the camp meeting movement to reform the church, it instead only amplified differences:

> During the last decades of the century, Methodist churches became more ornate. Worship, particularly in the cities, became more liturgical (that is, more "formal"), and traditional class meetings were gradually replaced with mission societies and service groups. At the same time, the leadership of the holiness movement encouraged the formation of regional, state, and local holiness associations modeled on the NCMA. . . . Holiness leaders insisted that the camp meeting was no substitute for the church; nevertheless, they had surrounded the camp meeting, which had never been a formal part of the Methodist church, with an array of associated structures. In so doing, they heightened rather than bridged the gulf between the local church and the camp meeting and unwittingly encouraged the formation of independent holiness denominations.[38]

35. Ibid.

36. Dieter, *Holiness Revival*, 98.

37. Taves, *Fits*, 232–5.

38. Ibid., 235.

The holiness streams that eventually merged to form the Church of the Nazarene sought worship structured after a revivalistic model that was spontaneous and free. They rejected many of the set forms of worship still found within the Methodist liturgy and other prayer book traditions, since they believed it was the chief cause of formalism. Ironically, in doing so they were further distancing themselves from the liturgy that Wesley loved and the essence of which he believed crucial in the pursuit of Christian perfection.

Discriminating Features of the Regional Denominations That Formed the Church of the Nazarene

When the Church of the Nazarene arrived on the scene at the beginning of the twentieth century, many of the limitations of eucharist observance faced by early Methodists did not exist. The days of the itinerant preacher were long past. Although the Lord's supper was valued by some segments of the denomination, the frequency of administering the eucharist did not uniformly increase throughout the denomination. Some of the merging bodies from the East and West were observing the Lord's supper monthly.[39] The testimonies of pastors and laity alike indicate that many had a high regard for the sacrament. However, these sentiments were by no means systemic. Most congregations celebrated communion less frequently and reduced it chiefly to memorial. Staples argues that the primary reason many of the descendants of the holiness movement observed the sacraments was because "Christ had commanded them"[40] to do so, and it was their practice in Methodism.

Wesley's sacramental theology and praxis did not become prominent in Nazarene theology and practice. Although the sacraments were valued by some of the churches, it was overshadowed by the revivalism of the day. The emphasis was upon Wesley's doctrine of Christian perfection and not upon his liturgical practice or sacramentalism.[41] The contributing cause behind this phenomenon finds its origins in the circumstances that led to

39. Prior to the merger the group in the East was known as the Association of Pentecostal Churches of America; the church in the West referred to itself as the Church of the Nazarene. Following the merger of the East and the West they were known as the Pentecostal Church of the Nazarene until "Pentecostal" was dropped in order for the denomination to distance itself from the tongues movement.

40. Staples, *Outward Sign*, 22.

41. Albeit this was a modified form of the doctrine, which diverged somewhat from Wesley's formulations and was influenced by the work of Phoebe Palmer and the American holiness movement.

the formation of the denomination. The Church of the Nazarene is not a split from Methodism or any other single denomination but rather involves the coming together of various denominational streams and theological traditions. Nazarene historian, Timothy Smith clarifies that the founding fathers came from a variety of backgrounds including: Baptist, Presbyterian, Congregationalist, Friends, and Methodist traditions.[42] Although this list is not exhaustive, it demonstrates the extent of the theological diversity present when the denomination was formed.

One of the problems the early leaders faced prior to merger was overcoming obstacles hindering the independent holiness streams from uniting. The various holiness denominations and associations seeking to merge differed in some areas of belief and practice, especially with issues concerning the sacraments and church order. One example of the extent of these differences is found in the conflicting baptismal practices of those regional denominations that eventually merged to form the Church of the Nazarene.[43] The New Testament Church of Christ believed that pouring should be the exclusive method of baptism. It rebaptized those candidates wishing to join their church who were previously baptized by another mode. Others insisted on immersion as the only appropriate mode.[44]

Horace G. Trumbauer records in his diary an instance of Bresee and the Church of the Nazarene negotiating over sacramental issues in order to facilitate merger. Trumbauer was presiding elder of the Pennsylvania conference of the Holiness Christian Church. It was a small denomination that had started in Pennsylvania and spread to Indiana. They were seeking to join the Church of the Nazarene when they were invited to attend the Chicago Assembly in 1907 as guests. The only significant hurdle revolved around the issue of infant baptism.

The Chicago Assembly was the first General Assembly of the Church of the Nazarene, which was organized to facilitate the joining of the Nazarenes in the West and the Association of Pentecostal Churches of America in the East. All holiness bodies open to the possibility of one day uniting with the Nazarenes were invited to send representatives to the Chicago

42. Smith, *Called Unto Holiness*, 21.

43. The three major regional groups that merged in 1907 and 1908 include the Church of the Nazarene on the West Coast, the Association of Pentecostal Churches of America in the East, and the Holiness Church of Christ in the South. There were, however, previous mergers from various holiness streams that united to form each of these regional groups prior to the larger mergers in 1907 and 1908.

44. Smith, *Called Unto Holiness*, 154, 171. The New Testament Church of Christ was one of the denominations in the southern stream. In 1904 it merged with the Independent Holiness Church to become the Holiness Church of Christ, which united with the Church of the Nazarene in 1908.

gathering.[45] Prior to an official committee meeting at the assembly Trumbauer met with C.W. Ruth and William Howard Hoople on October 9, 1907, to discuss the possibility of Trumbauer's Holiness Christian Church also uniting.[46] He makes the following entry into his diary: "Brothers Ruth and Hoople informed me that in the article on 'baptism,' our church was taken into consideration and that they believed it would be satisfactory to us."[47] When Trumbauer finally engaged Bresee and the legislative committee five days later, he raised the issue during the committee meeting: "In the afternoon I met with the 'Commission on Legislation,' to formulate articles on healing, baptism, etc. When I objected to infant baptism Dr. Bresee said to me, 'Would you object to other folks accepting it?' They struck out [of the *Manual*] for me the words 'for the remission of sins unto salvation.'"[48] Trumbauer in his diary entry is referring to the language of the article on Baptism which states,

> Baptism, by the ordination of Christ, is to be administered to repentant believers as declarative of their faith in Him as their Savior, for the remission of sins unto salvation, and the full purpose of obedience in holiness and righteousness. Baptism being the seal of the New Testament, young children may be baptized upon request of parents or guardians, who shall give assurance for them of necessary and Christian teaching.
>
> Whenever a person through conscientious scruples becomes desirous of again receiving the ordinance of baptism, it may be administered.
>
> Baptism may be administered by sprinkling, pouring or immersion, according to the choice of the applicant.[49]

The 1907 *Manual* reflects the changes noted by Trumbauer. The article on baptism underwent a significant reworking from the 1906 version to respond to obstacles posed by divergent beliefs of the various holiness streams. Alterations were made in response to the controversies over infant baptism, differences over baptismal mode, and rebaptism.[50] The issue was resolved

45. Ibid., 211.

46. C.W. Ruth was a Nazarene evangelist who had earlier been part of the Holiness Christian Church in Indiana. During his work as an evangelist he had been influential in negotiations between the various holiness groups. William Howard Hoople was, in 1907, a prominent leader in the Association of Pentecostal Churches in the East, which merged with the Nazarenes at the Chicago Assembly.

47. Trumbauer, "Horace G. Trumbauer Diary," 8.

48. Ibid., 14.

49. *Manual Nazarene* (1906), 23–24.

50. It is interesting to note that the Article in the 1907 *Manual* comes closer to

through compromise. Trumbauer was willing to accept wording which would allow infant baptism to be practiced by those who desire to do so in exchange for the removal of language that hinted at the idea of baptismal regeneration. The Pennsylvania Conference of Trumbauer's denomination joined the Nazarenes in 1908.[51]

Differences also arose in areas of church discipline. Streams from rural areas of the South were more concerned about outward behavior and "emphasized rigid standards of dress and behavior, and often scorned ecclesiastical discipline."[52] While all holiness streams were quite conservative in areas pertaining to behavior and appearance, the urban regions which were especially found in the heavily populated Northeast and West Coast were not as austere concerning "outward standards of holiness."[53] Surmounting these obstacles and others that were considered *non-essential* to the doctrine of Christian perfection could only be accomplished by compromise.

Essentials vs. Nonessentials and the Ramifications for the Liturgy

Due to the immense diversity of the merging streams, the early founders had to invoke a strategy to address disagreements. This is exemplified in the way they dealt with divergent theology and practices that were deemed *negotiable*. Stanley Ingersol points out that the leaders resolved these issues by focusing upon the Wesleyan doctrines concerning the *via salutis*, rather than upon practices and theological issues they considered standing on the periphery:

> Differences between and within the regional denominations remained, and these were reconciled by the principle of "liberty in nonessentials." The 1898 Manual of Phineas Bresee's Church of the Nazarene in the West makes clear that "essentials" were beliefs necessary to salvation. Particular eschatologies and

---

orthodoxy by eliminating the sentence in the 1906 *Manual* that allows for rebaptism. It originally appeared in the 1905 *Manual* and forever disappears by the 1907 version. The deleted line stated the following, "Whenever a person through conscientious scruples becomes desirous of again receiving the ordinance of baptism, it may be administered." However, Nazarene pastors have always been at liberty to rebaptize at their discretion and it is a practice that continues today. Ibid.

51. The Indiana conference of the Holiness Christian Church, along with a few members of Trumbauer's Pennsylvania conference, declined the invitation to unite with the Nazarenes. Smith, *Called Unto Holiness*, 230.

52. Ibid., 27.

53. Ibid.

baptismal views were nonessentials and required liberty of conscience. Were these doctrines then deemed unimportant? Hardly so. If educator A. M. Hills held staunchly to post-millennialism, Southern churchman J. B. Chapman and others were pre-millenialists with equal conviction. Did general superintendents Bresee and H. F. Reynolds affirm the importance of infant baptism? Rescue worker J. T. Upchurch disdained that doctrine and practice. In the newly organized Pentecostal Church of the Nazarene, liberty of conscience was required precisely because particular baptismal and eschatological views were affirmed strongly—so strongly, in fact, that it was pointless for those of one school of thought on these issues to seek prevalence in church councils over those who held contrary views. Pluralism was not indifference to these doctrines but the very opposite, though rooted in the belief that the focus of Pentecostal Nazarene unity should lie elsewhere—on the Wesleyan way of salvation, in particular.[54]

Ingersol insists that *liberty in nonessentials* in no way indicates that these issues were unimportant. Each of those who held divergent beliefs were extremely passionate about them. Therefore, the insistence to focus only on the essentials was the only plausible way to bring unity to these merging bodies. Otherwise consensus was impossible in certain theologies and practices where divergence emerged. They lived by the mantra *unity in the essentials and liberty in the nonessentials.*

While Ingersol's point is well taken, it is reasonable to suggest that these passionate and divergent beliefs might have provided one of the catalysts for the eventual devaluing of the sacraments, especially to subsequent generations of Nazarenes. The very fact that they were of such importance forced the acceptance of pluralistic beliefs and practices into a denomination bent on uniting. The only way to maintain unity was to ignore these privately held differences in corporate discussions, meetings, and gatherings, or unity would be impossible.

This potential threat which divergent baptismal practices posed for the union is demonstrated by the longevity of the tension they created. Even in later years when potentially divisive issues such as the mode of baptism or the validity of infant baptism consistently surfaced in denominational periodicals, the church leadership was forced to address this recurring controversy. Responding to a question submitted in 1946 to the *Herald of Holiness,* J. B. Chapman illustrates this phenomenon by requesting laity to demonstrate tolerance regarding variant baptismal practices:

54. Ingersol, "Christian Baptism Early Nazarenes," 162, italics mine.

> The Church of the Nazarene is very liberal on the subject of
> water baptism, seeing our people have come from many per-
> suasions on the matter, and seeing further that the subject is
> not in the nature of a necessary band of solidarity among us. . . .
> No one is supposed in our church to bring any pressure to bear
> upon any one on the subject of baptism, except to insist that
> all shall be baptized some time by some mode. . . . No one can
> have any trouble with us unless he is insistent on making others
> accept his interpretation. In that case he may find difficulty in
> that our people cannot see why there should be much argument
> about a matter on which everyone is given his own way.[55]

The unifying and dominant theology was Christian perfection. Even though some leaders did possess *passionate* beliefs regarding church order, eschatology, the sacraments, or other non-essentials, if it was not considered crucial to the *via salutis*, it was relegated to a lower status. This was a critical component in ensuring unity amid diversity. As Ingersol points out, their intention on many of these issues was not to devalue them, however it is likely that in later years their importance diminished. This was the residual effect of Nazarene descendants who had forgotten the passion of their forefathers. The ending result was that revivalism, evangelism, and the promotion of entire sanctification overshadowed other beliefs and practices, especially in those areas where divergence abounded.

James Fitzgerald explains that the early Nazarenes "strip-mined . . . [Wesley's sermons for] any reference to the doctrine of holiness"[56] but ignored other parts of his work that were critical to the practical application of the doctrine. Jeffery Knapp suggests that the rubric, *unity in essentials; liberty in nonessentials,* that characterized the early Nazarenes created a "pragmatic milieu,"[57] which still characterizes the denomination. This allowed the original groups to emphasize evangelism and promote the doctrine of Christian perfection, while having very diverse "baptismal views, eucharistic patterns, eschatological schemes and the like."[58] It appears that many issues were handled in this manner when consensus could not be reached (e.g., the sacraments, eschatology, church order, etc.).[59]

---

55. Chapman, "Question Box," July 29, 13.

56. Fitzgerald, "Weaving Rope of Sand," 229.

57. Knapp, "Throwing the Baby Out," 228.

58. Ibid.

59. The sometimes-volatile differences between the regional groups and holiness streams that formed them is demonstrated in the Seth Reese controversy. It occurred not long after Bresee's death, beginning in 1915 and reached its crescendo in 1917. Smith indicates that it nearly fractured the church union. Smith, *Called Unto Holiness,* 273–81.

This separation between sacramental practice and doctrine early in the denomination's history has significant implications for the ongoing development of worship practice, spiritual formation, and Christian identity. Other evidence in this text will indicate that what was true of the sacraments was also true of the Nazarene liturgy as a whole. Although the Wesleyan practices retained by Nazarenes were generally valued, there was an apparent failure to understand the relationship between various components of Wesley's practices (e.g., the liturgy, the means of grace, an emphasis on the spiritual disciplines, etc.) and the doctrine of Christian perfection. The primary instrument used for the promotion of salvation and entire sanctification was the revival, which nurtured the pietistic concerns of the movement. Practices that focused on the objective side of faith were among those that were deemed less important and thus considered debatable. The problem with this policy was that it made the separation between practice and doctrine even more distinct. The act of labeling certain practices as *nonessentials* failed to recognize the relationship between practice and doctrine.[60] These early Nazarenes were united by their desire to experience and promote the Wesleyan doctrine of Christian perfection, but there was no liturgical theology to illumine them about the essential relationship between *lex orandi, lex credendi* or to guide them in future decisions in orthopraxy.

This problem is illustrated by current sacramental practice in the church.[61] The sacrament of baptism does not function as initiation into the church, since it is not uncommon for the unbaptized to be church members or regular participants in the eucharist. Not only is it possible, but in some instances there have been unbaptized ordained clergy in the denomination.[62] Knapp goes as far as to suggest that the altar call became the sacra-

60. Ironically, in an effort to facilitate merger, Bresee and other early Nazarene leaders unintentionally communicated the idea that certain practices were unimportant (e.g. controversial issues related to baptism) or at least not as important as doctrine when they labeled them as nonessentials. This act of labeling can affect the value placed upon them and their implementation. This devaluing is especially relevant as it relates to the instituted means of grace and the sacraments which Christ ordained.

61. The devaluing of the sacraments can unintentionally occur in many ways. This includes the often-casual methods used for both sacraments of baptism and the eucharist. Such as when the rite is implemented spontaneously and absent from the proper prayers and ritual context that give it meaning (i.e. these rites are provided in the *Manual* and in other ritual resources). Other issues indicating a low sacramental practice include: low eucharistic frequency; the aesthetically impoverished nature of the elements sometimes used for the Lord's supper and the way it is administered; rebaptism; and the confusion between infant dedication and baptism. For more information on Nazarene sacramental practice, see Staples, *Outward Sign*.

62. Although an official record of baptized or non-baptized clergy does not exist, there are instances of unbaptized clergy being ordained. I am aware from personal

ment of initiation for the Church of the Nazarene, whereas the function of baptism was reduced to a personal testimony of a previous conversion experience.[63] Although Ingersol clarifies that the Church of the Nazarene continued to address its baptismal theology in later years, it is obvious from current practice that baptism has little connection to its historical function in either the early church or Wesley's ecclesiology.[64]

All of this suggests that the concessions which were made to make union possible had significant ramifications for both sacramental practice and the shape of the Nazarene liturgy. This is significant since Wesley's quest for inward holiness was inseparably linked to the liturgy he experienced in the Anglican tradition. Also, intimately linked to Wesley's pietistic concerns was his high sacramental theology and praxis.

Factors Influencing the Shape of Early Nazarene Worship

Tracing the Church of the Nazarene's historical roots is without question an essential component in understanding current liturgical practice and spirituality. Likewise, before it is possible to fully comprehend the challenges and obstacles the denomination now faces and how to respond to those problems, it is vital to know how the church arrived at its current bearing. Much history has already been written about the American holiness movement and the formation of the Church of the Nazarene. Likewise, the contributions of numerous Methodist historians have provided many valuable resources including: a thorough biographical portrait of John and Charles Wesley, details concerning the formation of Methodism, insight into John Wesley's liturgical theology and practice, and a description of worship within American Methodism. However, except for some research on the sacraments, minimal historical contributions exist concerning Nazarene liturgical practice.[65] The primary reason for this oversight is because the

experience and from correspondence with other Nazarene pastors that this phenomenon does exist. Concerning the case with which I am personally familiar, the ordained pastor was baptized a few years after his ordination. Most likely this is an unusual occurrence; however, it does not diminish the significance of this phenomenon, which indicates theological confusion and a reduction of the significance of baptism. Brook Thelander, e-mail message to author, May 22, 2011.

63. Knapp, "Throwing the Baby Out," 238.

64. Ingersol, "Christian Baptism Early Nazarenes," 161–80.

65. Except for the occasional and brief sections in Nazarene histories and biographies, little work has been done on the Nazarene liturgy. Contributions to this area of research have focused mainly upon the sacraments and reside in doctoral dissertations. The first liturgical theology published by the Church of the Nazarene, *Created to Worship: God's Invitation to Become Fully Human,* was authored by Brent Peterson and

Church of the Nazarene has always been part of the free-church tradition. Apart from the few rituals in the *Manual* there are no printed liturgical texts that were handed down through the ages. The prayer book was not only associated with those denominations whose religion was defunct, but it was viewed as *one of the primary* contributing factors to the absence of spiritual vitality within them. Therefore, Nazarene worship from the very beginning was driven not by liturgical theology but rather by the revivalism that gave birth and life to the denomination.

The last thirty years, however, have witnessed a dramatic shift in worship. Recently, there exists a growing sense that something is wrong. The revivalistic services, camp meetings, and evangelistic campaigns that gave birth to the Church of the Nazarene over a century ago have all but died out. The declining attendance at revival meetings became especially noticeable during the last thirty-five or more years of the twentieth century. The absence of revivalism created a vacuum in worship. Initially success in worship was measured by the number of seekers at the altar. Later the church focused upon Sunday school attendance and later counted the number of people in the pews for Sunday worship. The gradual but steady decline of revivalism meant that the church needed to shift directions if it was going to continue to grow numerically. The church-growth movement became the new method used to bring new prospects into the church. This had significant ramifications for the liturgy. Over time the revival pattern of morning worship shifted in a new direction.

The structure and content of worship ceased to be shaped by revivalism but instead was determined by the means and methods born out of the church-growth movement. The uniformity that existed in worship because of revivalism's influence was no longer available to shape the pattern of worship. Although some congregations have held onto traditional Nazarene patterns, they are becoming increasingly extinct. During the early 1990s Paul Basset reflected on this change by suggesting that Nazarene worship was experiencing a divide. Some congregations were departing from the worship traditions rooted in American revivalism and opting for a praise and worship style of music. Still others were attempting to return to their "Wesleyan and Anglican roots."[66]

Those Nazarenes seeking to return to their Anglican heritage, although gaining strength, remains a small minority. Furthermore, worship practices

---

published in 2012. For further reading, see Staples, *Outward Sign*; Bangs, *Bresee*; Cunningham, *Our Watchword and Song*; Estep, "Baptismal Theology and Practice, 1–224; Fitzgerald, "Weaving Rope of Sand," 1–258; Peterson, "Post-Wesleyan Ecclesiology, 1–316; Peterson, *Created to Worship*.

66. Bassett, "Church of the Nazarene," in Webber, *Renewal of Sunday Worship*, 37.

within the denomination are increasingly becoming more divergent rather than simply "moving in two directions."[67] Divergence itself is not a threat to Nazarene identity. Rather the absence of a robust ecclesiology and liturgical theology to guide clergy increases the possibility that many congregations and pastors will become lost in a liturgical quagmire.

It is my argument that one of the contributing factors to the loss of denominational identity, which Nazarene scholars have debated over the past decade, is the absence of a liturgical theology. It is also proposed that the absence of such a theology has led to the misguided changes and liturgical confusion that has transpired in worship over the last several years.[68] Traditionally liturgical theology has not been a typical Nazarene concern; however, developments over the last two to three decades has created a renewed interest in not only the sacraments, but also in the denomination's Wesleyan liturgical roots and the field of liturgical studies.[69]

Retracing history is an important step in assessing the present and planning for the future. As previously noted, other than the recent contributions to the field of sacramental theology, scholarly work examining Nazarene worship practice is minimal. Research in several academic fields, including liturgical theology, ritual studies, and the social sciences, demonstrate that over time the practices in which we engage are formative; often working at the subconscious level.[70] This means that the words, gestures, rituals, and actions that are a part of weekly worship shape our identity, often without our knowledge. Due to the formative potential of worship it is therefore

---

67. Ibid.

68. Although some congregations have retained more traditional forms of worship, at least some divergence is inevitable. Today there is significant variety in Nazarene worship encompassing a wide spectrum of forms. For example: A small minority of churches have sought to return to a prayer book model, which is similar and in some instances, nearly a complete adoption of the shape and content of Anglican worship. Others offer very *contemporary* worship, which generally is a reference to the type of modern music that dominates the services (i.e., pop, rock, or hard rock styles of Christian music). Some worship appears very disorganized and casual. It is at times characterized by lengthy periods of singing choruses followed by a sermon, with other elements such as a prayer, offering, the occasional hymn or a Scripture reading interspersed in between. In many congregations, the preferred medium for making the words available to the congregation is no longer the hymnal or printed sheet, but an overhead projection system, which reduces the need of the congregation to pick up a hymnal and turn pages but increases reliance on technology. Overall, the major focus and concern of contemporary worship trends appear to concentrate on music and the sermon.

69. While the number of those interested in and contributing to these fields is relatively small, interest does seem to be increasing.

70. Ellis, "Relationship Liturgical Practice," 36–117.

important to ask questions about current patterns in worship. What are our weekly rites and practices? What are the theological implications of the practices in which we engage? How are the practices that are part of weekly worship shaping one's identity? How did we arrive at these particular practices and why do we avoid certain others found within Christendom? Are there time honored practices we need to recover and others embraced that we should reevaluate? History can provide valuable insight into answering those questions and many others. We have already examined Wesley's liturgical praxis and theology, as well as the century-long period after Wesley and during the American holiness movement, that powerfully influenced the shape of worship for the holiness streams that would eventually merge to form the Church of the Nazarene. Now we will trace the characteristics, history, and development of worship practice in the Church of the Nazarene and the underlying thought that sustained those practices.

Influences of American Revivalism

Carl Bangs, in his biography of Bresee, notes several differences in Bresee's liturgical thought and practice distinguishing Nazarenes from other congregations in Los Angeles. He lists the following characteristics of Nazarene worship under Bresee's leadership. First, he suggests, that the atmosphere of worship at Los Angeles First Church was one of celebration for past spiritual victories as well as the expectation of additional transformative experiences to occur.[71] The early denominational periodicals and literature testify to very vibrant and lively forms of worship. Worship is described as containing emotion-laden testimonies, people raising their hands in praise, shouting, weeping, and various other vocal and bodily expressions. Early Nazarene worship reflected the camp meeting model of the late nineteenth century, which was characterized by the "spirited singing of gospel songs; fervent, spontaneous prayers,"[72] vibrant testimonies, shouting, and a sermon followed by an altar call. The altar call was an affectuous event, since the altar was often filled with individuals seeking conversion or entire sanctification.[73] This type of atmosphere occurred in multifarious services including those semi-regular occasions when they celebrated the Lord's supper and the love feast.

71. Bangs, *Phineas Bresee*, 231.
72. Bassett, "Church of the Nazarene," in Webber, *Renewal of Sunday Worship*, 37.
73. Ibid.

Next, Bangs notes that although Bresee and the early Nazarenes "respected [the] traditional forms of worship"[74] from the past and on occasion referred back to them, they were more interested in the "spiritual vitality that had produced those historic forms."[75] Bangs argues that Bresee was quite capable of implementing ritual, but "he was not ritualistic."[76] He continues this thought by stating that Bresee "regarded the fashionable formality in the old churches as stifling to the life that once enlivened the forms."[77] If this analysis is correct, then it pinpoints one of the major differences in liturgical thought between Bresee and Wesley. Wesley's view of the correlation between *spiritual vitality* and the ritual forms of the *BCP* liturgy was reciprocal. He believed an interdependent relationship existed between the liturgical means of grace and spiritual vitality. Wesley is noted for his high estimation of the Anglican prayer book. Therefore, according to Wesley, rather than the *forms* being a potential drain on inward religion, the opposite was true when appropriated correctly. God chooses to work through those very means and forms that Bresee and the early Nazarenes either avoided or used with reservation. When engaged in through faith, God uses these means to communicate his grace and cultivate authentic spiritual healing and growth.

While it is true that Wesley warned of the abuse of fixed forms of worship, since ritual misuse leads to the dead religion that Bresee feared, the same is true of spontaneous patterns of worship. However, Bresee, like the early American Methodists, was more interested in and comfortable with

74. Bangs, *Phineas Bresee*, 231.

75. Ibid.

76. Ibid. Bangs's use of the terms *ritual* and *ritualistic* is lacking in clarity. These words are interpreted differently depending upon one's church tradition. Outside of the sacraments and those items labeled "ritual" in the *Manual*, Nazarenes, like most individuals from the free-church tradition, would not consider the worship of their church to contain ritual. However, ritual is inherent to life itself and a part of every church and its worship. For example, movements, words, and actions surrounding the altar call encompass ritual. Ronald Grimes states, "Even the ritual-denying Protestant groups depend heavily on psychosomatically informed processes like 'being moved,' 'feeling the spirit,' or 'having a full heart.' As far as I can see, there is no escaping ritualization. . . . " It is because of this confusion over the use of *ritual* and its derivatives that Mary Douglas argues that instead of using the term to reference "empty symbols of conformity" ritual should be used in a neutral or positive sense. It is most likely Bangs is referring to those rituals Nazarenes associated with *written forms of worship* in the prayer book tradition. It is these forms which were avoided since they were considered an enemy to the spiritual vitality which Nazarenes sought. Grimes, "Modes of Ritual Sensibility," in Bradshaw and Melloh, *Foundations in Ritual Studies*, 135; Douglas, *Natural Symbols*, 2–3.

77. Bangs, *Phineas Bresee*, 231.

the spontaneous and free forms of worship characteristic of early American Methodism and American revivalism. Although Bresee did not completely disregard the use of ritual, he believed it should be approached with extreme caution. Prayer book forms appear to be limited to Bresee's sacramental practice.[78] Fitzgerald points out that even though the American holiness movement generally showed "very low regard for ritual, the Lord's Supper was an exception" to the rule.[79] However, other set forms of worship did not receive the same place of favor that was reserved for the eucharist.

Wesley, on the other hand, concluded that both the written and spontaneous forms were vital to the church's liturgy. They were essential for the propagation of inward holiness and to guard against the extremes of either formalism or enthusiasm. The exclusive use of written or spontaneous forms could readily lead to either of these distortions.

Finally, Bangs states that the mark of *spiritual worship* for Bresee and the early Nazarenes was determined by the number of individuals experiencing conversion or entire sanctification. Bangs states that, "Meetings were described less in terms of attendance or programs than in terms of seekers responding to gospel promises. It was expected that people would seek God wherever Christians gathered."[80] The shape of early Nazarene worship was modeled after the camp meetings and revival services of the American holiness movement. Revival meetings were the supreme vehicle for the promotion and propagation of an inward religion; therefore, worship in the holiness denominations was modeled after the movement that gave them birth.

78. Beyond the sacramental rituals in the *Manual* and information from the *Nazarene Messenger* on eucharistic frequency and the occurrence of baptisms, Bangs provides little insight regarding the actual ritual forms in Bresee's liturgy. Although Bangs states that Bresee had a "mastery of ritual," it is difficult to ascertain to what extent this assertion is a valid reflection of Bresee's reliance on prayer book forms for his liturgy. Bangs only references the prayer book forms Bresee implemented for his sacramental practice, but there is minimal data regarding his implementation of prayer forms, Scripture, the creeds, and other elements of Wesley's prayer book *ordo*. It is also significant to note that the Lord's supper was rarely a part of Sunday morning worship in Bresee's church. It occurred every other month mostly in the Sunday afternoon service. Therefore, available evidence indicates that spontaneous and free worship was the principle characteristic of Bresee's liturgy, while his primary connection to Wesley liturgical thought is found in the sermon, limited aspects of the hymnody, and extempore prayer.

79. Fitzgerald, "Weaving Rope of Sand," 155.

80. Bangs, *Phineas Bresee,* 231.

Avoiding the Extremes: Formalism and Fanaticism

Typically, practices characteristic of prayer book worship were avoided, since these forms were believed to be the enemy of inward religion. Bresee provides some insight into his thoughts on worship in a sermon published in the *Nazarene Messenger*. The prolonged quote provides an important window into the attitudes, thoughts, and concerns of Nazarene leadership as they relate to prayer book worship. Bresee based his sermon on a text from Rev 7:17:

> There is considerable thought given, in these days to forms of worship, men and women have wrought them out. We call them a litany or a ritual. Some churches are called ritualistic, because they have prepared forms of expression which are read from a book or recited from memory. The forms of worship in churches not ritualistic are sometimes considered "bald" and sometimes in their assemblies they almost cease to worship. Their meetings are seasons of instruction and entertainment and sometimes not much even of that. So while ritualism runs easily into formality—indeed seems to invite it—unritualistic meetings degenerate into education, or entertainment and sometimes folly.
>
> Worship rises high above all forms. If it attempts to find utterance through them it will set them on fire, and glow and burn in their consuming flame and rise as incense to God. If it starts out with the impartation and the receiving of the great thought of God; if it waits to hear His infinite will and eternal love, it spreads its pinions to fly to His bosom, there to breathe out its unutterable devotion. We have here the way of worship. They cry with a loud voice, saying "Salvation to our God which sitteth upon the throne and unto the Lamb." It is not the learning of some new thing; not a new shading of some thought which is a matter of interest; it is not the repeating, parrot-like of some written form. But is the cry of the soul, deep, earnest, intense, loud; the farthest removed from what might be regarded as cathedral service, with the intoning of prayer and praise, and where the light falls but dimly, the muffled music and sentiment rolling back upon the mind in subdued sensibility. I suppose this is about the best earth-born, man-made form of worship one can find. But that which is here described is something altogether different. It is also equally far removed from a gathering of the people, who, without solemnity or soul earnestness wait to be sung at, and prayed at, and preached at, until the time comes when they can decently go away.

The worship here seen rises from every soul; it is the out-
bursting passion of every heart; it breaks forth like a pent-up
storm; it rolls forth like a mighty tornado. One thing seems
certain; the worship of the Blood-washed company is not the
still small voice.

We often hear God speak to us as Elijah heard Him—"in
the still small voice;" but nowhere in the Bible is our worship
to Him described in that way. It is as a "great thunder" and "the
voice of many waters." One thing not to be lost sight of, the an-
gels do not sing the song of redeeming love; that they can never
do. But they do stand about the Blood-washed company and
fall upon their faces and worship God, saying "Amen," "Amen."
. . . If we really would worship as they worship, we'll do as they
do—fall upon our faces in the dust and cry as they cry "Amen"
and "Amen."[81]

Several significant aspects of Bresee's understanding of worship are
revealed in this passage. When he refers to ritual, ritualistic, or ritualism,
it is in reference to worship that includes written prayers, responses, and
other elements either read or memorized from a prayer book. Even though
God can work through the written forms of worship, Breese's preference is
worship that is spontaneous, since he believes rituals (i.e., written forms)
have a propensity toward formalism. However, he also indicates that free
forms of worship can, likewise, be meaningless when they are reduced to
entertainment or *foolishness*. This undoubtedly concerns the fanaticism
both Bresee and other Nazarene leaders avoided. While members of the *cathedral churches* erred because they lacked experiential religion, the conflict
that existed with the tongues-speaking segment of American revivalism was
an overemphasis on emotion or what opponents referred to as fanaticism.
Bresee refers to the problem of fanaticism in a December 1900 issue of *The
Nazarene Messenger*:

The work has its difficulties. The world, the flesh, and the Devil
are against us; and some difficulties more or less peculiar beset
our pathway.

A new movement, especially if it is successful, gathers to
itself some elements which become a hindrance. They come to it
for place and opportunity, and possibly for help which they have
been unable to get in other places. . . .

Fanatics of almost every kind expect a new movement to
embrace their particular fad; and when they find that it is the
same old gospel, made hot by the fire of the Divine Presence,

81. Bresee, "Lamb," 2.

which is fatal to all fanaticism, they rise up to declare that there is no special message, and betake themselves to more congenial climes; we have had some of these.[82]

Bresee proposes a middle way in his attempt to walk between the formalism of the mainline churches and the fanaticism found in some congregations born of the nineteenth-century revivals.[83] He describes authentic worship as one free from the repetitive, solemn, and lifeless written forms of the *cathedral* churches, while avoiding experience considered too extreme. His primary concern for worship is that the heart, mind, and soul of the worshipper are engaged in an experientially rich encounter with God. For Bresee, authentic worship "is the cry of the soul, *deep, earnest, intense, loud* . . . [since it] rises from every soul it is the out-bursting passion of every heart [breaking forth] like a pent-up storm."[84]

Descriptions of the experiential nature of the early revivals that occurred in the various streams of the holiness movement reflect this concern of Bresee and other Nazarene leaders.[85] Like Wesley's critique of the lifeless worship that he witnessed in the Anglican Church, the early Nazarenes were critical of a similar lethargy they observed in the religious life of contemporary Methodism and other mainline denominations. However, in contrast to Wesley, they believed that the only way to be faithful to Wesley's theological vision was to abandon the liturgy he deemed important. The following editorial in the *Nazarene Messenger* reflects that thought:

It is urged that John Wesley and his adherents remained in the Church of England. That was a State Church and everybody was

82. As quoted in Girvin, *Bresee Prince in Israel*, 166–7.

83. Nazarenes used the designation "fanaticism" to describe the undesirable behaviors they noticed in worship, which they interpreted as the same phenomenon encompassed by the term "enthusiasm" in Wesley's day. The undesirable behaviors included glossolalia, divine healings, and other activities associated with the tongues-speaking branch of the Pentecostal movement. This association is revealed in a *Nazarene Messenger* editorial in 1907, "In 1768 [Wesley] wrote to a friend, blessing God that if a hundred enthusiasts were set aside, they were still encompassed with a cloud of witnesses who have testified and do testify in life and death, the perfection he had taught for forty years. We find that the fanatics of those days had the same class of hobbies professed experiences, and prophecies, which they have in these days." "Fanaticism," 6. For a description of fanaticism, see "Fanaticism and Humbugs," 6.

84. Bresee, "Lamb," *Nazarene Messenger*, 2.

85. The early periodicals provide descriptions of various services that characterize the experiential nature of worship. For articles that reflect this emphasis, see "At the Tabernacle," October 8, 8; Girvin, "Seven Characteristics," 7; Scott, "Experimental Religion," 4; "School Notes," 7; Davis, "Experience Profession," 4; Dalton, "From Correspondents," 15.

in it. John Wesley did not see for a time how the people were to have the sacraments without the offices of the clergy of the established church. It was an almost life-long education for him to get rid of his High Church notions. Every student of the movement knows that Methodism in Great Britain has been greatly hampered and hindered by its subserviency to the State Church. In these days we have no excuse for High-Churchism. John Wesley organized societies—churches without the sacraments, urging his people to secure these from the State Church ministry—but in every other sense doing the whole work of the churches, preaching the word, building houses of worship, holding social meetings, licensing and sending out preachers, establishing missions, etc. At last it was found necessary to find a way out of High-Churchism and have the sacraments and all of the appurtenances to which they were entitled. It is ours to do again what Wesley did in the Eighteenth Century: Organize the people for the spreading of Scriptural holiness over these lands.[86]

This editorial theorizes that Wesley's connection to the Anglican Church was based upon two grounds. First, he was part of the state church, like all British citizens, out of necessity, rather than desire. Second, Wesley and the Methodists were bound to the state church because it was the only means that would allow them to celebrate the sacraments. However, the editorial points out, Wesley implemented all other ministries and work outside of the boundaries of the church.

Obviously, this early Nazarene understanding ignores Wesley's strong ties to the Anglican Church that he loved and which consumed his life's work, as well as his deep appreciation for the *BCP*. Significant to our understanding of early Nazarene liturgical thought is the perception that Wesley's primary ties to the Church of England were pragmatic in nature. He was a part of the church because it was expected of him as an Englishman, and it provided the sole means to administer the sacraments. Once he could work around those obstacles and celebrate the sacraments outside of the church, he did. This editorial provides compelling insight into the only redeeming quality that the early Nazarenes believed Wesley found in the Anglican liturgy—the sacraments. Therefore, it is no surprise that while written forms for the sacraments were retained, spontaneity and freedom were coveted in most other aspects of worship including the worship order, music, prayer, and the sermon.

Departing from Wesley there was a strong tendency to put at least partial blame on the rituals themselves as a contributing cause of formalism.

86. "Organize," 6.

They faced fears like those of the early American Methodists who believed "set prayer texts, a prescribed pattern of Scripture readings, and a tightly defined order of worship could lead to the kind of rote, monotone worship that failed to affect the heart, the arena for knowing God's saving touch."[87] Ironically, as Ruth points out, Wesley's prayer book "had deep resonance in the Scripture"[88] and it was for that reason that Wesley provided it to the Methodists. However, they failed to understand the importance of the *Sunday Service*.

Bresee was more accepting of using prayer book forms than many of his contemporaries, although his usage was primarily reserved for the sacraments. This is especially true when compared to those Nazarenes from traditions outside of Methodism. When the Lord's supper was celebrated, Bresee's language used to describe the people's experience indicates a great appreciation for it. However, the frequency of administering the sacrament in his Los Angeles church appears minimal, and it was separated from the Sunday morning liturgy. Even Bresee's practice was far from attaining Wesley's desire for *constant* communion. Available evidence indicates that he celebrated the Lord's supper every two months, and most often it occurred in the Sunday afternoon service.[89] However, the descriptive language used, as well as the frequency of practice, is reminiscent of those eucharistic celebrations depicted in early American Methodism.

Liturgical Pragmatism

Due to early Nazarene concerns over the propagation of holiness, the structure of worship took the shape of the revival service. Liturgical decisions were governed by implementing extemporaneous methods that would

87. Ruth, *Early Methodist Life*, 190.

88. Ibid.

89. Carl Bangs indicates Bresee celebrated the eucharist monthly in 1900 at Los Angeles First Church and observed it twice monthly beginning in 1903. However, the *Nazarene Messenger* reveals a bi-monthly celebration (every other month) of the Lord's supper beginning as early as 1900. Rather than the love feast being held in conjunction with eucharist, they were celebrated on alternating months. The *Nazarene Messenger* references this practice in a note referring to an upcoming change in the Sunday of the month that either the Lord's supper or love feast would occur: "Sacramental Service will be held next Sabbath at 3 p.m.—Hitherto the Sacramental Service and love feast have been on the *third Sabbath* of the month, held alternately, but it has been thought best to change to the *first Sabbath*." Bangs, *Phineas Bresee*, 236; "Sacramental Service," 5. Announcements indicating a bi-monthly eucharist are found in several issues of the *Nazarene Messenger*; see "Sabbath," August 8, 7; "Sabbath at First Church," October 9, 3; "Sabbath at First Church," July 7, 3; "At the Tabernacle," February 7, 8.

promote heart religion and yield seekers at the altar. Success or failure was determined by the number of those at the communion rail experiencing either conversion or entire sanctification. This sentiment is reflected in the following article:

> The average American preacher seemingly does not expect immediate results from his preaching, so that in a multitude of churches on the Sabbath day there is a PERFORMANCE with a religious coloring, which can usually be anticipated days before it comes off. The formalistic sameness is gone through it, the doors open and shut, and not a single soul is won for God. How any preacher who is called of God to declare the unsearchable riches of Christ to a lost and ruined world, can be satisfied with a mere performance, a mere preaching, or simply taking part in a program called worship, without pressing, yes, imploring, men to immediately flee from the wrath to come, and expecting to see somebody consciously and clearly converted, who has been moved to accept Christ through his preaching, is more than I can understand. . . .
>
> What is the preacher for? Is he to display brilliancy of intellect by the discussion of technical theological themes? Is he to entertain by his happy mannerism and smart way of putting things? . . .
>
> The only business of the preacher in the church or out of it is to earnestly seek the salvation of souls. . . .
>
> It ought to make a preacher weep with inexpressible grief to pass through a single week without seeing souls saved as a direct result of his preaching.[90]

Preaching was the dominant focal point of worship since it was the primary agent of harvesting souls. This most always transpired at the communion rail or what Nazarenes termed *the altar*. The number of souls seeking God could then be readily counted to reflect the success or failure of the service.

It is this sense of liturgical pragmatism that has characterized the church until the present day. Initially worship was driven by the means and methods that would lead to the conversion and entire sanctification of seekers. Since the virtual death of revivalism in the latter portion of the twentieth century, success was no longer measured in terms of the number of seekers at the communion rail but by the influences of the church-growth movement which replaced it.

A congregation's or pastor's success is still heavily determined numerically. Districts give awards and recognition to pastors and their

90. Cornell, "Preaching Without Results," 2.

congregations who demonstrate growth in membership and attendance during the previous year.[91] A pastor's salary is directly tied to the size of his congregation and the amount of money raised, which in turn reinforces the importance of church size and numerical growth. Positions of ecclesial authority and advancement are often reserved for clergy serving in larger congregations, since success is regularly (and perhaps subconsciously) determined numerically.

Thus, this philosophy permeates thought in the planning and implementation of the various ministries of the church, and it is inclusive of the content and structure of the liturgy. The shape of the liturgy in the past and present is strongly influenced by pragmatism. Decisions for worship are often based, not upon sound theological underpinnings, but upon methods that are perceived to return the greatest numerical increase either at the communion rail or in the pew. It is likely that this trait is so dominant in our *DNA* because determining success by numerical returns provides more immediate feedback, is far easier to measure, and is more rewarding than attempting to assess and address the spiritual climate of a congregation.

Challenges in Assessing Nazarene Liturgical Development

Bassett argued that the worship *ordo* in the Nazarene liturgy remained virtually unchanged until the middle part of the 1960s.[92] He indicates that the only Scripture read was the sermon text, which immediately preceded the sermon. The pastoral prayer was extempore. There would have been no tolerance for written prayers, while the benediction was predominately an "extension of the sermon."[93] The order included what Nazarene's refer to as *special music*. Special music is performed by select individuals (e.g. solo, duet, etc.) or a choir and the congregation does not sing. The congregational singing is dominated with gospel songs instead of hymns. Writing in the early 1990s Bassett indicated that his description was a current pattern.

Acknowledging that the church has retained the basic pattern of worship does not necessarily mean Nazarene worship has remained unchanged. Worship in the Church of the Nazarene has been in a gradual but constant

91. Not only does this practice recognize the churches with the most financial and numerical growth, but unintentionally it also places an unfavorable spotlight on those pastors and churches that are struggling and in decline. In recent years, this practice is in the process of change at many District Assemblies. The emphasis on a church's numerical increase throughout the year through awards and public recognition, for both pastor and church, is more subdued on many districts than it once was.

92. Bassett, "Church of the Nazarene," in Webber, *Renewal of Sunday Worship*, 38.

93. Ibid.

state of fluctuation over the past century. It was slight until the 1960s, and the basic *ordo* remained intact for many years. While this shape is still prevalent today, changes have occurred in certain aspects of worship. These modifications encompass several areas.

During the latter part of the twentieth century, there was a diminution in worship services ending with an altar call. Likewise, there was a decline in the number of congregants responding to the invitation on those occasions when one was given. Congregational response in worship with shouts of *Amen, Hallelujah,* or some other vocal response is at the very least minimalized in most congregations and is virtually extinct in others. Today the most common response is not vocal, but rather it is applause given by the congregation, in acknowledgment for some experience enjoyed in worship.

Additionally, a significant shift has occurred in the music. The Wesleyan hymns available in the hymnal have been greatly reduced over the years.[94] Many congregations essentially replaced the use of hymns with contemporary choruses, since the latter tend to be more self-affirming. Such self-affirming practices are highly coveted in contemporary society. Also, the eucharist experienced a devaluing when compared to the thought and practice of those early Nazarene leaders who highly regarded its use. While this list is by no means exhaustive, it illustrates the evolution of Nazarene worship, which has in the end undergone a dramatic transformation since the early twentieth century. The most notable modifications occurred in the last thirty to forty years due to the transition out of the era of revivalism, which gave the Nazarene liturgy its primary shape.

Sources for Tracing Liturgical History

Tracing the history of liturgical development within any denomination is fraught with difficulties. This is especially true in the Church of the Nazarene

94. Fred Mund indicates that *Waves of Glory* (No. 1), which was published by Nazarene Publishing Company in 1905, contained thirty-eight hymns attributed to Charles Wesley. This was more than 10 percent of the hymnal. *Waves of Glory* (No. 2), published in 1921, contained twenty-one hymns of Charles Wesley, which was a mere 5 percent of the hymnal. The first authorized Nazarene hymnal, *Glorious Gospel Hymns* (1931), included twenty-nine hymns from Charles Wesley or 4 percent of the hymnal. *Sing to the Lord* (1993), the most recent hymnal, did contain twenty-three Wesley hymns by Charles or John; however, it amounts to less than 4 percent of the hymns or choruses in the hymnal. Although the denomination did publish two hymnals composed entirely of Wesley hymns (i.e., published in 1963 and 1982), Fitzgerald indicates that their use by congregations was minimal. Mund, *Keep the Music Ringing*, 8–23; Fitzgerald, "Weaving Rope of Sand," 217–8. For additional information concerning Nazarene hymnody, see Cunningham, *Our Watchword and Song*, 439–41.

because it is part of the free-church tradition. Since a set pattern of worship, predetermined by the denomination, never existed, there is little remaining evidence that provides specific details. Apart from the few rituals in the *Manual* (i.e., Baptism, Reception of Members, the Lord's supper, and the Funeral Service), there is little enduring evidence of a liturgical structure.[95] Therefore only remnants of early liturgical patterns can be found.

These bits and pieces of information occasionally appear as descriptions of worship services in the early periodicals. Congregations reported into the church organs various details about Sunday worship. Such as, the occurrence of various meetings, services, activities, and other events, as well as the spiritual climate at their church. Occasionally included in these accounts were descriptions of worship, eucharistic celebrations, love feasts, baptisms, etc. However, even in these occasional references, it is rare to find detailed information about the worship *ordo*. This is because the focus of worship was the sermon and altar call, while all the other components were simply thought of as *the preliminaries*. Therefore, when worship is described, generally it will contain information about the sermon, the emotional atmosphere, and the results of the service but not the contents. The following article regarding a worship service and church dedication near Ballinger, Texas, exemplifies the nature of their reporting:

> The meeting was blessed and owned of God. Sunday was a great day. A large audience packed the house at eleven o'clock. A short prayer and praise service was conducted by Bro. West after which the Lord helped us in delivering the dedicatory sermon. After the message Bro. and Sister Mullenax, Bro. and Sister West and Bro. Roby read the Scripture references and the Trustees came forward, we offered the house to God. His glory filled our hearts and we were made to praise Him for another building in which naught but holiness and gospel truth shall ever be taught.[96]

Special services, like this dedication service, tended to provide the most descriptive accounts; therefore, this article does include some additional information about the service, but it is still extremely limited. Reference is made to the prayer and praise service, the sermon, and the Scripture. Concerning the content, the normal reporting method mentions only the sermon, Scripture text, and sometimes the sermon title in the report. The

---

95. These are the rituals included in the 1908 *Manual*. Additional rituals for the installation of officers and church dedications were added in later years. It was not until the 1997 publication of the *Church Rituals Handbook* by Jesse Middendorf that additional rites from the denomination were made available.

96. "Church Dedication," 7.

sermon, people involved, emotional and spiritual atmosphere, and the results of the service are typically the primary focus of worship descriptions.

Another source for determining the shape of worship is derived from church bulletins. Some bulletins do include an order of worship, whereas others do not. There is also the rare article or editorial in the denominational periodicals that provides a suggested order of worship; however, there is no confirmation that these were actually implemented by local clergy. The fact that they do appear is just as likely an indication that something else is taking place, and the article is an attempt to change some undesired practice or encourage the use of a liturgical element suffering neglect.

There is a further complication in determining actual liturgical practice. The number of pastors who employed the few available rituals in the *Manual* is questionable, since the tendency toward extempore worship has always been a potent force. A 2006 survey of Nazarene congregations in the United States indicated that only 50 percent of clergy use the *Manual* or *Church Rituals Handbook* for celebrating the Lord's supper. Two percent use other prayer book resources such as the *BCP* or *United Methodist Book of Worship*, while 29 percent of pastors stated that they speak spontaneously without a prepared ritual.[97] It is due to these complications, and others, that it is impossible to gain an exact and universal picture of the nature of worship in the Church of the Nazarene. Since the denomination is part of the free-church tradition, it is reasonably safe to assume that, while the basic order of worship may have remained constant for many years in the vast number of congregations, variations within the liturgy did occur.

While these obstacles make it extremely difficult to assess the liturgy, the available snippets of information do provide a rough sketch of Nazarene worship. It is therefore possible to examine some of the developments, characteristics, and concerns that occur in worship throughout the history of the church. Likewise, the strong influences of revivalism and the camp meeting services that gave Nazarene worship its distinctive form provide significant clues not only to worship's initial shape but to its continual development.

97. Ellis, "Relationship Liturgical Practice," 629–30. The statistics describing the use of Nazarene resources for baptism were slightly improved. Fifty-seven percent use the *Manual* frequently and nearly 15 percent of those who use the *Manual* also use the *Church Rituals Handbook*. Two percent stated that they use either the *BCP* or the *United Methodist Book of Worship* for the baptismal rite.

Influential Personalities in Liturgical Development

Prior to examining the Nazarene liturgy, itself, it is expedient to briefly discuss the human sources for the material in this text. The denomination's
periodicals contain various editorials, articles, comments, and questions
from a variety of Nazarene personalities that provide relevant information about Nazarene liturgical practice and thought. These resources are
more abundant during the formative years of the denomination. Some of
the contributions indicate authorship, while others do not. Due to space
constraints, it would be infeasible to discuss all the prominent leaders in
the Church of the Nazarene. However, two of those leaders who carried
enormous influence in the church are mentioned here: Phineas F. Bresee
and J. B. Chapman. Both men are important to point out not only because of
their extraordinary leadership roles within the denomination but also since
they are contributors to several of the articles cited.

Although ecclesial leadership has always insisted that the origins of
the Church of the Nazarene cannot be traced back to one leader but rather
its existence is the result of several holiness bodies uniting, it is without
question that during the initial years Bresee was the central figure in both
promoting the growing church and making future mergers possible. Bangs
points out that Bresee "did not so much 'found' a church as consent to be the
pastor of a church that a host of laypeople were bringing into existence."[98]
A series of circumstances had led Bresee into a very unsettling position in
which he was without a church to pastor. He had separated from the Methodist conference in Southern California in 1894, and, in 1895, he was ousted
from his ministry at Peniel Mission.

Through the work of strong lay leadership, friends of Bresee, a new
church was officially organized under California law with Bresee as its
pastor. As the church continued to mature and eventually grow into a denomination, Bresee was elected as a general superintendent and eventually
"became the *sole primus* of the new church."[99] Bresee also served as one of
the editors of the *Nazarene Messenger*. It is because of his leadership roles in
the origins of the church, his service as one of the first general superintendents of the denomination, and his work as the editor of the denomination's

---

98. Bangs, *Phineas Bresee*, 195.

99. Ibid., 215, italics mine. The circumstances surrounding the origins of the
Church of the Nazarene and Bresee's leadership role are quite complex and beyond the
scope of this discussion. For additional information, see Bangs, *Bresee*; Smith, *Called
Unto Holiness*.

periodical in the West that he was influential in shaping Nazarene liturgical thought and practice.[100]

As editor, Bresee certainly either contributed or influenced several of the articles and editorials reviewed in this text, many of which are anonymous. Bangs suggests that until it ceased publication in 1912, the "*Nazarene Messenger* was an extension of Bresee's person and ministry."[101] Therefore, it seems reasonable to assume that, in general, the opinions and thoughts shared in *Nazarene Messenger* editorials, if they did not come from Bresee's pen, were not incompatible with his own concerns.[102]

Included among the list of the many other contributors to the church's publications are Nazarene laypersons, pastors, evangelists, editors, professors, denominational leaders, district superintendents, and general superintendents. Some of the contributing personalities held more than one of these positions during their lifetime. J. B. Chapman served in several capacities; however, he was an anomaly. The positions of leadership he held allowed him access and influence that few other Nazarene leaders knew. During the formative years of the Church of the Nazarene, there was perhaps no one more influential, for as long a period of time, as J. B. Chapman. Not only did he serve in many important capacities within the church, but several of these positions placed him into contact either by print or in person with a substantial portion of Nazarenes across the denomination.[103] Writing in

100. The *Nazarene Messenger* was in print before the church in the West merged with other bodies in the East and South. It was one of the denomination's major organs. The others included the *Beulah Christian* in the East and the *Pentecostal Advocate* and the *Holiness Evangel* in the South. All the regional publications were eventually replaced within a few years after the Church of the Nazarene became a national organization. The new periodical began publication in 1912 in Kansas City, Missouri, and was entitled the *Herald of Holiness*.

101. Bangs, *Phineas Bresee*, 247.

102. Ibid., 247–8.

103. Chapman served as editor (or in some editorial capacity) of the following periodicals: *Highways and Hedges* (1906); *Holiness Evangel* (1908); *Herald of Holiness* (1921–1928); and *The Preacher's Magazine* (Chapman founded *The Preacher's Magazine* in 1926 and continued to serve as editor even after his election to the general superintendency). Furthermore, he served in various other denominational capacities such as president of the General Board of Education. He was elected General Superintendent in 1928 and ministered in that capacity until his death on July 30, 1947. Even after his election he was still a voracious contributor of articles to the various publications. He also maintained the column, "The Question Box" (previously titled "Questions Answered") in the *Herald of Holiness*, where he fielded answers to questions concerning theology, polity, practice, and a variety of issues that were submitted by Nazarene laity and clergy. These activities, in addition to his exposure as a preacher and evangelist, meant that he was extremely influential in the denomination. Smith, *Called Unto Holiness*, 324, 341; Messer, "Nazarene Leaders," 12–13; Corlett, "Three Million Words," in

Chapman's biography, D. Shelby Corlett expresses the enduring impact Chapman left on the church:

> Because he had a faculty of weaving human interest into his writings, making his readers feel that he was acquainted with their needs, Dr. Chapman became a popular editor. He always stated the great truths of the Christian life in a definite manner. He dealt with profound truths in a direct but simple style. His writings challenged the deep thinkers, yet they were stated in language common people could read with understanding. His editorials abounded in straightforward statements. Often one of his sentences was sufficient to make clear some great truth. He won a reputation for sound judgment, clear insight, and straight thinking until he was a recognized authority on the Nazarenes. Often a quotation from Dr. Chapman brought an end to a debate, for his wisdom was so widely recognized that few questioned what he said.[104]

Corlett's analysis suggests not only that Chapman had various avenues of communication with Nazarenes throughout the denomination, but the thoughts and opinions he voiced through his publications and positions of ministry were extremely influential upon laity, clergy, and other leaders within the church. It is because of the enormous influence he wielded within the denomination that numerous opinions, articles, and editorials from Chapman are cited. It is my task in the next chapter to describe and examine the structure and characteristics of the Sunday morning liturgy in the Church of the Nazarene and the implications of past and present practices upon spirituality and Nazarene identity.

Wiseman, *Two Men of Destiny*, 172–86.

104. Corlett, "Three Million Words," in Wiseman, *Two Men of Destiny*, 177–8.

Chapter 4

The Structure and Characteristics of Sunday Worship in the Church of the Nazarene

WORSHIP IN THE CHURCH of the Nazarene followed a revival pattern that was structured around the sermon and the altar call. This was the shape of Nazarene worship from the very beginning. Preliminaries, as they were referred to, preceded the sermon. Often, these included music, prayer, a passage of Scripture (i.e., normally the text associated with the sermon), offering, occasional testimonies, and announcements, but this form did vary somewhat. Former General Superintendent R. T. Williams, pointed out that the sole purpose of the preliminaries was to *introduce* the sermon, but they "do not constitute the main interest"[1] of the service. The amount of music and the type used differed (i.e., hymns, choruses, gospel songs). Often only one passage of Scripture was read, that being the sermon text; however, there were instances where additional Scripture was included, and sometimes it was read responsively. Prayer was extempore except on those occasions when the Lord's Prayer was included. Worship's basic shape was structured after the preaching service; however, its specific content changed depending on the church and the era.

When the church was in its infancy, orders of worship were not always written down. Whether this was to allow for the freedom of the Spirit in worship or if it was motivated by other reasons is difficult to determine. However, it was not uncommon for bulletins to have no printed order of worship. For example, one of the extant bulletins from Los Angeles First Church in 1914 does not contain an order of worship other than the sermon title. The main content of the bulletin is church news and announcements;

1. Williams, "After Which," 5.

it has nothing to do with the structure of worship on the Lord's Day. One exception is on the Sunday prior to Christmas in 1914, where the songs and participants for the Christmas *Musical Program* are listed.[2] An order of worship for Los Angeles First was provided in the March 26th, 1908, issue of the *Nazarene Messenger*. The article lists not only the pattern of morning worship, but the atmosphere as well:

> It was a glorious sight at 11 a.m. to see the tabernacle packed with a worshipful audience as Dr. Bresee gave out the opening hymn, "Stand up for Jesus." Bro. Haney, the venerable holiness evangelist, led in prayer, and surely heaven and earth met. The vast congregation was lifted into holy joy as they sang, "The Home of the Soul," and then when Dr. Bresee read a telegram from Bro. Hosley of Washington, D.C. stating that the Pennsylvania Conference of the Holiness Christian Church had just voted unanimously for union with our Church, the audience seemed to lose control of itself in the waving of handkerchiefs and glad enthusiasm.
>
> Bro. Bud Robinson was the preacher of the morning, and took for his text John 11:1 . . .
>
> After this unctuous, clear-cut sermon, several seekers came to the altar and were graciously blessed.[3]

A 1909 editorial in the *Nazarene Messenger* recognized the importance of the Spirit directing the course of worship, but in addition it made an appeal towards order. While avoiding universal conformity in the Nazarene liturgy, it emphasized to congregations and clergy alike the importance of moving towards a set order:

> We are warranted in believing from the usages of the Church, when it has been most blest of God, that the same things should ordinarily enter into worship in the sanctuary. There should be songs of praise, prayer, the reading of the Word, and the preaching of the Gospel, sometimes testimony, etc.
>
> We desire to suggest that our own Sunday morning hour of worship, after voluntary songs of praise, the minister should carefully and earnestly read one of the substantial hymns, and that it should be sung by the congregation, they reverently standing. That this should be followed by prayer, the people kneeling. That a verse of song, or an appropriate chorus should voluntarily follow. Then the reading of the Scriptures, at least a part of which might well be a psalm read responsively. Then

2. "Bulletin Los Angeles," December 13.

3. "At the Tabernacle," March 26, 8.

the offering, announcements, and if desired further song and prayer, and the preaching of the Word, with such opportunities for seeking the Lord as may be in accord with the conditions and as the Spirit may suggest.[4]

While Bresee is not specifically listed as the author of the article, at the very least, as editor, he most likely approved of it. The author of the editorial indicates this was an order of worship he used in his own congregation. Also provided are suggested postures for the hymns and prayers. The voluntary songs of praise and optional items allow for both spontaneity and flexibility in the worship pattern. The order suggested in the editorial is displayed in table 1.

This appeal for greater planning and an increased structure in worship was part of the continuing attempt to bring balance between formalism and fanaticism. Between these two problems, the concern over the propensity of fanaticism appearing in Nazarene worship was far greater than fear over formalism:

> There should be a form of church service, not a formal church service. We fear formality only less than fanaticism. But there should be a carefully and prayerfully thought out and prepared method of ordinarily conducting the great services in the house of the Lord. While the services should not be formal, neither should they be "without form and void." It is claimed that every service should be a fresh inspiration. Yes, and the Holy Spirit will inspire our careful thought and preparation much more surely and fully than our careless neglect.[5]

Songs of Praise (Voluntary)

Hymn (read by the pastor, then sung by congregation.)

Prayer

Song (one verse) or a Chorus

Scripture (an optional responsive Psalm may be added)

Offering

Announcements

Optional Songs or Prayer may be added

Sermon

Response to the Sermon

Table 1. Suggested order of worship in the February 11, 1909, *Nazarene Messenger*

4. "Forms of Worship," 6.
5. "Use of the Hymn," 6.

The burden of Nazarene leadership regarding the need for greater uniformity and an order of worship does not soon disappear. It resurfaces in denominational literature in later years. During the 1930s J. B. Chapman addresses this problem on two different occasions in less than five years. His editorial column in *The Preacher's Magazine* contained the following petition:

> I remember . . . that Dr. Bresee used to say there is a middle ground between the unplanned and the ritualistic service. He thought more people would be able to take part and get profit out of the worship if something of a regular program were followed from time to time.
>
> It was extreme, of course, but I have known a preacher who was called upon to lead in the Lord's Prayer in a Sunday school service, and his memory failed him at a vital place, so that the service was broken and hindered.
>
> Brother E. O. Chalfant was impressed . . . that the bishops at the General Conference of the Methodist Episcopal Church, South, spent considerable time before the devotional services in selecting the hymns and arranging for their use in proper order.
>
> If you have been an itinerant preacher you have no doubt often felt hindered because there was no sympathy between the plan of the worship service and the sermon you felt led to bring. If either you could have had charge of the service, or if the one in charge had consulted you, it would have been much better. . . . If there is a song leader, even then, especially during the Sunday morning service, the pastor should select the hymn and songs and should do this before the service starts and should make the whole service a unit.
>
> In our Nazarene meetings we seem to be almost enslaved to "special songs," and often these are rendered in such a way as to be a menace to [Sunday morning worship]. . . .
>
> . . . Chiefly I wanted to say that I believe it is worth any preacher's while to seek to improve his worship service. In doing this, I believe he should build around the sermon, and that he should select the Scripture readings and the hymns, and prepare himself for public prayer with this united service in mind. . . . Perhaps someone will answer that a plan of this kind will become a hindrance to the freedom of the Spirit. But I believe it will be a means of deepening the spiritual life, and when the Holy Spirit comes in special manifestation, surely all our preachers and people have the good sense to give Him free right of way, no matter what the plans had been. . . .
>
> I would not have any preacher give less attention to the sermon or to any other part of the service (unless it is to the

announcements, which are the ban[e] of a thousand good meetings), but I would exhort for more attention to the worship
"program."[6]

The tenor of Chapman's argument gives the distinct impression that the
content of the worship structure was loosely organized and often spontaneous. There may have been a common worship *ordo* that was used, but little
thought was given in finding unity between the various components, such
as integrating the music to the sermon text and theme. Part of the reason for
this dilemma seems to be the result of failing to plan the hymns or gospel
songs in advance.

 Chapman also indicates another tendency. When someone besides
the pastor was responsible for the music, often such persons did not communicate their selections to the pastor. A bulletin from Los Angeles First
in 1936 reflects this type of spontaneity. Although it does list an order of
worship, whereas some of the earlier bulletins do not, there is no indication
of the specific songs that will be used. The order from April 19, 1936, is
as follows: congregational singing, responsive reading, prayer, choir, offering, vocal solo, and preaching. There is a similar order in a 1940s order of
worship: congregational singing, responsive reading, prayer, choir, offering,
announcements, vocal solo, and sermon. Both instances provide the name
of the sermon, but the hymns or gospel songs are not listed.[7] So although
the sermon title is printed in advance, the songs are not listed. This could reflect the desire for flexibility in the music, which would facilitate the much-
coveted freedom in the Spirit.

 Chapman is more specific in addressing the lack of order in worship with the second article, which appears in the June 1939 issue of *The
Preacher's Magazine*:

> Spontaneity is wonderful for occasions, but is not dependable
> as a regular affair. The preacher should have a definite idea of
> where he is going from the time the first hymn is announced
> until the last handshake at the door. If an unusual outpouring
> of the Spirit directs the meeting in other channels, he should
> always be glad. . . . But if the meeting proves to be "usual," it
> should have order.[8]

Clearly he is indicating that spontaneity was often central in carving the
shape of both the worship *ordo* and its content. Apparently, Chapman

 6. Chapman, "Program of Worship," 1–2.

 7. "Bulletin Los Angeles," April 19, 16; "Bulletin Los Angeles," August 8, 32.

 8. Chapman, "Well Planned Worship Service," 2.

believed that the direction and shape of the liturgy was frequently determined while worship was occurring, rather than planned in advance. The
inclusion of this second article is perhaps both a sign of the extent of the
problem and a reflection of its persistence despite attempts to encourage
order and greater uniformity. Chapman even includes six sample orders of
worship. Three of the sample orders include suggested hymns one might
use, while the remaining three do not. Table 2 shows three of the orders
Chapman recommended.

Following his list of sample worship orders, Chapman enlists the following appeal to his readers:

> We do not, as a rule, select the hymns with sufficient care. We
> are largely overburdened with "special singing." We run our
> "preliminaries" too long. We dwell too much on the "announce-
> ments." . . . We do not read the Scriptures well. We often preach
> too long. We waste time getting started in the sermon. We
> scatter and spread and show want of concentration. We do not
> know how to conclude the service properly. We do not all have
> all these faults, but most of us have some of them, and there is
> nothing better than that we should look at the model and try to
> mend our ways.[9]

Although Chapman encourages pastors to find variations with these orders, it is evident that his purpose is twofold. He is admonishing pastors
to prepare for worship, rather than leaving everything to spontaneity, and,
by providing suggested orders, he is encouraging some uniformity in the
Nazarene liturgy.

A recent history of the Church of the Nazarene, *Our Watchword and
Song*, stated that in the years following World War II, the freedom desired
in the worship structure, which had existed since the beginnings days of
the denomination, gradually subsided. It became common to have printed
orders of worship in bulletins. The authors also suggest that the typical worship pattern in 1950s and 60s "began with a prelude, followed by a hymn
(or possibly two), a responsive reading from the hymnal, pastoral prayer,
the choir, announcements and welcome, the offering and offertory, a special
song (usually a solo), the sermon, and a closing hymn."[10] Bulletins from
the 1970s show a similar pattern as reflected in a printed worship order
from Kansas City First which lists a prelude, call to worship, invocation,
hymn, Scripture reading, hymn, pastoral prayer, choir selection, offering,

9. Ibid., 2–3.

10. Cunningham, *Our Watchword and Song*, 437.

announcements, solo, sermon, hymn, and benediction.[11] During the 1990s, several years prior to his election to the general superintendency of the church, Stan Toler offered the following suggested order of worship in *The Preacher's Magazine*: greeting, song, Scripture (one verse), hymn, hymn, special music, prayer chorus, pastoral prayer, offering, special music, message, benediction, choral benediction.[12] Obviously these orders of worship provide an extremely minute sampling of Nazarene congregations; however, what is important to discern is the commonality they share.

Despite the variance within these orders, there are also several similarities common to Nazarene liturgies. The placement of the sermon is typically located at the end of the service. This practice was modeled after American revivalism so worship could end in an altar call. Music is abundant in each of these orders, including the implementation of the choir or *special music*, which generally indicates the music is performed by trained or gifted musicians. Whenever this form of music occurs in the liturgy, congregational participation in singing is typically nonextant. The inclusion of Scripture in all three orders is minimal. Two of the orders indicate a passage of Scripture is to be read. It is likely this is in addition to the sermon text, but on one of these orders this extra passage is a single verse. Two of the orders include a time for announcements, which is another common feature of Nazarene worship. While all the worship orders list other prayers such as an invocation or benediction, the major prayer is referred to as the pastoral prayer. Often prior to the pastoral prayer, some individuals from the congregation will choose to gather at the communion rail to pray while kneeling. It is noteworthy that there are no litanies, collects, or other written prayer forms in any of these orders of worship. Finally, the predominant pattern, as exemplified in the above orders, is the absence of the eucharist from worship on most occasions.

11. "Kansas City First Bulletin," March 7, file 2262–04.
12. Toler, "Worship and Preaching Helps," 58.

Service Suggestion Number One (order only)	Invocation
	Hymn of praise to God
	Psalm and short prayer of thanksgiving
	"Our Father, which are in heaven . . . "
	Hymn of faith or prayer
	General Prayer
	Hymn of confidence or personal testimony
	Offering
	Song of willingness and receptivity
	Sermon
	Hymn of consecration or invitation
	Benediction
Service Suggestion Number Three (order only)	Hymn of Praise
	Devotional Scripture (Psalm)
	Hymn of Humility or Need
	Prayer
	Scripture lesson
	Song of Testimony
	Offering
	Hymn of readiness
	Sermon
	Hymn of consecration or challenge
	Benediction
Service Suggestion Number Six (order with suggestion of Psalm and hymns)	Hymn, "From All that Dwell Below the Skies" (12)
	Psalm 64
	Prayer
	Hymn, "Meditation" (104)
	Scripture Reading
	Offering
	Hymn, "Every Day and Hour" (249)
	Sermon
	Hymn, "A Charge to Keep I Have" (131)

Table 2. Suggested orders of worship in the June 1939 issue of *The Preacher's Magazine*

The Preaching Service

Traditionally the focal point of Nazarene worship was the sermon. Other elements in the service were often referred to simply as *the preliminaries*. Although most were deemed important to the liturgy, their primary function was to complement the sermon. Therefore, the structure of Nazarene worship is essentially a preaching service. It will be helpful to this discussion if each of the distinct components of Nazarene worship, and their function within the preaching service, is analyzed separately.

Music

Nazarenes have always regarded music as one of the most important features of worship. An analysis of church periodicals not only reveals a vast appreciation for music, but also it brings to light matters that some denominational leaders, clergy, and people found troubling. Very early in Nazarene history concern was voiced that the music not be selected and employed simply for its aesthetic qualities and emotive potential. It was essential that the message of the music be conveyed as well; therefore, steps were taken to communicate the content. One of the practices encouraged in a *Nazarene Messenger* editorial involved taking one of the "substantial hymns"[13] and reading it audibly to the congregation prior to the congregation's singing of it. The editorial provided the following guidance:

> At the moment of the beginning of the great service on the Sabbath, the minister should announce a carefully selected hymn, which he should clearly and impressively read. . . . This reading should not be an extempore affair. The hymn through which the congregation is to pour its praise and worship and adoration, should be thoroughly studied and mastered by the pastor, and its great thoughts and rhythm should be poured upon the minds and hearts of, the people preparatory to their using of it. . . . When the hymn is sung by the congregation, in which every person in the house should join, from the pulpit to the back pew, saying devoutly and earnestly the words, if they are by nature or condition deprived of joining in the tune, but as far as possible and as earnestly as possible, all the people should sing. This may not be without art, but it is not a matter of art; it may be full of

13. "Forms of Worship," 6.

sweetest entertainment, but it is not entertainment. It is united
praise and adoration, when the people see God and worship.[14]

The editorial highlights several points which voice concern over the
proper use of music in the liturgy. Its author wants to ensure that the words
are understood and that the music is not utilized for emotive reasons alone.
The editorial states that the purpose of music is for the congregation to
praise, worship, and adore God. Therefore, knowing the content of what is
sung is crucial, since cognitive recognition is essential to prevent the spoken
words from being uttered mindlessly and to ensure that they flowed from the
heart. Additionally, the singing must be the praise and worship of the entire
congregation; therefore, the participation of everyone was essential.[15] If in
the unlikely event someone was unable to sing, they could at least *devoutly
and earnestly* say the words. To summarize, the primary purpose of using
music in worship is not for its aesthetic or entertainment value, but rather as
a means to prepare the listener for the preaching of the Word.

Other issues of the *Nazarene Messenger* reverberate similar concerns,
like an article on hymnody that appeared in 1901:

Certain qualities are necessary in a hymn. Firstly, it must have
some sense in it. If we are to "sing with understanding," there
must be something to understand. It must not be a mere jingle
of sound, it must contain thoughts and ideas. Secondly, the
words used must express truth. Singing is worship, and men are
to worship in spirit and in truth; but how can man worship in
truth by singing a falsehood? . . .

There are words the reading of which would provoke laugh-
ter, and tunes set to them which do not subdue and chasten the
soul, but rather excite worldly emotions and passions. Such
hymns as these do not soften, convict or convert men; they do
not cast down high thoughts, nor bring minds into subjection to
the gospel of Christ. . . .

There are hundreds of hymns that have been tested for
generations. There is no question about their character or their
tendency. . . . And while we hail the new songs which come to us
like bird notes which herald the dawn of day, we cannot spare,
we must not forget, these grand old hymns; sound in teaching,
rich in melody, full of heavenly pathos, blessed of God to the

14. "Use of the Hymn," 6.

15. *The Holiness Evangel* also included an article reflecting this concern of congregational participation in the singing; see "Reports from the Field," December 9, 3.

salvation of sinners, the upbuilding of saints, the advancement
of religion, and the glory of our common Lord.[16]

Identified within this article are the objectives of effectual music. Proper
songs and hymnody should glorify God, edify the saints, and lead to the
conviction and conversion of souls.[17] Bresee and the early Nazarenes published their own hymnal in 1905. Bangs indicates that "One hundred twenty-four of the 308 songs [in *Waves of Glory*] were . . . 'standard hymns'[18] and
forty of these were by Charles Wesley." Obviously, there was an appreciation for the older hymns of the church, like those from eighteenth-century
Methodism. There was also an awareness of the potential dangers of music
that lacked substance but served only to move the emotions. A consistent
theme throughout denominational literature is the disquietude regarding
the potential for worship music to degenerate into entertainment.

During the 1915 General Assembly, a committee was appointed for
the purposes of producing an official hymnal for the denomination. Due to
financial restrictions, the production of an authorized hymnal was delayed
until 1931.[19] However, this action prompted an article that voiced both
excitement and apprehension over the contents of the anticipated hymnal:

> We were delighted at the movement put in operation by the
> leadership of Brother W. M. Creal at the recent General Assem-
> bly for the production of a suitable hymnal for the Pentecostal
> Church of the Nazarene. We sincerely trust that Brother Creal
> and his committee may succeed in financing the enterprise and
> the new hymnal may appear. It is far more important, however,
> that the new song book may be of the proper character than that
> we may have a new one. We need and ought to have hymn book;
> not a book of ditties and light-natured songs, such as we have
> heard in religious meetings and even in holiness meetings. . . .
>
> There is a lack of depth and gospel truth and gravity and
> dignity in many of these songs. There is a lightness and a rapid-
> ity and swagger of movement in them which is not conducive
> to devotion, but only stir the merest surface of the lighter emo-
> tions and tend to dissipate real devotion. We have often seen in
> the song services these emotions so stirred and such a sway of

16. "Good Old Hymns," 7.

17. An article in the *Pentecostal Advocate* argues that the only purpose of music
in worship "is to assist the soul in its devotion toward God. . . . Away with the song, no
matter who composed it, if it does not lift the soul toward God and make the heart and
life better." London, "Music and Education," 2.

18. Bangs, *Phineas Bresee*, 239.

19. Mund, *Keep the Music Ringing*, 14.

excitement on the lines of the energy of the flesh that the congregation was practically worn out before the preaching hour arrived, and the deepest purposes of the preaching practically defeated before it began.

> The remedy for this is in the character of hymns we are to train our people to sing. . . . We earnestly trust that the grand old hymns of the Wesleys and others are not doomed forever to be ignored by the Holiness Movement.[20]

The fear that worship should digress into entertainment because of inappropriate music was not new. Such concerns were addressed in various denominational publications.[21] One article even suggested that people, evangelists, leaders, and preachers preferred such music instead of hymnody with greater substance, since the "light, lively, humorous songs . . . produce a stir"[22] of the emotions and are what people most desire. Criticism of contemporary music was wide ranging. Songs that lacked sound theology; music that was poorly composed and arranged; words that were misspelled or songs containing grammatically incorrect construction; songs with repetitious verses; and services being turned into a performance were among some of the complaints filed against church music.[23] The fact that this dilemma is addressed continuously is an indication that the use of unsuitable music was not only a perceived problem but likely a common occurrence within Nazarene congregations. Ironically, despite these perils, there was still the persistent desire to appropriate more contemporary music that transcended some of the perceived limitations of the classical hymns.

Even though many recognized the potential dangers of modern songs, there appeared to be an interest among denominational leaders to adopt music that reflected the victorious experience of those who had claimed entire sanctification. J. B. Chapman addresses this tension that existed:

> While the Wesleyan movement [i.e., John Wesley's eighteenth-century movement] was so mature doctrinally that no advance beyond it has been either desirable or possible, the songs of those times, as they have come down to us, indicate that the dominant feeling with reference to holiness was that of "pursuit" rather than of "possession." This is not entirely true, of course,

20. Haynes, "Great Hymns for Holiness," 2.

21. Several articles voiced similar concerns over the music used in worship and the future of Nazarene hymnody; see "Good Old Hymns," 7; Barbieur, "Old-Time Singing," 13; Day, "Church Music," 7–8; Wordsworth, "Singing with the Spirit," 11–12; Lillenas, "Literature of Hymnology," 7–8.

22. Marsh, "Release the Accelerator," 9.

23. "Singing Church Service," 2; Ciprico, "Church Music," 7.

but it is dominantly so, and the best songs and hymns of that day which have lived are those which express the sentiments of mourners and of those who are seeking to become holy. Their contribution to the hymnology of "Assurance" and "Victory" was small and uncharacteristic.

And though some would wish it could be done, the hundreds of songs and hymns of that "Penitential" day which have died during the century and half which separates us from the time of their birth cannot be revived; not only because they sound droll, unpoetical and unmusical to our ears, but principally because they emphasize heart hunger, whereas, we want poets who can teach us the song of victory.[24]

Chapman indicates an appreciation for the older hymns of Wesley and others but at the same time believes they are inadequate for the current age. Despite his suggestion that such music is not appropriate for contemporary worship, since "they sound droll"[25] and are found wanting in their poetic ability, this is not his main area of contention. He finds the Wesleyan hymns limited in being able to adequately reflect the religious experiences of the Nazarenes. He does not blame the Wesleys themselves but argues that the spirituality of the twentieth-century holiness movement exceeded that of Wesley's day. In other words, Chapman is suggesting that the experience of Christian perfection was not as prevalent in Wesley's day as it was in Chapman's own time. Chapman concludes that the Wesleys did not write more victorious songs because even though the eighteenth-century Methodists were seeking entire sanctification—they were not attaining it. Therefore, the Wesley's hymnody reflected penitence for sin rather than victory over it. However, because individuals are being sanctified entirely at Nazarene altars, Chapman insists that his age requires victorious songs, a quality he finds lacking in the hymns of John and Charles Wesley.

Chapman's assessment of Wesleyan hymnody not only has theological implications beyond our intentions here, but it reveals a distinct quality that he finds essential in modern music within the holiness movement. He makes it clear that the hymnody used in Nazarene worship needs to express the subjective experiences of those who are entirely sanctified. The words and imagery of hymnody should provide assurance for attaining Christian perfection and be descriptive of the victory one experiences once original sin is vanquished. Chapman states that the holiness movement requires music that contains "distinctive holiness songs in which the triumphant note

24. Chapman, "We May Sing," 1.
25. Ibid.

is dominant."[26] He believes that the Wesley hymns are deficient since they focus primarily on penitential attitudes and seeking to be holy, rather than achieving it:

> Every proper thing has its dangers. That of the Wesleyan hymnology was the dominance of the doleful and the mournful. The demands on the minister of that day were fulfilled when he testified that he was "groaning" after perfect love, and there seemed to be a somewhat unwritten prejudice against his claiming that he had "attained" that for which he groaned. The hymns, likewise, express the prayer for perfect holiness; but too frequently they left the singer standing on Jordan's stormy bank and looking with wistful eyes to "Canaan's fair and happy land where my possessions lie." So long as they were the language of a true, earnest, expectant seeking, the old hymnology was all right, but the tendency was to make seeking the goal and to live always in the attitude of striving for a practically unattainable goal.[27]

An excerpt from Bresee's sermon, "The Lifting of the Veil," reveals that he had similar sentiments to Chapman. Although he valued older hymnody, such as those from early Methodism, Bresee was also seeking music that would proclaim the current sense of victory that was part of the experience of Nazarenes who were entirely sanctified:

> I have examined with a good deal of interest, Charles Wesley's hymns on consecration and sanctification, as given in the Methodist Hymnal. . . . Over and over is repeated the deep, impassioned cry, the promise of God, and the way to enter in. That men are to enter now, by faith, is plainly taught. These hymns give rare, little glimpses of experience which comes after one has entered, but viewed more as a hope. . . .
>
> But why the fact that all, or nearly all, of those hymns deal only with the transitional period, if it be not that this was the place where the church at that day largely lived?
>
> The hymnology of the worship of holy hearts is scarce. The great hymns—those most familiar to us, which the fathers and mothers have sung—are mostly a cry out of the darkness, a cry for help, the cry of need. "Rock of Ages," "Jesus Lover of My Soul," And among another class of singers, "Nearer My God to Thee," and "Lead, Kindly Light," are all prized, but are they not chiefly a cry out of the darkness for light and help?

26. Ibid.

27. Ibid., 1–2.

I hardly know where to turn for singable hymns of real devotion. We have what is called a rich hymnology. But the hymns are so largely, simply sentimental, or descriptive, or the cry of an imprisoned soul for deliverance, or an endangered one for help! I admit, good in their places, but hardly the songs to be sung by holy hearts at the feet of Him whom we love better than all else. The songs of worship and adoration—where shall we find them?[28]

On the other hand, there were also voices challenging Chapman's view of the older hymns, especially those of John and Charles Wesley. J. Glenn Gould responded to this position a few years later in an article in the *Herald of Holiness*. He stated that Chapman may have been correct in his assertions with some of the Wesleyan hymnody, but the Wesleyan hymns which were still used in the holiness movement *did exert* a triumphant tone. He also indicated that the older hymns were often Christocentric, which was a distinct contrast to the very subjective music characteristic of modern songs, "These old hymns . . . revolve around the person and work of Jesus: His mission and message, His suffering and death, His triumphant resurrection, His glorious atonement, His shedding forth of the Holy Spirit."[29] Gould acknowledged that some of the contemporary gospel hymns were quite valuable to the holiness movement, but he also sounded a warning of the dangers posed to the church focused upon overly subjective music.[30]

Chapman also recognized such dangers. Even though he believed that earlier hymnody was inadequate in expressing the religious experiences of the twentieth-century holiness people, he concluded his editorial by issuing a caution on the use of more recent music. He argued some contemporary songs portray a false version of Christian experience with its "'jiggy' music and light words."[31] For Chapman the future of Nazarene hymnody rested in the tension between finding hymnody as theologically robust as the contributions made by Wesley and other time-tested hymnists, but also reflected the subjective experiences of twentieth-century holiness people.

Perhaps one of the soundest perspectives was voiced by Nazarene theologian, H. Orton Wiley. He called for a reevaluation of the hymns that congregations were implementing in public worship. Wiley argued God should be the object of our worship and the music should reflect that liturgical orientation. He also suggested it was proper for "the church with

28. As quoted in Girvin, *Bresee Prince in Israel*, 364–6.
29. Gould, "Music Church Service," 8.
30. Ibid.
31. Chapman, "We May Sing," 1.

her means of grace"[32] to be a theme of the hymnody. He writes, "A study of those hymns of acknowledged and enduring worth in the public worship of the church reveals two characteristics—*first*, they are objective in the sense that they direct the worshiper's thought to something outside of, and beyond himself; and *secondly*, they deal with the group rather than with the individuals."[33] Wiley states that the place of more subjective and individualistic forms of music was not in public worship but rather in other contexts such as the evangelistic service. It is in the non-liturgical settings where it would be appropriate for "hymns and songs of warning or comfort, songs of exhortation and appeal, or songs depicting the peace and joy of the Christian life."[34] Despite Wiley's recognition that there was a place for some of the more subjective songs, he found no value in "meaningless jingles."[35] The test of all music is it should "minister both truth and grace to the hearers."[36]

The tension among Nazarenes in finding appropriate music, and the ensuing arguments that followed, did not begin with Chapman. An 1893 article in the *Beulah Christian* included the following excerpt from *Bennett's History of Methodism* to support what it views as inappropriate music in worship:

> Mr. Wesley watched over his societies with the care of a father, and corrected every error among the Methodists as soon as he saw it. "I put a stop" he says, "to a bad custom which I found creeping in at Warrenton. A few men who had fine voices, sang a psalm which no one knew, in a tune fit for an opera. . . . What an insult upon common sense! What a burlesque upon public worship! No custom can excuse such a mixture of profaneness and absurdity."
>
> We commend this passage to the notice of those who are engaged in the work of changing the grand old tunes of Methodism into the ear-stunning operas of the present day.[37]

Ironically another type of tampering with the traditional hymns had already occurred at the hands of American revivalism. Some of the beloved hymns of eighteenth-century writers such as Isaac Watts and John Wesley were modified to fit the concerns of the camp meeting atmosphere during the Second Great Awakening. Verses were added and/or the lyrics were "set to

32. Wiley, "Public Worship," 2.
33. Ibid.
34. Ibid.
35. Ibid., 3.
36. Ibid., 2.
37. "Wesley and Singing," 4.

more contemporary and improvisatorial music."[38] Often imagery and language characteristic of earlier evangelical hymnody was borrowed; however,
it consistently "reflected an individualized, pietistic emphasis."[39]

The preferred music for the camp meeting and revival atmosphere was
the "popular, simple, repetitive revival music"[40] like that found in the gospel hymn (i.e., gospel song), which was born of that era. It was a "new genre
of popular hymnody that arose after the Civil War, [and] became ubiquitous
through urban revivalism."[41] Gospel hymns were highly subjective in nature and designed to stimulate an individual spiritual experience. It has even
been suggested that gospel songs, "unlike other forms of hymnody, have
the childlike quality of nursery rhymes."[42] Gospel hymnody took its name
from the collection of songs Dwight L. Moody employed in his revivals. His
songbook was entitled *Gospel Hymns*.[43] Contributors to this style of music
included hymn writers such as William Kirkpatrick, Fanny Crosby, William
Bradbury, and Thomas Hastings, all of whom wrote gospel hymns that are
still found in last published Nazarene Hymnal, *Sing to the Lord*.[44]

Originally they were used exclusively in camp meetings and revivals,
but during the latter part of the nineteenth century, gospel hymns infiltrated
the liturgy of many congregations. This invasion, however, did not come
without resistance. It created tension within several denominations, including Methodism. Critics of this new musical style were convinced that it was
a counterfeit form of hymnody that served primarily to corrupt the liturgy.[45] Others, however, believed that gospel hymns were an essential music
genre for converting the lost. Tucker not only addresses the conflict within
late nineteenth-century Methodism that was created by the gospel hymn,
but also warns of other potential liabilities:

> Concerns that hymns of doctrinal depth (e.g., the Wesley
> hymns) form the core repertoire, rather than popular but theo-
> logically bankrupt "ditties," were met with the argument that
> the salvation of souls could be accomplished only with recently
> composed songs of sound sentiment and fervent devotion, and
> for that reason denominational hymn books were rarely used

38. Van Dyken, "Singing the Gospel," 18.

39. Ibid., 17.

40. Ibid., 19–20.

41. Rothenbusch, "Is This Beulah," 53.

42. Larson, "When Heaven," 171.

43. Rothenbusch, "Land of Beulah," 53.

44. Van Dyken, "Singing the Gospel," 19.

45. Ibid., 116–8.

at revivals. . . . the gospel hymn's stress upon personal, autono-
mous religion and freedom of choice accentuated, perhaps un-
wittingly, one of the basic tenets of liberalism.[46]

Tucker is not alone in critiquing the effects of the gospel hymn upon both
worship and spirituality. Esther Rothenbusch, in her analysis of the gospel
hymn, points out another troublesome result of its use within the holiness
movement:

> The third significant shift in early twentieth-century Holiness
> hymns is the greater emphasis on supernatural manifesta-
> tions, power, and personal experience. The new texts tend to
> marginalize the Spirit's person, character, ministries, and Deity.
> God's power and glory become separated from Him, and the
> distinction between spiritual gifts and commodities that could
> be "prayed down" becomes blurred. . . . Hymns more often refer
> to "the glory," and "the power" rather than to God in His glory,
> or to "the fire," rather than God as a consuming fire. The trend,
> in a word, was a sensationalization of the Spirit in the Holiness
> movement that ironically seemed to overlook God in His holi-
> ness, a neglect of the worship of God in the quest for one's expe-
> rience of Him—that which He could give and do.[47]

Although some of the Wesley hymns were used by the Nazarenes,
there was a much greater usage of the gospel hymns. Mund points out that
"Nazarene hymnody has always been of [an] American Tradition rather
than European and therefore, more gospel song-oriented."[48] Tamara Van
Dyken states that gospel hymns are responsible for the development of
many styles found in contemporary Christian music.[49]

The gospel hymn has had a significant influence in the evolution of
music used in a substantial portion of Nazarene congregations. Contemporary musical forms are often highly subjective in nature. Regularly they
lack the theological depth found in eighteenth-century hymnody, and their
focus is upon one's personal experience of God. While the intent both of
gospel hymns and much of contemporary music is to facilitate "individual
conversion,"[50] it has wielded an adverse effect on spirituality by contributing
to the individualism and narcissistic psyche commonly found in American
Christianity. Marva Dawn addresses the problems caused by those mu-

46. Tucker, *American Methodist Worship*, 170.
47. Rothenbusch, "Is This Beulah," 69.
48. Mund, *Keep the Music Ringing*, 24.
49. Van Dyken, "Singing the Gospel," 234.
50. Ibid., 235.

sic forms that shift the focus off God; it is a dramatic change from older hymnody. Dawn charges that this narcissistic shift is both "dangerous . . . [and] subtle"[51] and one that the modern church at worship encounters:

> When God is the subject, our character is formed in response to his.
>
> In contrast, focusing in worship on me and my feelings and my praising will nurture a character that is inward-turned, that thinks first of self rather than God. Though many modern songs actually praise not God but how well we are loving him, this tendency isn't found only in modern music. The old camp song "We Are Climbing Jacob's Ladder," for example, does the same thing. We sing that we are climbing higher in our relationship with God, rather than that God comes down to us in his revelation of himself. Such a theme teaches us to depend on our feelings or efforts, rather than on God's gift of grace, in assessing our relationship with God. . . .
>
> It is urgent that the Church recognize how easily we assume the self-centered mind-set of culture that surrounds us and work more deliberately to reject it.[52]

The early Nazarenes did identify with Wesley on the importance he attributed to the role of music in worship. Music was a critical ingredient in the liturgy for many of the groups that came out of the holiness movement. However, much of the music used by the holiness movement differed significantly from the hymns the Wesleys implemented in their revivals and society meetings. The hymns of John and Charles Wesley were saturated with doctrinal teaching, which followed the *via salutis*. John compiled and edited Charles's hymns for the specific purpose of not only promoting inward religion, but to provide complete and balanced doctrinal instruction. The Wesley hymns were experiential in nature, yet they were also objective—embedded with words and biblical imagery that held a much richer theological content than most of the gospel songs of American revivalism. Former General Superintendent William Greathouse, in a 1989 paper he presented at Nazarene Theological Seminary, addressed what he considered to be a crisis in worship. One of the problems he identifies concerns the music:

> More than 40 years ago General Superintendent Chapman complained that many Nazarene services had more of the atmosphere of "an old-fashioned mountain corn husking," than of the

51. Dawn, *Reaching Out*, 107.

52. Ibid., 107–10.

worship of Almighty God. He was struck by the fact that many
pastors did not know the difference between hymns (which are
addressed to God—or at least are God centered in content) and
gospel songs (which are subjective and experience centered).
The latter may be appropriate, he said, as the service moves into
a more intimate and personal mood, but a service of worship
should open . . . with the acknowledgement and adoration of
God, with hymns like "Come, Thou Almighty King" or "O For
a Thousand Tongues," music and words that enable the soul to
rise into God's presence. . . .

Not many months ago I was in one of our larger churches
in the Midwest; a truly great and influential church. I was disap-
pointed and grieved in the Spirit not to be able to join in singing
a single hymn of worship that morning. It was a gospel song
service throughout. And although the people sang lustily, I
sensed little of the "wonder, love, and praise" my heart yearned
to experience. The entire service was experience centered.[53]

Music in the Church of the Nazarene is the catalyst for at least part of
our current liturgical orientation. When pastors and people refer to worship
style, they are predominately referring to the music. Many of the worship
wars that occurred in Nazarene congregations over the past forty years were
over the issue of music. Even the liturgical diversity that is found among
Nazarene congregations was in many ways driven by the decisions made
over musical options. Troublesome tendencies in our culture, which have
infiltrated the church, such as individualism and trends toward narcissism,
was reinforced by music that has tended to be overly subjective and often
lacking in scriptural integrity. While this is not true of all contemporary
music it does characterize a significant portion of it. Pastors, worship leaders, and musicians need to be equipped with the tools and resources to adequately evaluate the music employed in worship.

Current music trends in Nazarene worship did not emerge out of a
vacuum. Although culture has played a significant part in influencing worship in a highly subjective direction, the seeds were already sown years
earlier. Since the focus of worship was evangelism, the gospel hymn became
the main staple of Nazarene worship. This preference for the gospel songs
is evinced not only in the early Nazarene hymnal but continued with the
release of later hymnals. Fred Mund, in describing the 1972 release of the
Church of the Nazarene's third authorized hymnal, *Worship in Song*, characterizes it as a "Jesus-oriented hymnal."[54] He states that almost all the songs

53. Greathouse, "Present Crisis in Worship," 4–5.
54. Mund, *Keep the Music Ringing*, 24.

made some reference to Jesus, while less than twenty-four of the hymns addressed God.[55] Mund's description exemplifies the fact that the balance in biblical imagery, doctrine, and experience characteristic of the Wesley hymnals was missing from Nazarene hymnody. The genre of music known as gospel hymns reflected the overall liturgical concerns of the evangelical movement. Worship's fundamental purpose was to use the means available to facilitate crisis experiences at the altar. Music was employed not only to set the mood for worship but also served as a vehicle to transition from the sermon to the altar call. While the altar call was initiated during preaching, the music was essential in accomplishing the task.

Significant changes in music began to occur in the mid to late 1960s, with the shift in culture, diminishing of revivalism, and advent of the church-growth movement. Whereas previously one of the primary roles of music was to create an atmosphere conducive to spiritual experiences, music gradually became the medium to attract people into the church. Thus, congregations began to search for music styles that would attract their targeted demographic. Towards the end of the twentieth century and into the twenty-first, some contributors to the *Preacher's Magazine* echoed similar calls as that of previous generations. There was a growing sense that much of the music incorporated into public worship lacked substance and tended in the direction of entertainment. Some felt that the church needed to return to the older hymns of the church. Others argued that *not all* contemporary music was deficient. Much of it *was* theologically grounded and for the church to be culturally relevant modern forms were indispensable. Pastors were urged to find ways to encourage congregational participation in singing and reduce the amount of music that was given over to "special music"[56] or reserved for choirs or professionals, since it diminished congregational participation in the liturgy.

As the culture changed, new tensions arose in worship and much of it surrounded the new forms of music which were appearing. Some argued that the church needed to embrace the new styles of music, which included everything from southern gospel to rock.

Advancements in technology meant that there was less reliance on a printed hymnal and greater access to current musical forms. Many churches inserted copies of contemporary choruses and popular music into the bulletin. Others turned to projection systems, which in some cases eliminated

---

55. Ibid.

56. *Specials* or *special music* is the term the Church of the Nazarene has given to music that is sung by one or more individuals where the congregation serves as spectators and does not participate. It is a frequent part of many Nazarene worship services and has been since the beginning.

the use of the hymnal altogether. Gradually congregations stopped turning pages in the hymnal and instead often gazed at the words of the music as it was projected onto a screen. While seemingly insignificant, many of these changes, and others, have had important ramifications for Nazarene worship. The question we should be asking is what are the resulting consequences of the changes we make in worship?

Prayer

Throughout the Church's history Nazarenes have typically regarded public prayer as a spontaneous event. There are minor exceptions to this rule such as the occasional use of the Lord's Prayer or the rarely used written prayers found in the rituals section of the *Manual*. Even so, spontaneity is the hallmark of the holiness movement and thought essential if the Spirit of God is going to be free to work amongst his people. Nazarenes attributed the set forms of worship, including written prayers, as a chief cause for what they perceived as spiritual decay in the *cathedral* churches.[57] An article in the *Beulah Christian* reflects the sentiments of most in the holiness movement: "Formal prayers are tombs for the backslidden in heart. But *praying in the Holy Ghost* is the mightiest revival force on earth."[58]

Although extempore prayer was generally seen as the only legitimate form of prayer, it was not without its defects. Articles consistently surfaced in the *Herald of Holiness* and *The Preacher's Magazine* to address the chronic problem of incompetent prayers. The articles most often referred to the prayer considered the fundamental prayer of Nazarene worship, the pastoral prayer. Critiques included problems such as "vain repetition,"[59] the use of endearing names for God, protracted prayers, employing meaningless words, and the pastor's lack of preparation for prayer.[60] S. L. Morgan's article included the following complaint: "The poor form and lack of fervor in our public prayers in general are a reproach to us. Now and then some pastor delights me with the fervor, the dignity, the noble form of his public prayer. But this is rather the exception."[61]

57. Bresee, "Lamb," 2. A *cathedral service* or worship was the label Bresee and others gave to the liturgy of the mainline denominations from which many in the holiness movement emerged, especially those churches of the prayer book tradition. This includes Methodists, Presbyterians, Roman Catholics, Lutherans, etc.

58. "Revivals," 4.

59. "Maintaining the Form," 1.

60. Ibid.; Chapman, "Leading the Public Prayer," 1; Wordsworth, "Pastoral Prayer," 23.

61. Morgan, "Our Poor Public Prayers," 34.

Responses to this problem included various remedies. Although some suggestions hinted at the idea, none of them actually proposed that the denomination should consider returning to Wesley's practice of using both written and extemporary prayers to address this dilemma.[62] J. B. Chapman states that public prayer should be modeled after the Lord's Prayer: "Form is distinguished from formality in that form is capable of vitality. Good taste suggests that the public prayer should pattern somewhat after the 'Lord's Prayer,' and contain its elements of thanksgiving, as well as petition, and that it should close with praise and adoration in both words and spirit."[63]

A. M. Hills suggests that clergy compose their public prayers to include adoration, praise and thanksgiving, confession, supplication, and intercession.[64] Others argue that to resolve the issue of deficient prayers the pastor should prepare in advance before praying publicly.[65] However, this corrective was carefully distinguished from writing the prayer in advance and then praying it:

> There were reformers who gave their lives over the principle that the minister should pray an extemporaneous prayer rather than a set, liturgical one. And many of the students of public worship today, even among groups that lean toward a more ritualistic form of worship, will contend that the "poorest extemporaneous prayer" prayed in the Spirit and from the heart is better than the best liturgical prayer ever uttered. Certainly this is our heritage and our concept of public prayer. While there is perhaps a place for short liturgical prayers in ceremonies—marriage, baptismal, the Lord's Supper—other prayers within the church should be extemporaneous. Let those who would seek to modify this position remember that in so doing they are calling into question their entire philosophy of worship. This is a point to be guarded, if necessary with our lives. . . .
>
> Public prayer is of such significance that it warrants some thought ahead of time. At first glance this seems contradictory to what our concept of public prayer has been. And it is at this point that many of the "free" traditions have erred. Just because public prayer is to be extemporaneous and given by the one

62. The practice of using written prayers familiarizes the individual with the great prayers of Scripture and Christian tradition; such use often breeds knowledge and can serve to correct erroneous theology common to spontaneous prayer. Therefore, written prayers can be a tool of instruction enabling one to pray more robust extemporary prayers in both structure and content.

63. Chapman, "Leading the Public Prayer," 1.

64. Hills, "Pastoral Theology," 7.

65. Morgan, "Our Poor Public Prayers," 34; Wilcox, "Pastoral Prayer," 14.

doing the praying is not to say that it should not be given some thought ahead of time. This will in no way defeat the purpose of the "prayer in the Spirit" but rather make it more significant both to the minister and to the people.[66]

Lauriston Du Bois suggests that pastors make the following preparations: attain an awareness of people's needs, review in advance the ideas and thoughts the prayer will encompass, and, prior to worship, the pastor should spend time with God to ready himself spiritually.[67]

Besides the issue of poorly prayed prayers, there were other concerns. A 1931 article by C.W. Ruth addressed the issue of *concert praying*. A form of prayer most likely associated with tongues-speaking churches of the holiness movement, Ruth provides the following explanation:

> [Concert praying refers] to a congregation all engaging in audible prayer with a loud voice simultaneously. This we think is confusion and wholly unscriptural. . . . Where all pray aloud at the same time, certainly no one can be edified, as no one can understand what the other is saying. . . .
>
> If speaking in tongues without giving the interpretation thereof is forbidden, lest they "speak into the air," and be regarded as "a barbarian," and the "unlearned believers" say that "ye are mad" because it could not be understood, why would not the same be true of concert praying when it cannot be understood?[68]

It is probable that the objection to concert prayer is closely tied to concerns over fanaticism, which was associated with tongues-speaking groups. Ruth also clarifies the difference between praying in unison and concert prayer: "United praying does not mean that all must pray aloud at the same time. . . . A number of persons may unite in the same prayer, and for the same object in the prayer, without personally and individually voicing the prayer. . . . We most certainly believe in united prayer."[69]

Church leaders also believed that some pastors were not tending to the pastoral prayer as carefully as they should. Evidently clergy were passing off this responsibility to others, such as visiting ministers who were not prepared to pray or expecting ill-equipped laity to offer the prayer. Pastors were discouraged from this practice for several reasons but primarily because

66. Du Bois, "Prayer and Worship," 6.

67. Ibid., 6–7.

68. Ruth, "Concert Praying," 5.

69. Ibid.

Nazarenes viewed the pastoral prayer as a privilege reserved for the pastor as well as the pastor's responsibility as the *shepherd* of the people.[70]

Extant orders of worship indicate that in addition to the pastoral prayer, three other types of prayer are found in Nazarene liturgies with regularity. These include invocations, offertory prayers, and benedictions.[71] Not all congregations consistently use all of these prayer forms. However, the pastoral prayer is constantly found in nearly all worshipping congregations. It has traditionally functioned as the primary prayer of Nazarenes.

Recently the church has appeared more open to written prayers than it was in earlier years. Although a small minority, those congregations who adopted a prayer book worship form are likely using written prayers. However, other congregations appear more willing to accept written forms as well. This is still a rather small movement, and complete spontaneity in all prayers is still expected in most congregations. However, the church is more accepting of this change than previously in its history. An article in a 1996 issue of *The Preacher's Magazine* stopped short of recommending that pastors use some type of written guide in their preparation for the pastor prayer, but it did stress the necessity of careful planning:

> Without question, a spirit of freedom should characterize the pastoral prayer. Pastoral prayers lack intimacy if they sound like form letters or do not engage the heart of the person who prays. . . . However, because it is an awesome thing to lead people into conversation with God, a prayer must wed careful planning to spontaneity. . . . A well crafted pastoral prayer will engage the heart and the mind of the pastor and, through him, the hearts and minds of parishioners who rejoice that their pastor, on their behalf, says to God the things they want to say to Him. Scripture discourages empty forms, it also encourages thoughtful prayer.[72]

Ironically, a stringent attachment to spontaneity can cripple the ability of clergy to improve the quality of extempore prayers. A review of classical Wesleyanism would reveal that the careful and strategic use of both extemporaneous and written prayers can ameliorate the quality of praying by

70. Corlett, "Pastoral Prayers," 4. See also Morgan, "Our Poor Public Prayers," 34–35; Wynkoop, "Rules for Public Prayer," 30; Wordsworth, "Pastoral Prayer," 23.

71. A historically important part of Nazarene prayer is prayer which occurs around the altar (e.g. communion rail) in response to an altar call. This practice was especially prominent in the beginning years of the denomination until revivalism began to wane. It is not listed as one of the types of prayer, since it will be covered in the section that discusses the sermon and the altar call in Nazarene worship.

72. Green, "Pastoral Prayer," 16; italics mine.

avoiding trivial and theologically deficient prayers, while at the same time guarding against formalism. Both Scripture and church tradition provide a very rich history of prayer that would prove beneficial if adopted into the Nazarene liturgy.

Scripture

Liturgical theologian, Gordon Lathrop, clarifies the role of Scripture in the Christian liturgy. He states that Scripture's purpose goes far beyond the notion that the biblical texts merely serve as "archaic imagery for our current situation."[73] Some suggest that in hearing the biblical narratives persons can identify with the characters in those stories through the shared feelings of human sorrow and hope. Lathrop argues that the biblical canon's function in worship has a more profound intent. Scripture is transformative and speaks of God's grace, action, and "of a new thing not yet imagined."[74] It works in conjunction with the other aspects of the liturgy to communicate God's presence and grace.

> Hearing the Bible, we are gathered into a story . . . the liturgical vision is that these stories mediate to us an utterly new thing, beyond all texts. Juxtaposed to this assembly, the texts are understood by the liturgy to have been transformed to speak now the presence of God's grace. In this way, the texts are made to carry us, who have heard the text and been included in its evocations, into this very transformation: God's grace is present in our lives. Texts are read here as if they were the concrete medium for the encounter with God. . . .
>
> Christian corporate worship is biblical, then, or at least Isaian, in much of the way it uses texts and understands them to be meaningful. That use is complex. The texts are not simply read, as in a lecture hall or even a theater. They are received with reverence, yet they are criticized and transformed. They become the environment for the encounter with God and with God's grace. They become language for current singing.[75]

John Wesley believed that Scripture functioned as a means of God's grace. This includes, but is not limited to, the hearing of Scripture publicly read within the context of worship.[76] Hearing the Word also comes through

73. Lathrop, *Holy Things*, 18.
74. Ibid.
75. Ibid., 16–20.
76. Knight III, *Presence of God*, 2, 3, 130–32, 44, 150, 159, 167.

the sermon, but preaching does not serve as a substitute for reading the actual texts. Scripture shapes our own identity as the people of God, since it reveals to us God's true nature and character, while challenging our false assumptions of him. Therefore, it has a critical function within the liturgy.

Operating without a liturgical theology as a guide has made it difficult for many pastors and denominational leaders in the Church of the Nazarene to understand the interaction between the various elements of the liturgy and their purpose. The objective of the preliminaries was to direct everything toward the main feature of worship, which Nazarenes identified as the sermon and subsequent altar call. This liturgical confusion is especially evident as it relates to the reading of Scripture. Strangely enough, a tradition that holds a very high estimation of Scripture, regarding it as divinely inspired and revelatory of God's will, has for the most part minimized opportunities to hear the reading of substantive portions of Scripture in the liturgy.[77] Rather than Scripture being the primary locus of hearing God speak in worship—that focus has shifted to a more subjective approach mediated through the sermon, extempore prayer, testimonies, and music. All of which have a tendency, if left unchecked, to concentrate largely upon human experience, rather than directing attention upon God as the object of our affections. What is needed is a more balanced approach to worship. The incorporation of a planned pattern of Scripture readings for use in the liturgy is an essential component in achieving balance.

While it is likely they did not fully comprehend the reasons, some Nazarenes were cognizant enough to realize that the failure of congregations to incorporate more Scripture into the liturgy was problematic. Occasionally articles appeared in denominational periodicals stressing this need.[78] Appeals were made for pastors to read more substantial portions of Scripture in addition to the sermon text. Often sermon texts were limited to a very brief passage of one or two verses. Some offered practical solutions that included reading larger portions of Scripture as a background for the sermon text. Others suggested adding a responsive reading to worship

---

77. *Manual Nazarene* (2009), 29. The *Manual* also admonishes members to faithfully attend to all the ordinances of God, including the means of grace. Among those means listed by Wesley is the mandate to *search the Scriptures*. Wesley believed that this included hearing the Scripture in the liturgy, which was inclusive of both the public reading of Scripture and the sermon. The morning prayer in Wesley's *Sunday Service* for Methodists included a Psalm, one lesson from the Old Testament, and one from the New Testament. Evening prayer incorporated both an Old and New Testament reading along with the sermon.

78. Corlett, "Public Reading," 3; Brown, "Scripture Lesson," 12, 18; "Question Box," February 6, 17; Du Bois, "Scriptures in Worship," 2; "My Complaints," 11, 55.

whereby Scripture was read responsively.[79] Chapman provided several suggested orders of worship for pastors to follow. Five out of the six orders he
suggested included a Scripture reading listed separately from the sermon.[80]
Bresee also encouraged clergy to implement an order of worship that he
used. It included "the reading of Scriptures, at least a part of which [could]
be a psalm read responsively."[81] This was followed by the offering, announcements, and the sermon. Whether Bresee read a separate sermon text
in addition to these suggestions he made for incorporating Scripture into
worship is not clear. However, even if no additional Scripture was included,
his practice seems more substantial than most.

Despite these petitions, the typical practice of clergy was to read only
the Scripture text that served as the basis for the sermon. Scripture functioned in the Nazarene liturgy as a constituent of the sermon, rather than
having a distinct contribution of its own. This is exemplified in some of
the articles that either describe or critique the various segments of worship.
Contributors often speak of music, prayer, testimonies, and the sermon,
without mentioning the Scripture reading:

> Every part of the service should be edifying: the songs should
> be appropriate: the sermon full of spiritual food, of encourage-
> ment, of scriptural truth. Let the prayers be full of supplication,
> thanksgiving, and pointed pleading. The testimonies should be
> from real, present, up-to-date experience, full of spicy, interest-
> ing, edifying thoughts of what the Lord really does for one. . . .
>
> Now assuming that the songs, prayers, testimonies, and
> sermon are in themselves edifying, for fear they lose their ef-
> ficiency, the apostle admonishes, "Let everything be done de-
> cently and in order."[82]

Although the author refers to an order that contains scriptural truth, he
makes no mention of the reading of Scripture as part of the worship *ordo*.
It is assumed that it will be read with the sermon, since a frequent practice
was to read only the Scripture that was used as the sermon text. Often small
portions of text were read, rather than larger bodies of material encompassing a more significant portion of the canon. Ironically, while Scripture is
minimal, it is not uncommon for the announcements to be considered part
of the order of worship:

---

79. Stowe, "Responsive Reading," 23; Du Bois, "Scriptures in Worship," 3; Corlett,
"Public Reading," 3.

80. Chapman, "Well Planned Worship Service," 2–3.

81. "Forms of Worship," 6.

82. Marsh, "Method of Divine Worship," 6; italics mine.

The third element in a satisfactory worship service includes atmosphere but it also includes much more. It is a combination of
those positive means which assist the worshiper in turning aside
of the beckoning things of this world, and which produce such
a response in his heart as will enable him in genuine sincerity
and diligence to definitely resolve and insistently endeavor to be
fully Christian in every attitude and expression of life.

> With such an objective for our worship services, there is
no room for preliminaries. All must be blended together in the
building of a whole. The song service, the prayer, the announcements, the offering, the message, the altar service should be
planned in such a manner as to become a vital and integral part
of the means and method of accomplishing the desired end.[83]

Even the announcements are included in the list of those *positive means* in
helping one become fully Christian; however, Scripture is not mentioned.
This evidence reinforces the argument that the reading of Scripture was
both minimal and perceived to be a part of the sermon.

There are instances when worship accounts do reference the use of
Scripture. Such accounts demonstrate that on occasion some clergy included a passage of Scripture in the worship *ordo*, which was in addition to the
sermon; however, this tends to be the exception. The following report, by a
layman, mentions the Scripture reading:

> For fifty-seven minutes we sat in one of the most enjoyable ser-
vices it has been our privilege to attend in recent years. Nothing
was omitted; it was a complete program, and it was all good—
the call to worship, three congregational songs, four verses each,
special duet, Scripture reading, prayer, offering, introduction
of out-of-town guests, emphasis of one bulletin announcement, and an inspirational and challenging twenty-five minute
sermon. . . .
>
> On behalf of laymen, I make a plea for services of this type.
I have known a few pastors who were able to conduct a service
in such a manner . . . but I regret to say that most pastors I have
observed cannot seem to engineer the service without wearying
their audience and making them sluggish.[84]

It is important to note that the author specifies that this was an unusual service. We do not fully know all the elements that made it differ from typical

---

83. Finch, "Church in Worship," 7; italics mine.
84. "Fifty-Seven Minutes," 13; italics mine.

worship, other than the fact that it was *brief* and *well organized*. However, it does denote that the above account is atypical of Nazarene congregations.

The problem with the use of Scripture in the Church of the Nazarene is not limited to its meager quantity incorporated into worship. The quandary is far more complex. If a pastor chooses to include more Scripture, he or she lacks the underpinnings of a liturgical theology or ecclesiology to provide real direction. The only guidance is to choose texts that contribute to the theme of the sermon.

Additionally, the Christian calendar, which is followed by churches in the prayer book tradition, is largely ignored. The Christian Year has been replaced with a church calendar highly infiltrated by the civil calendar. It focuses on some of the major Christian holy days but is conflicted with its recognition of national celebrations and commemorative days, such as Memorial Day, Mother's Day, and Independence Day. Traditionally, the church has rejected any manifestations of prayer book worship including the use of a lectionary.[85] Therefore, when Scripture is read, it often lacks a sound theology to guide it and to enable it to work in conjunction with the liturgy throughout the yearly cycle. Regularly the choices made are based on a whim or a pastor's limited vision. Therefore, it is easy to neglect the whole counsel of God, which time-tested sources, such as a lectionary, help to guard against.

Most articles from denominational periodicals addressing the use of Scripture in Nazarene congregations criticized its limited inclusion in the Sunday liturgy. Such criticism was an attempt to correct this faulty practice.[86] Critiquing the minimal use of Scripture in worship is valid for several reasons. The propensity for worship to fail at reflecting biblical truths increases if insignificant amounts are read as part of the liturgy. Wainwright points out that "the constant reading of the scriptures in worship bears testimony to the fact that Christianity considers itself a historical religion centered upon the revelation of God in Jesus Christ."[87] The reading of both the Old and New Testaments is an essential means through which the congregation comes to know God. The New Testament canon provides "our

85. Although the clear majority of pastors still do not use a lectionary, there is more openness among some in the higher echelons of the denomination for its use. During the last several years, and especially in the twenty-first century, *The Preacher's Magazine* has suggested the lectionary pattern as an option for choosing Scripture and sermon texts; and it has been more sympathetic to the Christian Calendar than in previous years. See, Busic and Rowell, "Preacher to Preacher," 1.

86. One exception is an article by Carl Leth that challenges James White's critique of the minimal use of Scripture readings in evangelical congregations. See, Leth, "In Spirit," 13.

87. Wainwright, *Doxology*, 165.

closest witness in time to Jesus and to the impression which he created. It is part of the ministry of teaching in the Church to help Christian worshippers listen with a discerning ear to the scripture readings in order at the very least to catch 'a whisper of his voice' and 'trace the outskirts of his ways.'"[88]

The greater use of Scripture, which the church holds as God inspired, provides content, reflection, and critique for other elements of the liturgy including prayer, the music, testimonies, the sermon, etc. Listening to the Word of God as it is publicly read serves to guard against the secularization of worship including individualism, materialism, and nationalism that always threatens the church and can remain unchecked in liturgies that are scripturally deficient. The liturgy provides the context that "keeps the 'original' scriptures before the attention in a way that is partly independent of current interpretation and application, so that there is always the possibility of a critical challenge to the present-day Church, whether pastors, theologians or people, in the name of the primitive authenticity to which the scriptures bear witness."[89]

No doubt Scripture can be used thoughtlessly and inappropriately or even ignored by the congregation—it is possible to have the forms without the power, but that does not justify worship that fails to provide a healthy diet of God's Word. Quantity, or lack thereof, does not say everything, but it is indicative of something. The essential question is not whether worship can be effective with a minimal use of Scripture, but rather why one would choose not to give it a place of prominence in the church's liturgy. The reduction of Scripture in worship is most likely pragmatically driven rather than the result of a carefully weighed theological decision. It is a causality of the quest for forms of worship that are both spontaneous and hold the appeal of an entertainment-driven culture.

The Creeds

Even though both appear in the most recent hymnal (*Sing to the Lord*, 1993), it is doubtful that either the Apostles' or Nicene Creeds saw widespread or regular use in Nazarene worship. This is due to their association with the prayer book tradition. Relatively recent research indicates that 72 percent of Nazarene congregations recite the Apostles' Creed once a year or less. Only four percent of congregations recite the Nicene Creed more frequently than once a year.

88. Ibid., 167.
89. Ibid., 168.

Chapman acknowledged in 1935 that the Apostles' Creed was employed by some congregations: "Some local churches of our denomination have tried the formal service, including the reciting of the Apostles' Creed, for certain periods of time, although I do not know of any that are following this order just now."[90] In the same article he provides his own estimation, and apparently that of some of his colleagues, of worship they labeled as formal: "The consensus of opinion among us seems to be that this method of conducting a service is too clumsy and too fixed for our free spirit. It is like trying to put new wine into old wineskins."[91]

Earlier in his ministry Chapman appeared to reflect a more positive tone towards the creeds. Responding to a subscriber who asked if the Apostles' Creed was of Roman Catholic origin, he stated, "I believe it is perfectly adapted for use in Protestant churches."[92] This opinion appears to have changed. Writing to a subscriber several years later Chapman indicates that while the creeds had value in the past, they were too ancient to be of much use to contemporary congregations:

> [The Apostles' Creed] was used in the early, medieval and modern periods for the instruction of prospective church members, as well as an instrument of reaffirming the principle tenets of faith in the public services of the church. But in its ancient form the symbol is, according to my judgment, of doubtful service. Its language is not the language of the modern Christian. . . . The usefulness of the symbol is marred by the fact that it is no longer familiar. Just about the best way, I think, is to let this creed rest in the archives of the past.[93]

A year later Chapman wrote, "I believe much of that time-honored creed (i.e., the Apostles' Creed) is unintelligible to our present generation, and on this account it has largely lost its usefulness."[94] Chapman's critique has been voiced by others who argue that "the language of the traditional creeds depends on an ancient . . . perception of reality which the modern world has abandoned."[95] The assumption is, therefore, that the creeds have lost their ability to function as a statement of faith. This was essentially the same critique Rudolph Bultmann made of Scripture when he began to "advocate

90. Chapman, "Question Box," October 12, 12.

91. Ibid.

92. Chapman, "Questions Answered," May 31, 3.

93. Chapman, "Question Box," October 14, 8.

94. Chapman, "Question Box," October 21, 13.

95. Wainwright, *Doxology*, 193.

'demythologization.'"[96] Wainwright states that similar to poetry, the linguistic nature of the creeds, while needing interpretation, contains a quality that transcends both time and culture. Like Scripture, in a condensed form the creeds embody "the primary and fresh experience of the first believers"[97] and therefore become essential to identity.

> The traditional creeds are the concise verbal forms of the Christian community's identity in time and space. . . . When the believer confesses his baptismal faith, he is being initiated into a people of God which has a historical identity undergirded by the Christ who is 'the same yesterday, today and for ever.' As long as the believer goes on recapitulating his confession, he may be assured of his own identity in the identity of the Christian people. The liturgical use of the traditional creeds is a sign that it is indeed the Church of Jesus Christ to which the believer belongs. . . .[98]

Originating in the context of ancient baptismal liturgies, the creed was primarily a response to God's initiative of grace experienced in baptism. Berard Marthaler states, "The creed, like the *shema*, serves both as a chant of praise (in Greek, *doxa*) and as a witness of faith. Christians confess before their Maker and their fellow human beings the wonders God has done for them. Although there are important differences between creeds and hymns, the two genres have much in common."[99] The creed is both doxology and a profession of faith, and as such it serves to shape our identity as the people of God. It applauds "the work of the Triune God in our lives and in the world. It calls to mind the mystery of salvation, and, in the context of worship, Christian doctrines become statements of Enlightenment, truth, and praise. The old axiom *lex orandi, lex credendi*—'prayer is the norm of belief'—is still valid. . . . Doxology precedes doctrine; practice comes before theory; the church before ecclesiology."[100]

The timelessness and ecumenical nature of the creeds serve to remind us to whom it is that we belong. Marthaler points out that modern people often find the creeds to be oppressive and controlling; however, for the early Christians, the creeds provided an important standard to measure sound teaching against heretical thought. The observations of both Wainwright and Marthaler suggest that the utilization of the creeds in contemporary

96. Ibid., 192–3.
97. Ibid., 195.
98. Ibid., 189–90.
99. Marthaler, *Creed*, 8–10.
100. Ibid., 379.

liturgies is vital. This is especially relevant in an age that has witnessed the infiltration of individualism, materialism, relativism, narcissism, and other secular philosophies and beliefs into the church.

The Sermon and Altar Call

The archetype of Nazarene worship finds its roots within the revivalism of the late nineteenth century. The sermon was the core component of this liturgical model from the beginning, since it was the chief means for the conversion of the heathen and the entire sanctification of believers. All other elements of worship were referred to as the preliminaries, since their purpose was to build an atmosphere that would amplify the potential effect of the sermon upon the congregation. The concern was for an environment that was conducive to the work of the Spirit. Therefore, the preliminaries of worship needed to be free of activities that served only to stir the emotions, since it interfered with creating an atmosphere of awe and reverence.[101] These preliminaries typically included music, testimonies, prayer, announcements, offering, and occasionally a Scripture reading that was not directly connected to the sermon. The *sermon text* itself was considered part of the sermon and often included only a brief passage, rather than a larger segment of Scripture.[102]

Consistently Nazarene periodicals reflect a disquietude that the preliminaries would fail at their primary function. This could occur if they proved inadequate in building momentum towards the sermon or if the preliminaries consumed excessive liturgical time and space, which should be reserved for the pastor's message. An editorial in the *Nazarene Messenger* provides the following guidance to clergy:

> The main thing in the hour of worship is usually the presentation of the truth of God, and the gathering of the fruit of the message. The one thing of attraction in which the interest of the hour gathers, is the preaching of the Word and the gathering by its power of men and women to God. The singing is

---

101. Chapman, "Getting Service Ready," 1.

102. An article in the *Nazarene Messenger* describing a sermon by Bresee exemplifies the common practice of preaching from very brief biblical texts. This also meant that the only text read with the sermon were the few verses exposited. This resulted in the congregation hearing the word removed from its scriptural context, "Sunday was a blessed day of victory from beginning to close. Dr. Bresee preached in the morning to a packed house. He read three texts from the fifth chapter of Acts, verses 20, 25 and 42." "Sabbath Services," 4. Also, see "At the Tabernacle," November 22, 8; "At the Tabernacle," July 25, 8.

preparatory and helpful; the waiting prayer opens heaven and brings strength and unction for the Word of Life.

No preacher should allow anything to eclipse or discount the sermon. If there are songs, they should go before or follow in its wake. Are there prayers, they bring the undergirding arms for the proclamation of the Word of God. Everything should center in and cluster about the preaching of the Gospel—all help exalt the ministry of the Word of Life. If anything comes into the service more attractive than the preaching of the Word, something is wrong.[103]

The author of this editorial believes that the sermon, while serving a primary function in worship, is still a mechanism used to achieve the intended goal of lifting men and women "God-ward."[104]

Due to the central place the sermon occupied in worship there was also much discussion as to the amount of time a pastor should preach. Although guidance is continually given through several publications, contributors are cautious in providing an exact number of minutes for fear that setting a fixed time would limit the Spirit's movement in worship. Speaking in very general terms J. B. Chapman indicates that "the thirty-minute sermon is short, and the hour sermon is long."[105] However, these recommendations for the proper length of a sermon can be less strenuous depending on the mitigating circumstances. Chapman theorizes that it is the preacher who unintentionally preaches long sermons who is at fault, whereas it is generally permissible for those clergy who prepare to preach longer sermons to do so:

> A preacher must be allowed to follow the plan which in his judgment promises the best success. If he has decided that the long sermon is better, and has elected to pursue that plan, he must be allowed to fulfill his own ideal: his hearers will be the best judges of his wisdom. But the average preacher does not intend to preach long sermons.[106]

103. "Suggested Rules for Preachers," 6. Also see, Oliver, "Sermon," 6; Chapman, "Make the Sermon Prominent," 2.

104. Ibid.

105. Chapman, "Why the Long Sermon," 7. Other recommendations ranged from forty to sixty minutes. Goodwin argued that young preachers should only preach twenty minute sermons in their first year or two of ministry. Haynes stated that "preaching is, or ought to be, the 'center and soul' of the service. It is what people go to church to hear." See, Haynes, "Proper Length," 3; Goodwin, "Plain Words to Preachers," 25.

106. Chapman, "Why the Long Sermon," 7.

Chapman theorizes that it is the ill-prepared preacher who is caught un-aware who preaches long sermons. Since he has not planned adequately he does not know how to end his message to get the desired results.[107]

The main concern was that Nazarene clergy were adequately prepared to preach. The general theory was that preachers who had not studied and planned sufficiently tended to preach longer sermons while a "sermon well prepared is likely to be condensed and brief."[108] Concern over preparation and the destructive consequences if clergy fail to prepare is voiced in the following editorial:

> Long sermons often show lack of preparations. There is in them no proper condensation and method. A sermon—so called—may be an exhortation or rambling talk, whether it be long or short. If short, it may be enjoyable and effective, but if drawn out, it is likely to become unendurable.
>
> Many of our evangelists cripple, some almost destroy their usefulness by the length of their sermons. The first half hour is enjoyed, the second half hour is tolerated, and the time that follows is endured, or those who have not the power of endurance leave, and when at last the over-due amen arrives, the people are too weary to stay longer and hasten to get away as soon as practicable. If the sermon had closed at the end of the first half hour . . . some of them could have been caught; but now they are too tired, if not disgusted with the discourse and the preacher who has so trespassed upon their patience, that nothing can be done.[109]

Apparently, this problem of long sermons and the resulting complaints was common to Nazarene congregations.[110] Bresee acknowledged that in his travels and in meetings with laity, he found that most believed *lengthy sermons* ranked high among those homiletical defects that impeded worship. He argued that "this habit of long sermons"[111] characteristic of some of the most influential preachers had become a poor example to young ministers.

Denominational leaders believed that the effort to combat the various maladies related to impoverished preaching began with adequate sermon preparation. Chapman notes that Bresee, even in his advanced years, wrote sermon manuscripts. As part of an effort to assist a struggling pastor,

---

107. Ibid.

108. "Suggested Rules for Preachers," 6.

109. "Short Sermons," 8.

110. Pierce, "Some Suggestions on Peaching," 6.

111. Bresee, "Further Suggestions to Preachers," 5.

Chapman indicated that Bresee shared the following advice about his own methods of preparation. "'Write your sermons carefully; do not try to prepare more than one a week. Old as I am, I do well to prepare two; put your best into that sermon; prepare it diligently; write it out carefully and then pray and meditate until the sermon possesses you and becomes your message.' Surprised as the young preacher was, for he had supposed that Dr. Bresee preached by free spontaneous inspiration."[112]

Although pastors were admonished to be prepared, they were also expected to preach extempore sermons. Writing a manuscript was accepted, even encouraged, but preaching from that manuscript was considered simply an act of reading the sermon, a practice that was frowned upon. Chapman suggested that clergy even memorize their outlines instead of taking "their notes with them into the pulpit."[113] The pastor's reliance upon reading the outline while preaching could hinder the Spirit by limiting spontaneity and curbing the interest of the congregation. Practices that were reminiscent of formalism, such as using written texts, were the enemy of a vibrant faith. Chapman believes that "notes may add to the preacher's dignity, but they detract from his effectiveness."[114] Extemporaneous acts were expected in all aspects of worship because it allowed for the free movement of God's Spirit, while fixed forms whether in prayer or preaching tended towards formalism and were to be avoided.[115]

Although the documented evidence is rare, there were instances when preaching was absent from the worship service. This was due to the movement of the Spirit sensed by the pastor and/or congregation:

> At the 10:30 service no preaching was possible. It was a stormy morning and only one sinner had come out at the time. He was one that had sat under Gospel fire in our church for fifteen years with rejection and open defense. Of late he had shown a little tenderness. On being questioned, after a glorious march by about the whole church, he said he would like to be a Christian. That was enough. The saints gathered about him and for an hour or more literally took "Heaven by violence" for his conviction and salvation. He surrendered and God met him.[116]

112. Chapman, "Preaching Preacher," 1.

113. Chapman, "If Preachers Would Try," 3.

114. Ibid.

115. Haynes, "Helpful Suggestions," 3; "Where Written Sermons Failed," 4; Chapman, "Why the Long Sermon," 7.

116. Pierce, "Great Day," 4. Also, see Dalton, "From Correspondents," 15.

Services were altered, and, in some instances, the sermon dispatched on those occasions when "glory swept over the congregation"[117] and seekers came to the altar prior to the preaching of the Word.

Chapman acknowledged that the normal practice for clergy was to "preach to the church on Sunday mornings and to the unconverted in the evening services."[118] During the early years of the denomination, the Sunday Evening service tended to attract the church's more detached prospects. Therefore, it was the prime opportunity to reach the unconverted. However, he argued that clergy should be open to including altar services in the morning as well.[119]

Pastors were not always expected to give an altar call; still the ultimate purpose of the sermon was to gain tangible results.[120] This was evinced through conversions and other spiritual experiences at the altar. Literature often admonished pastors to improve their preaching skills to achieve the desired outcome. The determining standard for measuring successful preachers was marked at the communion rail. Great preachers were those who were "great in bringing souls to God."[121] One editorial in the *Herald of Holiness* equated the ideal preacher to a master salesman who can convince their listeners to desire what they have to offer.[122] Chapman also argued that the main homiletical purpose was to persuade individuals to make a decision for either salvation or sanctification:

> It is the preacher's task to bring on the crisis and compel people to make their decisions. We are greatly in need of more men who can "draw the net" and land souls into the kingdom. . . .
>
> I have received great personal profit from the study of prophecy and God helps me to preach on the Second Coming of Christ and other such themes until my own soul is blessed and refreshed; but I always regret to see a preacher announce himself as a specialist on these lines and regret to find him giving more than due emphasis to the importance of such studies. There should be an occasional sermon on "Heaven," but there

---

117. Domina, "Harvest Hallelujahs," 8.

118. Chapman, "Question Box," July 31, 7.

119. Ibid.

120. The most prominent means for measuring the success of the sermon was pragmatic. The sermon's ultimate purpose was the conversion of the lost and entire sanctification of believers. This was determined by the number of souls who lined the altar. See, Cornell, "Long-Winded Preachers," 5; Haynes, "Missing an Opportunity," 3; Chapman, "Word Preached Power," 1; Young, "Lengthen That Altar," 1.

121. "Where Written Sermons Failed," 4.

122. Chapman, "Colorful Preacher," 2.

should be constant insistence upon the importance of getting ready for heaven. . . . But let a preacher preach anything he will, only let him remember that preaching sermons and establishing doctrines are but secondary matters. Getting souls is the main concern.[123]

The importance of preaching to facilitate the desired results was often stressed; yet pastors were discouraged from invariably effectuating the altar call.[124] It was essential that no opportunity was missed; however, there was fear that if a pastor repeatedly gave an altar call that yielded no results, it would harden people to the work of the Spirit. Chapman declared that if a pastor gives an altar call and receives no response, it will become more "difficult to get a move"[125] on another occasion. He then reminds his readers the altar call was one of various methods to win souls. Therefore, if a pastor was unable to create a revival atmosphere in any given service, he should conclude it and dismiss the congregation. Although Chapman declared the sermon and altar call to be "simply a method,"[126] in practice it was an essential and primary method of Nazarene evangelistic efforts.[127]

The decline of revivalism in the latter part of the twentieth century resulted in a gradual but consistent reduction of the number of seekers at the altar. The inability of the sermon and altar call to generate the results it once did created a vacuum within the church. Towards the end of the twentieth century focus shifted from revivalism to church-growth methods of bringing people into the church. Even though the denominational leadership continued to emphasize the importance of the altar, its effectiveness as a tool of evangelism continued to wane.[128] Currently the altar is still an important part of Nazarene worship. People in many congregations still frequent the communion rail for times of prayer, and, on occasion, they pray at the altar

123. Chapman, "Word Preached Power," 1; italics mine.

124. Ironically, J. B. Chapman who often encouraged clergy to improve their preaching in order to "get results," also suggested that that sort of thinking could also pose problems. He writes, "We are inclined to believe that our preachers have in many instances been influenced by the general demand for 'immediate results,' and have 'preached to sinners' directly until their preaching has become shallow and hortatory to a weakening extent." Chapman, "Making Special Point," 4.

125. Chapman, "Concluding the Service," 2.

126. Ibid.

127. Haynes, "Missing an Opportunity," 4; Chapman, "Concluding the Service," 2.

128. Several articles appeared in the 1960s, and occasionally in years that followed, promoting the altar by addressing various concerns, such as proper altar design, the biblical basis for the altar, and appropriate methods for an altar service. See, Ruth, "Altar Service," 7–8, 37; Huff, "Altar Service," 3–4; Reid, "Altar Service," 10–11, 21; Adams, "Mourners' Bench" 10–11; Dodge, "Evangelistic Invitation," 11; Lint, "Altar," 10–11.

in response to the sermon. Some congregations kneel at the altar to receive communion. However, the days of determining the success or failure of a pastor's preaching ability by the number of seekers at the altar is past.

Another apparent problem faced by many pastors was the absence of a well-defined preaching calendar. As one would expect from a denomination that distinguished itself by its promotion and proclamation of the Wesleyan doctrine of Christian perfection, a significant number of articles stressed the importance of preaching holiness from the pulpit.[129] Others noted an overall decline in doctrinal preaching and argued that preachers needed to concentrate on addressing the fundamental creeds in their sermons. Pastors were admonished to resist the temptation of overemphasizing the "inspirational and ethical [sermonic] themes."[130] Although some pastors chose to preach a series of sermons and planned their preaching schedule in advance, others did not. Contributors to the denomination's periodicals encouraged pastors to develop a plan for preaching ranging from three months to a year. One article encouraged pastors to develop a plan so that preaching would not be careless. The author appealed to the examples left to us by preachers such as Chrysostom, Augustine, Wesley, Spurgeon, Moody, and Bresee, and provided the following guidance:

> Our preaching should be purposeful rather than haphazard and hit-or-miss. Therefore, why not draw up a fairly comprehensive plan. . . . May I suggest a broad outline? We have New Year's, Palm Sunday, Easter, Mother's day, Children's day, Rally day, Thanksgiving, Bible Sunday, Christmas; nine Sunday mornings, if you observe them all; and each with a vital appeal. Then there are missionary sermons—at least once a quarter, and preferably once a month; communion meditations; sermons on stewardship, on holiness, on practical living; sermons corrective, inspirational, prophetical, doctrinal, biographical and instructional. And if we are to do justice to these engaging themes we must prepare a program where each shall have its proper place. . . . Plan for sermons on sin, on repentance, on conviction, on the baptism with the Holy Spirit, on judgment, on the atonement, on personal responsibility, on heaven, on hell, on influence, on prophecy, on grace, on glory, on eternity, on punishment, on Christ, on man, on God.[131]

129. See, Corlett, "Preaching Holiness," 3; Wiley, "Strongly, Constantly, Explicitly," 3; Chapman, "Making Special Point," 4.

130. Haynes, "Doctrinal Preaching," 3; Corlett, "Notes and Comments," 4; Chapman, "We Must Preach Doctrine," 4.

131. Byron, "Preaching," 15–16.

Noticeably absent from this extensive list are holy days such as Pentecost, the Baptism of the Lord, and Ascension Sunday. Equally as significant as the missing items in the list are the *special days* included in this preaching plan: Mother's Day, Children's Day, Thanksgiving, etc., all of which are derivatives of more secular influences than a preaching plan guided by Scripture and early church tradition. The place of the sacraments is also reduced with the communion message listed as a meditation and the sacrament of baptism omitted altogether. The lectionary, the time-honored resource that could have provided the guidance necessary for balanced preaching and the incorporation of Scripture into the Nazarene liturgy, was excluded—most likely because it lacked the freedom Nazarenes required and was inextricably linked to formalism.

During the latter part of the twentieth century, issues of *The Preacher's Magazine* started including suggested orders of worship. An article encouraging the use of a lectionary to determine the preaching calendar appeared in a 1989 issue. It was written by a pastor in the Wesleyan Church. Early in the 1990s a few Nazarene clergy started submitting preaching resources based upon the lectionary. One contributor defended the use of the lectionary in his sermon resource submissions against potential opponents, who argue that the lectionary stifled the Spirit. Randall Davey states:

> I haven't experienced it that way. On the contrary. The more ordered we have become, the more informal and spontaneous we have become. . . .
>
> For the past several years, I have submitted to the discipline of preaching through the lectionary. I continue to be amazed at the ways in which the Spirit works to address timely and sensitive issues throughout the year. I have found it to be demanding and stretching. For that I'm grateful.[132]

Eventually the complete structure of the *Preacher's Magazine* was arranged to conform to the church year, but ironically the sermon resources did not follow the lectionary, nor were the lectionary texts provided. This change first appeared in the Advent/Christmas issue of 2000–2001. Several

---

132. Davey, "Worship and Preaching Helps," 54. A public declaration of lectionary use by Nazarene clergy was somewhat precarious. Some pastors even appear apologetic in using it; however, it is probable that their caution was justified. Although an unwritten rule, historically any resemblance of formality was suspect within Nazarene congregations. Mary Paul seems to communicate such vigilance in the preface to the worship resources she submitted: "I use the Common Lectionary as a base of my Scripture choice, but I am not confined to it. It is a tool, not a jail. I feel that it has been helpful to me in unveiling the richness of the church year." See, Paul, "Worship and Preaching Helps," 54.

months later, in the Lent/Easter 2002 issue, the editors provided the following guidance concerning the lectionary:

> The use of a lectionary doesn't need to be viewed as giving way
> to cold ritual or formalism. To the contrary, I have been amazed
> at how often the reading of a lectionary passage has precisely
> fit the need of the congregation on that particular day. There's
> nothing sacred about the lectionary. It's simply a tool that we
> can use to help guide our people to the Word of God in a way
> that will be intentional and comprehensive.[133]

Concern over how this change would be accepted by a denomination that
valued its freedom and was highly suspicious of anything that resembled
fixed forms of worship is evident. This is not only revealed in the editors'
comments, but also in the conflicting messages sent by structuring the periodical pursuant to the church year but failing to include sermon resources
that coincide with the lectionary texts. The Lent/Easter 2002 issue was the
first to suggest an outside lectionary resource that pastors could consult,
but the lectionary texts were not listed in the magazine. Beginning with the
Advent/Christmas 2006 issue, the lectionary texts were finally designated;
however, the sermons only occasionally corresponded to a lectionary passage. Most likely the probability of the sermons following the lectionary was
dependent on the preferences of the contributing pastor.[134]

　　This liturgical confusion was no doubt fueled by the reluctance of the
Church of the Nazarene to accept a resource associated with the *cathedral
worship* that the denomination has considered dead and lifeless. Traditionally Nazarenes have assumed that fixed forms impeded the work of the
Spirit. There is, therefore, a tension that exists. Pastors are encouraged to
plan their worship, but spontaneity is still highly valued. The lectionary's
relationship to prayer book worship and the corresponding denominations
known to utilize it (e.g., Roman Catholic, Anglican, Lutheran, etc.) makes
the lectionary even more difficult for Nazarenes to accept. Even with these
inconsistencies, the restructuring of the *Preacher's Magazine* required a dramatic attitudinal change in denomination leadership. Despite this evolution
of thought among some denominational leaders the lectionary's current use
among Nazarene clergy is still minimal.

　　133. Busic and Rowell, "Preacher to Preacher," 1.

　　134. The *Preacher's Magazine* was no longer available in print after 2007 and was
available only on the web in a digital format. It did retain the same *church year structure*
that was instituted at the beginning of the twenty-first century. However, the *Preacher's
Magazine* virtually ceased to exist in its former construction following the Lent/Easter
2010 online issue. Currently preaching and lectionary resources are available at www.
preachersmagazine.org.

Observance of the Christian Year

Appropriation of National Holidays

Like other evangelical denominations, the yearly cycle in the Nazarene calendar has typically consisted of the observance of the major Christian holy days of Christmas and Easter (and in some instances Pentecost) in combination with a selection of culturally relevant commemorative days and national holidays. Some of these festive days were viewed as opportunities to evangelize the lost and spread the doctrine of inward holiness. The following article appeared in a 1928 issue of *The Preacher's Magazine*, advising clergy of ways to utilize special occasions throughout the season:

> There is nothing improper about making the "times and seasons" of the year help you in building the interest in your services. Christmas and New Year are past. But there are Washington's birthday, Easter, Decoration Day, Independence Day, Labor Day, Thanksgiving, etc., yet to come. And the wide-awake pastor will not fail to use every occasion possible to draw special attention to the services of his church, and he will not fail to use such occasions to drive home special doctrines, privileges and duties of his people.
>
> Some may object on the ground that you are "becoming like other people," but you will see to that by maintaining a genuinely spiritual atmosphere amidst all the "occasions." I was once holding a revival in a community of coal miners. The night services and the meetings of the Sabbath were well attended, but only a few came to the meetings on week days. But the Fourth of July came and we announced well in advance that at ten o'clock on the morning of the Fourth we would have a special "Fourth of July Holiness Sermon." We had six hundred people out that Monday morning and had a wonderful salvation time. And I have seen the same thing done on other anniversaries. Labor Day, coming on Monday, provides a good opportunity for a brief, intense convention.

In fact, to "Be instant in season and out of season" would seem to us to require the preacher to make the very best possible use of every unusual day and season that comes on during the year.[135]

Chapman's article stresses to Nazarene congregations the importance of appropriating national holidays and some of the major holy days for pragmatic purposes. This was not a new practice, but one that churches in some of the merging bodies had implemented from the beginning. These celebratory days provided the opportunity to hold evangelistic services that drew larger numbers of attendees and in some instances yielded higher spiritual dividends than other occasions.

Bresee was also known to implement this strategy. The following article describes an Independence Day celebration in 1902:

> As is our custom, an all-day meeting will be held in First Church on Friday July 4th beginning with a sunrise prayer meeting at 4:57 a.m., to continue throughout the day. In former years we have witnessed some marvelous tides of salvation on this, our National Independence Day, and we shall pray and expect that this day shall be even more signally owned and blessed of God. Let the friends pray for a mighty outpouring of the Spirit, and come prepared to spend the day with us.[136]

A later issue of the *Nazarene Messenger* described the above Fourth of July meeting as an event-filled day, lasting until 10:00 p.m. The numerous services were well populated throughout the celebration. Even the sunrise prayer meeting had approximately 150 present. Other events included a "Prayer and Promise service,"[137] testimony meeting, preaching service, an open-air service, and several other activities with a strong evangelistic emphasis. The report indicated that throughout the course of the day there were a total of five altar services with several seekers at each: "Many declared this was the best day of all their lives."[138]

Other national holidays also provided occasions for special services in Nazarene congregations, including Thanksgiving, Washington's Birthday, Lincoln's Birthday, Decoration Day (Memorial Day), and New Year's Day.[139]

---

135. Chapman, "What Church Year," 2.

136. "July 4th 1902," July 3, 6.

137. "July 4th 1902," July 10, 4.

138. Ibid. The Nazarene Messenger also referred to other Independence Day celebrations; see "Fourth of July," July 5, 6; "Fourth of July," July 11, 6–7; "Fourth of July," June 27, 8.

139. "Notes and Personals," December 4, 3; "West Somerville," 6; "Hyde Park," 4;

Comparable to Bresee's Independence Day celebration, the purpose of these meetings was evangelistic and frequently encompassed the entire day. Available descriptions of these services suggest that they were frequently well attended and often resulted in seekers at the altar.

Civil Influence Upon the Christian Year

During the early years of the denomination, typically congregations observed Christmas, Palm Sunday, Easter, and Pentecost. However, most of the liturgical calendar was either ignored or was forced to compete with national holidays and commemorative days. A 1931 article on sermon planning, appearing in *The Preacher's Magazine,* noted the various days in the calendar providing topics for pastors to preach upon: "We have New Year's, Palm Sunday, Easter, Mother's day, Children's day, Rally day, Thanksgiving, Bible Sunday, Christmas; nine Sunday mornings, if you observe them all."[140] Although the observance was not obligatory, the article suggests that it was an acceptable practice for worship to focus upon commemorative days and national holidays.

Several years later James McGraw, then editor of *The Preacher's Magazine,* provided additional insight into this continued practice:

> Some pastors take them in stride, with never a hint of pressure. Some fret and chafe under them, wishing they would go away. Some are slaves to the custom, following it in minute detail as though driven by an overwhelming compulsion. Others are "free," even to the point of ignoring them completely. We refer here to the "special days" in the church year, the "seasons" during which the pastor is expected to produce a masterpiece which is directly related to the occasion.
>
> At the top of the list is Easter, and this could include the entire Lenten season. Christmas stands also at the top in importance. Some might argue Pentecost should head the list. Regardless of their order of importance, the list of special days is long. There is the New Year, Reformation Sunday, Mother's Day, Father's Day, Promotion Day, and Laymen's Sunday, to name only a few.
>
> The ideal is for the pastor to USE these special occasions, but not let them make him a slave to their demands.[141]

Brown, "All-Day Meetings," 8; "Decoration Day," 5; "Tuesday New Year's Meeting," 4–5; "Chicago," 16.

140. Byron, "Preaching," 15.

141. McGraw, "Seasonal Sermon," 1.

McGraw's article is helpful in that it adds to the seemingly endless list of
special days on the Nazarene calendar. However, McGraw also reveals an
important insight into the Nazarene perception of the church year. Little
distinction is made between the holy days of the Christian calendar and the
various commemorative days and/or days of special emphasis recognized
by the denomination. He also states that the intent in observing these special days is for the pastor to *use* them for his purposes. Often the intended
goal was pragmatic in nature. During the early years, it was a means to gain
seekers at the altar. Chapman states,

> Do every legitimate thing to get the people out to the house of
> God. . . . If you really want to get ahead and build up the church.
>
> There are the annual festivals and holidays. No matter
> whether Christ was born on the twenty-fifth of December or
> not, Christmas is a good time to get people together and preach
> Christ to them. Easter Sunday and Thanksgiving Day are splen-
> did occasions to have "Something extra" in your church. I once
> got six hundred people out on Monday morning to "A special
> fourth of July service."[142]

Following the decline of revivalism and the advance of the church-growth
movement some of these special days often served to increase attendance
and provide more contacts for the local congregation.

Wiley suggests that evangelical denominations resisted following the
Christian calendar due to its tendency to move congregations toward formalism, therefore destroying the work of the Spirit: "As days and seasons are
observed there develops gradually a ritualistic attitude of mind in which the
form of the service is substituted for the spiritual realities. The observance,
therefore, becomes formal and the real significance is too often entirely
lost."[143] Wiley also notes that overloading the Christian calendar with too
many observances had contributed to its decline, since the plethora of special days made worship *too ritualistic.*[144]

Cautiously, in a 1932 editorial, Wiley calls the church to observe
Christ's life and ministry as reflected in the season of Lent. He first warns
of the peril of placing too much emphasis on the Christian calendar but
encourages the recovery of that which was of value in Lenten observance.[145]
The following year Wiley was bolder in his apologetic of the season:

142. Chapman, "Capitalizing the Incidentals," 1.

143. Wiley, "Value," 3.

144. Ibid.

145. Wiley, "Protestants and Lenten Observance," 2. Wiley's editorial appears to go
against the current thought of the day in the Church of the Nazarene. Most in the

The Church very early observed the anniversary of our Lord's suffering and death as a time for special humiliation and prayer. By meditating upon the awful price paid for the world's redemption, men's hearts were quickened into new love and devotion. During the dark ages of the Church's history, when spirituality was all but lost from the world, these beautiful spiritual practices became merely outward and formal observances. More than this, with the development of sacramentarianism, these observances became, not a means of grace but a substitute for grace. As a result, spiritual people have reacted to them as being valueless. . . .

But the perversion of a practice does not necessarily mean that it should be discarded—rather that it should be purified. God has commanded us to fast and pray. The early Church tarried in prayer when opposition arose, and God granted new power and increased success. The world has commercialized our Christmas and Easter; but Lent kept as the earlier Church kept it, would hardly appeal to the commercial interests.[146]

Other articles supporting the practice of Lent followed those of Wiley. This included an article by D. Shelby Corlett, a subsequent editor of the *Herald of Holiness*. Corlett states,

There is no more appropriate season of the year for heart examination, for soul inventory and the practice of self-denial and sacrifice for Jesus' sake than this period preceding the commemoration of our Lord's passion and resurrection. If more of us would prepare ourselves for these great Christian commemorations they would be of much more spiritual value to us, and there would be a consequent deepening of our devotional life and a greater manifestation of saintliness in our living.[147]

It must be remembered that these articles supporting Lenten observance were appeals to personal piety rather than a call for Lenten observance in corporate worship. This included prayer and fasting, self-examination, and the reading of and meditating upon Scripture. Corporate observance of

Lent avoided! Catholic —

---

church avoided the larger portion of the Christian calendar. This was especially true of Lent due to its observance being equated with Catholicism. A 1920 article written to children on the topic of Lent portrayed it as an unspiritual outward form of religion; see Benson, "Home," 8.

146. Wiley, "Observing the Lenten Season," 4.

147. Corlett, "Lenten Season," 3. For examples of other contributors to the *Herald of Holiness* who encouraged Lenten observance, see Kiefer, "Lenten Retirement," 8; Barber, "Spiritual Significance," 8–9.

Lent through Ash Wednesday worship would have been avoided, especially as expressed by the prayer book tradition. Even the solemn themes of Holy Week, found in prayer book worship, would appear *too Catholic* to many Nazarenes. Many of these perceptions persist among modern Nazarenes where Anti-Catholic sentiments are tenacious.

The holiness movement's association of Spirit baptism with the entire sanctification of the disciples meant that Pentecost was viewed as one of the most important of the holy days in the Nazarene calendar. This was more characteristic of the first several decades of the denomination than it is representative of current practice where Pentecost's meaning and importance are mostly lost along with a distinctive Wesleyan identity. Wiley refers to the importance of Pentecost in the Nazarene calendar:

> While the denominations generally observe Lent and make much of Easter, it seems appropriate that those whose chief doctrine centers in the gift of the Holy Ghost, should make much of Pentecost and events leading up to it. The Church of the Nazarene in its earlier beginnings celebrated Pentecost annually as "Victory day" and many are the times when the Spirit of God was poured out in new power and glory.
>
> It is admitted by Superintendents, pastors and people that the younger generation of Nazarenes . . . are not so thoroughly grounded in the doctrine as they should be.[148]

Wiley reveals that the primacy Pentecost should occupy in the calendar is due to the connection Nazarenes made between Pentecost and entire sanctification. One also gains the sense that Wiley believes the emphasis upon entire sanctification and therefore the celebration of Pentecost is already in decline.

Corlett, writing eight years after Wiley, references the neglect of Pentecost observance. His article also exposes the existing conflict in the Church of the Nazarene between the Christian calendar and the civil calendar:

> One day in our church calendar which is not given the prominence it deserves is Pentecost Sunday, the seventh Sunday after Easter. This year May 12 has the distinction of being both Pentecost Sunday and Mother's Day. Perhaps it is unfortunate to have both of these features fall on the same day, but why not at least emphasize the feature of Pentecost in the evening service.
>
> Nothing is more important in the history of the Christian than Pentecost.[149]

148. Wiley, "From Easter to Pentecost," 2.
149. Corlett, "Pentecost Sunday," 4.

Corlett's comments not only indicate that Mother's Day was observed in the Nazarene calendar, but it reveals its prominence. On those occasions when the two collide in the calendar, Corlett assumes that Mother's Day will be celebrated and Pentecost ignored. Ironically, instead of arguing the theological importance of celebrating Pentecost rather than Mother's Day, Corlett simply suggests that Pentecost be relegated to the evening service. His comments, even though not necessarily shared by all, demonstrate the tremendous influence of the civil calendar upon the church year. Important holy days are replaced by commemorative days. Even days in the calendar that Nazarenes valued were willingly surrendered to certain civil events. It appears this tendency to celebrate civil events at the cost of holy days in the Christian calendar was often driven by the pragmatism that repeatedly-governed decisions about worship practice. In other words, the days selected to observe in the calendar were frequently chosen for their ability to attract the unchurched, for evangelistic purposes, without considering the theological implications of this calendrical approach.

Deviations from the Christian calendar to a civil calendar are not inconsequential. Emphasizing commemorative days or national holidays shifts the focus of worship from the story of God to a fixation upon subjective human experience, achievement, or interests. When these rest at the heart of the liturgy, worship veers dangerously close to idolatry. On the other hand, journeying through the life, work, and ministry of Christ by the observance of the Christian calendar challenges secularism and helps to reorient us toward God. Don Saliers warns if we abandon the benefits of the Christian year we do so at great cost. "The images, and the themes of the incarnation, and the death and resurrection of Christ brings new discipline and accountability. The liturgical year is not a matter of 'playing church,' it is a matter of integrity and formation in the grace of the Christian Gospel."[150]

The observance of and participation in the festivals of the yearly cycle allow us to participate in the life of Christ. They bring both the salvific events from the past and the hope we have in God's future into our own time. "While the church's worship is always an offering to God, worship is also a great gift bestowed upon us by God; for *liturgical anamnesis* and *prolepsis* constitute a primary means by which we maintain contact with the past and the future, both so integral to our identity and sense of mission in the world as a people of the resurrection."[151] Activity in the life of God is transformative. It reshapes us into his image and imprints upon us that identity as his children.

150. Saliers, "Seasons of the Gospel," 13–14.
151. Stookey, *Calendar*, 29–33; italics mine.

The Christian Year and Identity

More recent years have pointed to a renewed interest in the Christian calendar. Articles in *The Preacher's Magazine* in the 1980s and 90s were attentive to seasons such as Lent and Advent.[152] Simultaneously contributions to the denominational periodical revealed a lack of understanding over the seasons of the liturgical year. Such misconceptions were exemplified in a sermon series appearing in the 1994 summer issue of *The Preacher's Magazine*. The series was prefaced with the following words of introduction:

> I am mindful that it is immediately following the celebration of Pentecost. I'm on a campaign to raise to a higher level the awareness, appreciation, and celebration of this third great "divine exclamation point" of the Christian faith! Advent and Easter are adorned with careful planning and traditions. However, Pentecost often slides past in the shadows without a notice. It would seem that the holiness churches would see Pentecost Day as a grand opportunity to highlight the work of the Holy Spirit in the church.[153]

While John Hay Jr. mentions the seasons of Advent and Easter, noticeably absent is Christmas. Since, he mentions three *divine exclamation points* (Pentecost being the third), it seems reasonable to assume that Hay's failure to mention Christmas is not because he thinks it is unimportant, but rather he is equating the season of Advent with the season of Christmas.

The loss of distinction between the seasons of Advent and Christmas is not unusual for Nazarenes. Other issues of *The Preacher's Magazine* intermingled the two seasons as if they were one and the same. The sermon by C.S. Cowles entitled, "The Astonishing Christmas Miracle," was labeled as an Advent Sermon. The table of contents in a 1984–85 issue listed "An Advent Meditation" under the Christmas heading.[154] Comparable mistakes were repeated in other issues. Beyond preaching and the influences of secular culture, Advent is also regularly lost in the many Christmas celebrations

---

152. McCall, "Heritage of Lent," 4–6; Cowles, "Advent Sermon," 42–44.

153. Hay, "Introduction," 54; italics mine.

154. Cowles, "Advent Sermon," 42–44; "In This Issue," 1; Brokhoff, "Make the Advent," 30. The article by John Brokhoff (professor from Candler School of Theology) does provide a corrective to misconceptions of the meaning of Advent; ironically it was placed under the heading of Christmas by the editors of *The Preacher's Magazine*. Brokhoff states, "Of all the seasons, Advent is the most difficult to observe because of the competition with the commercial world. The world celebrates Christmas during Advent rather than on Christmas." The very magazine in which the article was placed made the mistake Brokhoff alludes to—confusing Advent with Christmas.

of the local church, which congregations commonly inaugurate following the celebration of American Thanksgiving. During Advent, the church life is all too frequently inundated with various programs such as the children's Christmas program, Christmas cantatas, caroling, and other celebrations. Due to these complications and others, the recovery of a robust understanding of Advent becomes difficult.

There is a significant difference between the themes of Advent and those of Christmas. The common misconception is that Advent is concerned foremost with the *past* expectation of the coming Messiah born in a Bethlehem manger. Instead Advent is "primarily about the *future*, with implications for the *present*."[155] Advent points to the end of time as the church awaits the second coming of Christ. Therefore, it urges both expectation and celebration. Christians are charged to self-examination of their spiritual life in order that they are prepared for the risen Christ who will come to "judge wickedness and prevail over every evil."[156] Stookey argues that it is these themes that provide the counterbalance to corrupting influences that assail the Christmas season: "Only this focus on the central purpose of God in history can keep the story of Jesus from falling into the superstitious or almost magical understandings that often afflict the Christian community, on the one hand, or into the trivialization and irrelevance that characterize secular interpretations, on the other hand."[157]

Obstacles Inhibiting Change

The confusion and problems that surround attempts at an authentic Advent observance illustrate the importance of the Christian year in forming and nurturing Christian identity. Philosophies and the sweeping tides of secularism found in modern culture seek to distort the gospel by reshaping the church into something less than faithfulness to the divine call that God has placed upon it. Observance of the core values of Christian faith as expressed in the yearly cycle provides a voice that opposes those forces threatening the body of Christ. However, the recovery of the Christian year for Nazarenes will involve some significant hurdles.

Pervasive anti-Catholic sentiments and fear that adherence to the yearly cycle is too akin to Roman Catholic practice and threatens the freedom coveted in Nazarene worship is but one of the obstacles. Another is the deeply imbedded traditions of both culture and nationalism that make

155. Stookey, *Calendar*, 158; italics mine.

156. Ibid., 121.

157. Ibid., 121–2.

change difficult. The suggestion that worship is not the appropriate place to celebrate Independence Day or honor one's mother brings accusations of being unpatriotic or indifferent. Encouraging the church to observe Advent and to wait for the celebration of Christmas, instead of being caught in the commercialism of the secular observance of the season, brings criticism from those who assume that in waiting the excitement of Christmas is being lost. Such changes can prove to be a tedious task. Transitioning from current practice to an observance of the Christian year requires patience, careful planning, and catechesis, and would need to be implemented both gradually and methodically. Despite these obstacles the rescue of the Christian year from the influences of secular culture is a prudent task for the church if it desires to recover a distinctively Christian identity.

Religious Experience in Worship

The accounts describing the worship practices of both British and American Methodists portray very rich and transformative religious experiences.[158] Like the early Methodist movement, those holiness streams that eventually converged to form the Church of the Nazarene also depict vibrant encounters with God. Taves states that as one might expect those who "experienced religion . . . explained their experience in religious terms."[159] Expressions such as power, presence, the indwelling of God, or the witness of the Spirit, as well as other terms were often used. The early Nazarenes also employed terminology to express their experience of God in worship. Some of the language and expressions are comparable to those found in descriptions of early Methodist worship experiences.

Religious experience was also central in confirming that the Spirit was at work. It provided tangible evidence that their worship of God had not become empty and dead, as they believed it had in many of the *cathedral* churches. However, they were cautious that their pietism did not go to extremes. Denominational leaders were continually on guard against the problem of fanaticism, which was often associated with many of the more ecstatic experiences of the Pentecostals including speaking in tongues,

---

158. For examples and discussion of the experiential nature of these society meetings and multifarious worship services, see Wesley, "Journal May 1760 to October 1762," in *Works* (BE), 21:381–2; Wesley, "Journal August 1738 to November 1739," in *Works* (BE), 19:106–7; Wesley, "Journal July 1749 to October 1751," in *Works* (BE), 20:293–4; Tucker, *American Methodist Worship*, 71–2; 76–7; Ruth, *Little Heaven Below*, 63, 74–8.

159. Taves, *Fits*, 3.

prophetic utterances, and concert praying.[160] It will be of value to examine some of the bodily expressions used in Nazarene worship as well as the unique language they employed to describe their encounters with God. This will provide understanding not only about the characteristics of the early Nazarene liturgy, but also it will give insight into the evolution of liturgical patterns, experiences, and practices.

Language

Ruth points out that within Methodism there existed a collection of terms employed to express religious experience. This vocabulary encompassed "words and phrases universally understood and used across the scope of early Methodism. . . . The general thrust of the whole repertoire was to emphasize an affective assessment of God's presence and of the ways in which humans experience grace."[161] Ruth suggests that the most common word they chose to describe people's experience of being "deeply affected by the presence of God"[162] was the term *melting*.

Melting or one of its derivatives, such as *melt* or *melted*, repeatedly appears in Nazarene descriptions of worship experiences where God was encountered in profound ways. The following account describes a Sunday morning worship service in Lowell, Massachusetts:

> God met us there in a mighty way. . . . Holy fire fell and melted the saints and sinners. Confessions were made, and the tide did rise higher and higher. They kept coming to the altar and owning up, and God blessed them out of themselves and gave a real old fashioned time in the Holy Ghost. Glory to God for ever! I came up again in the afternoon, and the saints led by Brother Riggs in the Holy Ghost were still praying and holding on. Glory! Glory! Glory![163]

Consonant with its usage among eighteenth-and nineteenth-century Methodists, when Nazarenes employed the term it implied a sense that the power of God was at work. *Melted* in the above account is followed by descriptions of people praying at the altar offering confession for sin. This indicates that when the term *melted* is used, it is because the affected individual has

---

160. As described earlier, concert praying was the practice of several people praying audibly at the same time.

161. Ruth, *Little Heaven Below*, 79.

162. Ibid.

163. Dalton, "From Correspondents," 15; italics mine.

experienced a rich and transformative experience with the Divine. This is
further exemplified in another detailed report of worship:

> Truly the Lord is visiting Peoria in a most wondrous manner
> and Sabbath April 12, was a crowning day. The anointing fell on
> the saints in the morning service and continued all day. At 2:30
> in the afternoon Bro. H. M. Swangle spoke from Heb. 12:15,
> amidst shouts and groans of the saints, and a remarkable spirit
> of testimony came on the people and conviction on the sinner,
> melting them to tears.[164]

Once again melting is in reference to God's presence. The anointing was
accompanied by other signs that God was at work, including "shouts and
groans . . . and a spirit of testimony."[165] All of this eventually led to a melting.

Nazarenes also used other expressions to describe their heartfelt
encounters with the Spirit. Vibrant liturgical experiences were at times referred to as a *feast* or the act of worship often called *feasting*, such as "we had
a feast of good things"[166] or "a delightful feast of fat things."[167] *Red hot* was
occasionally used to articulate emotion-laden services when people were
emotionally stirred. The following account exemplifies this trend: "At about
2:30 the service began anew with what is common in a holiness meeting,
red-hot songs, prayers and testimonies, after which the writer preached his
first sermon."[168] The Nazarene vocabulary was not limited to these words
alone; there were others. When they reflected upon their religious encounters with God, Nazarenes often incorporated biblical imagery to describe
their experience. Since the use of that imagery was frequently followed by
descriptions of vocal and bodily response within the context of worship it
is addressed next.

Vocal and Bodily Response

Nazarenes were often impulsive in both their vocal and bodily expressions
of religious piety. The responses commonly documented include testimonies; trips to the altar (i.e., communion rail) to kneel and pray; the waving
of handkerchiefs; shouting—generally a loud audible response using words

164. Peel, "Peoria," 4; italics mine. For additional accounts where melting language
is used, see "Los Angeles," 4; Dunn, "First Church," 8; Milligan, "Harvest Hallelujahs,"
8; "Bible School Notes," 7.

165. "Ibid.

166. "School Notes," 7.

167. Carey, "Harvest Hallelujahs," 8.

168. Collins, "Reports from the Field," 3. Also, see "Installation at Malden," 6.

such as *Amen, Hallelujah, Glory,* or a similar expression; weeping; clapping; hand-shaking; leaping; running in the aisles; and marching in and around the church and sanctuary. Enthusiasm in worship was encouraged, but with limits, since there was always concern it would evolve into fanaticism.[169] D. Rand Pierce provides the following description of a service where such enthusiastic response was exhibited:

> At the 7 o'clock, and last, service the writer spoke from I John 4:8, "God is love." At the close of the sermon four were at the altar for prayer, and testified clearly to having been sanctified wholly. Some entirely new cases. The order was changed to song and testimony. Soon a grand "Jericho march" followed, in which nearly every Christian participated. The audience was so large that the aisles, front and back, were seated with extra chairs, and so many were in the march that things were somewhat congested, but we marched, and sang, and shouted, while the air was white with waving handkerchiefs. This over, song and testimony rolled on until another felt led to march around the church, which was the signal for another landslide of the Jericho besiegers. Thus, the meeting rolled on in wonderful freedom and power until the farewell handshaking had begun, when a former male member, backslidden for seven years, wended his way to the altar and was soon happy in the arms of the prodigal's waiting Father.[170]

The biblical imagery used to describe religious experience closely resembles early Methodist patterns. Taves indicates that the shouting Methodists interpreted "their bodily experiences in light of biblical typologies."[171] Metaphorical language was drawn upon to delineate profound encounters with God.[172] Pierce's worship depiction speaks of the *Jericho march,* which is clearly imagery reminiscent of the Book of Joshua account when God's power was manifested during the Israelite invasion of Canaan (Josh 5:13— 6:27). Other images were used as well; the following expressions provide a sampling of the descriptive language that appeared in denominational peri-

169. An article in the Beulah Christian exemplifies this tension, "There are two classes of religious shout. The other is the superfluous demonstration, which is not of the Spirit of God. . . . 'Demonstration will not produce the Holy Ghost, but . . . the Holy Ghost, when He comes, will produce demonstration.'" "Shout!," 5–7.

170. Pierce, "Farewell at Lynn," 7. For other examples of vocal and bodily response in worship, see Norberry, "Portsmouth Campgrounds," 5; "Brooklyn," August 1902, 8; "Texas Holiness University," 5; "Stockton," 10.

171. Taves, *Fits,* 78.

172. For a description of the Methodists' use of biblical imagery to describe religious experience in worship, see Ruth, *Little Heaven Below,* 76–81.

odicals: "feeding on the milk and honey,"[173] "some wept their way through to Calvary,"[174] and "Pentecost broke forth."[175] The metaphorical language of *Pentecost* was used in abundance because it became the primary biblical image for the experience of Christian perfection. The baptism with the Holy Spirit that the disciples received at Pentecost was interpreted as disciples' experience of entire sanctification and cleansing from original sin.[176]

Taves states that during the revivals of the late eighteenth-century Virginia, many Methodists identified bodily expressions such as "falling to the ground, crying out, and shouting for joy . . . as specific manifestations"[177] of God's power and presence. Early in the nineteenth century, Methodist quarterly meetings and camp meetings "emerged as primary contexts in which Methodists might expect to see the power of God manifest through bodily experience."[178] Influenced by the early Methodist traditions of the revival and camp meeting atmosphere, early Nazarenes perceived bodily expressions during worship in like manner. Shouting and other forms of response were at times accompanied by conversions and other experiences of divine grace:

> The afternoon service was a veritable Pentecost. Brother Clark brought the message, his subject being "Free Grace." He was peculiarly helped and blessed in speaking the Word, and when the testimonies began the fire began to fall. The blessing was in scriptural measure, "filled full, pressed down and running over." Many shouted aloud the praises of Jesus; many wept and laughed in holy joy. Some were converted during the testimony meeting and others came to the altar seeking pardon and purity.[179]

Shouting was quite prominent in Nazarene worship. No doubt it was passed down to the Nazarenes from the early Methodist camp meeting traditions. Articles periodically appeared both encouraging and defending the

173. "Brooklyn," August 1902, 8.

174. "Sunday," March 24, 3.

175. "Texas Holiness University," 5.

176. The equation of Pentecost with the entire sanctification of the disciples is a traditional Nazarene position. The *Manual* states, "We believe that entire sanctification . . . is wrought by the baptism with or infilling of the Holy Spirit, and comprehends in one experience the cleansing of the heart from sin and the abiding, indwelling presence of the Holy Spirit, empowering the believer for life and service." *Manual Nazarene* (2013), 32–33. For a more in-depth explanation of this position, see Grider, "Spirit-Baptism," 31–50.

177. Taves, *Fits*, 78, 86.

178. Ibid., 78.

179. "Sabbath," September 6, 4.

use of shouting.[180] This would suggest that there was at least some resistance to its use in worship. Writing in 1926, Cornell indicates that shouting by Nazarenes was in decline in some congregations:

> There seems to be an apparent lack of liberty in a number of churches. The responses to an "Amen" point are noticeably absent. There is lack of spontaneity, lack of liberty and the result is that formality and coldness predominate. If the Nazarenes lose their "shouting attachment" we will soon be as dead as those in the graveyard. There is no service more gracious and blessed than one where freedom exists and exuberant, happy people shout the praises of God.[181]

Cornell believed that the lack of vocal response in worship was indicative of a church that was growing spiritually cold. This thought appears consistent with Taves's argument concerning early Methodists who believed vocal and bodily expressions were evidence of the manifestation of God's power. It seems reasonable to assume that the early Methodists would also equate the continued absence of such expressions evincive of the absence of God's presence and power. Cornell clearly thought that any congregation without some measure of shouting Nazarenes was as "dead as those in a graveyard."[182]

Another indication that shouting was commonly held as a manifestation of the Spirit's work is revealed in theories surrounding its impulsive nature. Defenders of the practice argue that the natural "outward expression"[183] of a victorious Christian was shouting. Some even suggest that shouting was instilled by the Spirit, and, therefore, it was an unavoidable response: "You can not [sic] 'put on' shouting like you put on your shoes. It is not something put on, it is something that God *puts in*. When it really gets in, nothing can keep it down."[184] Another proponent of shouting's compelling nature recounts the story of a woman who testified, "I have had to bear the cross of shouting all my Christian life. When I was converted, God saved me wonderfully; I could not restrain my shouts of praise."[185] It seems that

180. Lehman, "Shouting," 7; Cornell, "Shouting," 6; Cowan, "Shouting or Rejoicing," 6.

181. Cornell, "Nazarenes and Shouting," March 10, 7. Cornell's article reappeared in a later issue of the *Herald of Holiness*; see Cornell, "Nazarenes and Shouting," January 24, 8.

182. Cornell, "Nazarenes and Shouting," March 10, 7.

183. Morgan, "Shouting Christians," 8.

184. Cornell, "Shouting," 6. Trowbridge also suggests that "a spontaneous shout of praise cannot be stopped." Trowbridge, "Why Shout," 5.

185. Cornell, "Shouting Not the Fashion," 3.

shouting was not only understood to be an individual's natural response to
the inward workings of God's grace, but if God had "put in"[186] the shout—it
was irresistible.

Even though bodily response, such as shouting, was believed to be a
necessary and essential part of worship for any congregation that was alive
and well, its proponents did not insist that all Nazarenes should shout. It was
recognized that there were some who simply had a quiet temperament and
yet were still deeply devoted to God.[187] As one contributor to the *Herald of
Holiness* recognizes:

> It may not be physically possible for all to express themselves in
> shouts and leaps and bodily exercises, and yet the joy of salva-
> tion may be present, and the glory of God fill the soul which is
> fully yielded to Him, without shouts or a loud voice. . . .
>
> Some may shout and leap and clap their hands, others may
> weep, or laugh, or shake hands with their fellowmen, or just sit
> still and let their cup of rejoicing run over as the Spirit fills and
> wills.[188]

Even with this allowance for diversity, it was expected there would be persons within each local church who would express their piety vocally or
bodily. Such response was a necessary consequence of a spiritually healthy
congregation and important in the pursuit of inward religion. They based
the value of these practices upon the Methodist tradition from which many
descended, but more importantly they believed that vocal and bodily response had both scriptural precedence and support.[189]

Contemporary Patterns of Response

Bodily response in worship, as well as the entire complexion of the Nazarene
liturgy, has changed significantly since the beginning days of the denomination. While the basic worship *ordo* may remain intact in many congregations,
the dynamics and characteristics of Nazarene liturgical practice common to

186. Nazarenes were aware that some shouting could be merely a human contriv-
ance rather than a manifestation of God's presence. Such activity was discouraged.
"Shouting just for shouting's sake has no meaning. But there is nothing that clears the
atmosphere and makes for a good meeting more than a good Holy Ghost shout. I think
it is a mistake to try to 'work up' a shout, just as it is a mistake to quench one when it
appears." Chapman, "Question Box," February 3, 13.

187. Wordsworth, "Shouting," 6.

188. Cowan, "Shouting or Rejoicing," 6.

189. Ibid.; Trowbridge, "Why Shout," 5.

worship during the early years of the denomination have changed dramatically. The once primary forms of vocal and bodily response are now either no longer extant or greatly diminished. Altar response consists primarily of those going to the altar during prayer time or to receive the Lord's supper, rather than the result of an altar call following the sermon. The shouting of a vocal response such as *amen, hallelujah,* or something similar has also been minimized both in intensity and frequency. The waving of handkerchiefs, marching in or around the church, jumping, running, and other vigorous forms of bodily response, which was at one time the required affirmation of spiritual vitality within congregations, virtually never occurs in contemporary worship.

Today one of the most common responses in Nazarene worship is applause. When the church was in its infancy, congregations rarely responded with applause, and, if they did, it was discouraged by denominational leadership. The clapping of hands was mentioned in a 1928 General Assembly resolution. Reasoning that the clapping of hands threatened a spirit of awe and reverence within worship, the resolution stated that the practice was to be avoided. It is not clear if the "clapping of hands"[190] includes applause, or if it refers to the Pentecostal practice of clapping the hands in rhythm to the music, or both. Staples states, regardless of which type was intended, the resolution would have censured each type.[191]

Although applauding congregations did not become epidemic until the end of the twentieth century, it is specifically mentioned much earlier. Writing in 1949, Bangs indicates that *applause in worship* was a new problem and one that he witnessed in a revival service:

> I was gratified to hear the old-fashioned shouts of praise which have so markedly characterized our church and contributed to its success. Shouts, amens, and hallelujahs were attendant upon the music and preaching. In the same meeting, however, I witnessed a new feature which was a bit disturbing. Too many times the shouts faded away, to be replaced by applause. Thus, the special singers were applauded at the end of their numbers, and the preacher was occasionally interrupted by it during his sermon.[192]

190. Staples, "What About Applause," 48.

191. Staples indicates that "the clapping of hands" alluded to in the 1928 resolution could have referred either to applause or the Pentecostal practice of the clapping of hands in rhythm to music, which "was prominent in the religious environment of that day." However, Staples argues that both forms of clapping would have been censured in the resolution. Ibid.

192. Bangs, "Spiritual Vocabulary," 7.

Bangs continues by suggesting that the use of applause in worship is inappropriate, since it directs attention toward the person speaking or singing, rather than God. Additionally, he finds applause a threat on two other levels. First, it tempts the minister or singer to seek even greater applause or it could create a sense of competition among other individuals who are utilizing their gifts in worship. Secondly, it could lead to the diminishing of authentic response to God by providing a false substitute that is directed toward a performer.[193]

During the late 1980s Rob Staples contributed an article to the *Preacher's Magazine* addressing this same problem. Based upon one's intent, he distinguishes applause in worship from other forms of clapping. According to Staples, clapping the hands "in rhythm to the music"[194] differs significantly from the applause that follows some form of musical performance such as a solo or a song by the choir. He argued that the problem with the *ritual of applause* is not only its lack of any real scriptural support,[195] but also in what it points to, the fact that

> applause is a symbolic action, signaling one's approval of what he has seen or heard. It is a ritual. . . .
> Now what signal are we sending when we engage in the ritual of applause? What message are we communicating? Almost without exception in Western culture . . . applause is an expression of praise for the performer, appreciation for the performance, or agreement with what the performer has said or done. . . .
> But the worship of God is not a performance! We do not enter God's house to be entertained. When in the gathered congregation the Word is read and preached, sacraments administered, hymns sung, prayers made, and offerings given, these actions are not mere performances. They are acts of praise and worship of the holy God.[196]

Both Bangs's and Staples's concern over the dangerous nature of applause seems both well-founded and prophetic. Previous forms of expression in worship from both the shouting Methodists and the early Nazarenes were focused upon God's action. It was believed that vocal and bodily responses

193. Ibid.

194. Staples, "What About Applause," 48–49.

195. Ibid., 49. Staples indicates that clapping is unknown in the New Testament and that the Old Testament references to clapping are both "ambiguous and extremely scant."

196. Ibid.

were expressions that not only signified God's presence and power but were also envisioned as the legitimate and appropriate response of gratitude for God's gracious activity in the lives of his people. Legitimate response always pointed toward God or his movement. However, as Staples indicates, applause instead is directed towards human action; it highlights the performance of the creature rather than the divine movements of the creator.

Generally speaking, applause, rather than being motivated by attitudes of gratitude, awe, and reverence in the worship of God, is generated in response to the congregation's sense of satisfaction with what is perceived as performance. Therefore, applause is the result of the performer's ability to entertain the congregation. This creates a vicious cycle. Performers are encouraged to entertain the congregation to receive the reward of the applause, which reciprocates an increasing expectation by modern congregations to be entertained in worship. Thus, the temptation to structure the liturgy to please people accrues, since an entertained congregation is more apt to increase attendance. Regrettably, the end result of worship designed primarily to entertain is the creation of a congregation that is cultivated to seek self-affirming experiences. Left unchecked this will eventually breed both individualism and narcissism.[197]

Summary

The next chapter will examine the sacraments. The Lord's supper and baptism are treated separately since they are not a regular part of weekly worship. Although the eucharist is celebrated weekly by many congregations in the prayer book tradition, this has not been the situation for the overwhelming majority of Nazarene congregations. The decision to place the eucharist in the next chapter should not be interpreted as an approval of its neglect and devaluation in some congregations; quite the contrary is true. Rather the motivation for its placement is twofold. First, it reflects both past and present practice in many Nazarene congregations. Secondly, for organizational reasons, it was placed with baptism to treat the sacraments together.

197. Contemporary society is already inundated with what David Wulff terms "the rising cult of self-centeredness." He argues that narcissism can even "exist on the group level." This may be evinced in worship that mirrors back "one's own 'self-love'" through the "affirmation and admiration of others," thereby creating a gathered community that is self-absorbed. This danger is evinced in various aspects of overly subjective worship. As noted earlier, much of the contemporary music focuses upon the *human subject's devotion* to God and experience of God, rather than pointing to God as the object of worship. Applause given in response to music that tends to be excessively subjective only amplifies this preoccupation with one's self. Wulff, *Psychology of Religion*, 354–5.

Chapter 5

The Sacraments

OPINIONS AMONG NAZARENES CONCERNING both the practice and theological implications of the sacraments are mixed. This variance is the result of the diversity inherent to the merging holiness streams. Many of those originating from Methodism possessed a substantially higher eucharistic theology and praxis than those proceeding from other traditions. Former Quakers and Anabaptists perceived both baptism and the Lord's supper in a different light than the sacramental theology embedded in classical Wesleyanism. Some groups, such as the Quakers, "viewed the sacraments as hindrances to the inner life of the Spirit,"[1] while the Anabaptists diluted "the Wesleyan doctrine of baptism"[2] and diminished the significance that John and Charles Wesley placed on the eucharist.

This divergent mix of sacramental practice and thought served not only to devalue the sacraments, but it disoriented laity and clergy alike as to their purpose in Wesleyan theology and praxis. Staples points out that in the beginning the sacraments were "administered sincerely and with some degree of regularity,"[3] but an exhaustive sacramental theology was never established. Even though many of the first-generation Nazarenes valued the eucharist and emphasized the importance of baptism, the sacramental confusion created by the divergent holiness streams served to further relegate the sacraments to a place of secondary importance or beyond. This becomes most obvious in the sparse eucharistic observance and in the frivolous manner that both sacraments are often administered.

1. Staples, *Outward Sign*, 22.
2. Ibid., 15–16.
3. Ibid., 22.

The Eucharist

Frequency of Observance

Brent Peterson points out that there was a moment in the early stages of the church that "the *Manual* encouraged members to partake of the Lord's Supper as much as possible."[4] The language is reminiscent of Wesley's call to constant communion. However, the wording was changed in 1928, thus removing any such appeal for frequent eucharistic celebrations within Nazarene congregations.[5] Although this change in language is striking, the frequency at which the Lord's supper was received within Nazarene congregations was never in danger of being deemed *constant communion*. Evidence suggests that the most prevalent practice occurred on the East Coast, where some pastors with Methodist backgrounds celebrated monthly.

The frequency of eucharistic celebration only occasionally appears in church documents and in reports from local congregations printed in denominational periodicals.[6] Eastern churches that designate the periodicity of observance often speak of a monthly practice. Prior to their merger with the Nazarenes some churches in the Association of Pentecostal Churches of America included a requirement for monthly observance in their statement of belief.[7] It is possible there were other congregations in the East, who provide no documentary evidence of the regularity of their observance, that were following a similar practice. Louis A. Reed[8] supports the notion that, overall, churches in the East celebrated with the greatest frequency:

> In the early days of the Church of the Nazarene, especially the Eastern group, the Communion service was commemorated monthly; but when the union took place, it was mutually agreed that it should be held quarterly. Some churches still hold to the old custom, but the rule requires the quarterly practice as a minimum expression of acquiescence to a liberal degree.[9]

4. Peterson, "Post-Wesleyan Ecclesiology," 19.

5. Peterson, "Post-Wesleyan Ecclesiology," 19; Wesley, "Duty of Constant Communion," in *Works (BE)*, 3:427–39.

6. Churches indicating monthly celebration in the *Beulah Christian* include Lynn, MA; Beverly, MA; Lowell, MA; and Lincoln Place, PA. See "Lincoln Place," 14; "Mission Church," 4; Waldie, "Beverly," 15; Riggs, "Lowell," January 22, 6.

7. *Church Manual First Peoples' Brooklyn*, 10; *Manual First Pentecostal Lynn*, 14.

8. Reed had served in various capacities within the denomination including pastor of Kansas City First and Chicago First; columnist for the *Herald of Holiness*; and professor of preaching and pastoral ministry at Nazarene Theological Seminary. Purkiser, *Called Unto Holiness*, 2.

9. Reed, "History Lord's Supper," 11.

Most references describing eucharistic practice among local congregations come from the *Beulah Christian* and the *Nazarene Messenger*, the periodicals from the East and West. Reports detailing eucharistic practice in the South are not found in the abundance characteristic of the other two geographical regions. Fitzgerald suggests that the Holiness Church of Christ was among those holiness streams that "practiced more frequent communion."[10] His argument is based upon the statement in their church discipline and their ecclesial roots with the Disciples of Christ. The Disciples of Christ followed a weekly observance. The *Manual* of the Holiness Church of Christ makes the following statement:

> It is the duty of all Christ's followers to commemorate His death until He comes again, by often meeting and partaking of the emblems of His broken body and shed blood.
>
> In the absence of the Pastors, Elders, or Deacons, it may be administered by any person whom the congregation may select for this purpose. No fermented wine shall be used.[11]

Although the text urges individuals to commune *often* and allows any member of the congregation to administer it, there is nothing that indicates how frequently they actually celebrated. Certainly, they came from a tradition with a robust eucharistic practice, but it was not uncommon for the various holiness groups to abandon practices from the very denominations they departed, especially if they considered certain practices to impinge on their liturgical freedom. Therefore, it is tenuous at best to assume that the Holiness Church of Christ communed with greater frequency based solely on their *Manual* statement and ecclesial background. There is simply not enough information to judge one way or the other.

While some of the churches in the East and West practiced monthly observance, at least one church in the West followed Bresee's pattern by celebrating the Lord's supper once every two months. The Grand Avenue Church exceeded Bresee's practice with a monthly observance.[12] Even though it has been appropriately noted that Bresee held the Lord's supper in

10. Fitzgerald, "Weaving Rope of Sand," 152–3. Fitzgerald does not qualify what he means by "more frequent"; therefore, it is difficult to fully comprehend his intentions. One can only definitely assume he means more than a quarterly observance, but whether he is pointing towards a bimonthly, monthly, weekly, or some other measure of observance is impossible to determine.

11. *Manual Holiness Church*, 20.

12. The Grand Avenue Church indicated that "the first Sabbath of each month" was reserved for the Lord's supper; it immediately followed the sermon. The Compton Avenue Church followed Bresee's pattern of bi-monthly communion. "Grand Avenue Church," April 9, 8; "Compton Avenue Church," December 23, 8.

high esteem, the regularity of his eucharistic celebration does not appear to be more ambitious than those in New England. Available evidence indicates that he celebrated bi-monthly in his Los Angeles congregation.[13]

Even the minimal requirement of quarterly eucharist was not adhered to by all pastors as the following report demonstrates:

> A local preacher who called on us yesterday said he had been a member of the Church of the Nazarene for about three years and that he had never yet had the privilege of celebrating the sacrament of the Lord's Supper in his own church. His case may, perhaps, be rather exceptional, but nevertheless, there are churches in our connection that are not very regular and not very frequent in their observance of this holy sacrament, and we believe they are falling short. . . . It is possible to subtract from the sacredness of this Christian ordinance by observing it too frequently and with too small and amount of preparation for it. But no church should be content with less than the observance

13. Both Timothy Smith and Carl Bangs argue that Bresee's celebration of the eucharist was at minimum a monthly observance. Bangs even indicates that at least for a period of time Bresee celebrated the Lord's supper twice monthly at Los Angeles First. However, the *Nazarene Messenger* states on several occasions that the eucharist was celebrated bi-monthly at Los Angeles First. Bangs's assumption appears to be a misinterpretation of the meaning of bi-monthly, which refers to every other month rather than twice a month. He states that after Los Angeles First moved to their new location Bresee started observing the eucharist twice a month. The following quote from the May 3, 1900, issue clarifies the correct understanding of bi-monthly, "Sacramental service will be held next Sabbath at 3 p.m. Hitherto the Sacramental Service and love feast have been on the third Sabbath of the month, *held alternately*, but it has been thought best to change to the first Sabbath" (italics mine). Apparently Bangs also errs in his understanding of this passage and interpreted it to mean that initially the love feast and eucharist were held together on a monthly basis. However, the phrase "held alternately" indicates that the eucharist and love feast were held on separate months, rather than together. As the reference in the *Nazarene Messenger* states, previously, either the love feast or eucharist occurred on the third Sunday of the month, but it was in the process of being changed to the first Sunday of the month. This evidence as well as numerous descriptions of the eucharist and love feast in the *Nazarene Messenger* do not support the practice of a combined love feast and eucharist in Bresee's church. Timothy Smith stated that the eucharist and love feast celebrations were both "monthly" occurrences and alternated "biweekly." He references six issues of the *Nazarene Messenger* from 1902 and two issues from 1903 to support his claim. However, these issues demonstrate that the eucharist alternated with the love feast on a monthly basis; and do not support claims of a biweekly practice. Additionally, other reports of the eucharist in the *Nazarene Messenger* consistently speak of the eucharist occurring bimonthly, rather than being a biweekly celebration. Smith, *Called Unto Holiness*, 134; Bangs, *Phineas Bresee*, 235–6; "Sacramental Service," 5; "Sabbath," August 8, 7; "Sabbath at First Church," October 9, 3; "Notes and Personals," December 11, 6; "Sabath at First Church," July 7, 3; "Sabbath at First Church," May 11, 10; "At the Tabernacle," April 12, 8; "At the Tabernacle," February 7, 8.

once every three months, and this should be a regular and not
an intermittent matter.[14]

Other articles and communications from local churches also demonstrate the problem of clergy celebrating the eucharist less than the *Manual*
stipulation.[15]

The account above also signifies another belief that became characteristic of many clergy and laity and a notion still prevalent today. This is
the assumption that a too frequent celebration of the eucharist diminished
its sacredness. Wesley himself addressed similar objections in *The Duty to
Constant Communion*. He responded to those who suggested that communicating too often lessened one's reverence for the sacrament. Wesley
argued that the sacredness of the eucharist is only diminished for those who
approach it inappropriately; however, for those who truly love and fear God
more frequent participation in the Lord's Supper serves to increase one's
reverence for it, not reduce it.[16]

J. B. Chapman is one who not only admonished pastors about the
importance of celebrating communion in accordance with the *Manual*
mandate, and the need to adequately prepare for the communion service,
but he also warned of decreasing its value by celebrating too often. His response to a letter written to the *Herald of Holiness* provides the following
recommendation:

> I believe the sacrament of the Lord's Supper should be observed
> at regular set times—in connection with the regular services of
> the church, I think once every three months meets the demands
> about the best. Too often has a tendency to make the service
> common, and too seldom gives the impression that it is not very
> important.[17]

While the older Chapman admonished pastors to follow the *Manual*
stipulation, his earlier preferences were different. Writing in 1925 Chapman
indicated that he would be satisfied with an extremely exiguous observance
if the adequate preparations were made:

> I do think that this blessed institution loses much of its sacred-
> ness when a congregation receives it too frequently. Every week,
> as some receive it, or even every month is too frequent for the

14. "Observing the Sacrament," 3.

15. Chapman, "Question Box," March 25, 2; Chapman, "Question Box," January 3,
2; White, "Question Box," December 19, 9.

16. Wesley, "Duty to Constant Communion," in *Works (BE)*, 3:437.

17. Chapman, "Question Box," January 24, 2.

maintenance of the spirit of reverence. Once every six months, or even once a year with full preparation and announcement and with the service gathering pretty much about this holy sacrament is, I think, fully Scriptural and of the greatest profit, though I would certainly condemn the carelessness that would permit longer periods of elapse.[18]

The crucial issue for Chapman was not celebrating more often but rather making certain that adequate preparation was made. This included preparing the people to receive it by announcing well in advance of the date it would be administered and orchestrating the whole service around the eucharist.

Ironically, although Chapman thought clergy should limit the eucharist to a quarterly observance, he indicated that he discovered it beneficial to participate in the eucharist whenever it was served, even in other denominations. Such sentiments are exemplified when he writes, "I make it a rule to take every part in any service I attend that is open for the participation of Christians in general. So I take the sacrament with any who do not forbid me, and as often as they offer it. It does me good and I think it is a good example to others."[19] Chapman does not offer any other explanation for this practice. It is difficult to ascertain why Chapman believed the Lord's supper risked its sacredness if churches observed it too frequently but at the same time felt that it was beneficial for him to partake of it whenever he had the opportunity.

Peterson argues that the elemental cause for the infrequent celebration of the Lord's supper and the absence of a *sacramental vitality* can be traced to the denomination's rationale for celebrating the eucharist. The church has "emphasized the Lord's Supper more consistently . . . as an ordinance, rather than a sacrament."[20] This seemingly subtle distinction has in the end marginalized the eucharist both in theology and praxis. Peterson suggests that as an ordinance, clergy celebrate communion in order to comply with church polity, rather than being driven by a "sacramental vision,"[21] which

18. Chapman, "Questions Answered," March 18, 6.

19. Chapman, "Question Box," April 15, 12.

20. Peterson, "Post-Wesleyan Ecclesiology," 17–18.

21. Ibid., 17. Ted Campbell clarifies that in "Wesleyan practice and thought" the terms ordinances and means of grace "are closely related" to each other. Additionally, ordinances and means of grace are somewhat broader and more inclusive categories than that of sacrament. The eucharist is a chief means of grace which is both sacrament and ordinance. Peterson highlights the nuances between an ordinance and a sacrament as it relates to sacramental practice. He states that an *ordinance* focuses upon the command to perform the sacrament, which means an ordinance is primarily focused on

hungers for the therapeutic benefits that God offers in the meal. Consequentially the Lord's supper is celebrated only to fulfill the minimal requirements the church demands. Often it does so in the absence of thoughtful preparation and care.[22]

Converting Ordinance

Bresee typically celebrated the Lord's supper in the mid-afternoon service, rather than in the morning liturgy. Reports of worship at Los Angeles First depict experientially robust and meaningful sacramental services. It is possible that in some of the services the eucharist was a converting ordinance: "In the afternoon the bi-monthly Sacramental service was held. There was a large gathering of the saints, and the presence of the Master at the feast was very blessedly manifest. Four seekers came forward at the close as persons and in answer to the united prayers of the people of God were very blessedly saved."[23] It was not uncommon for an altar call to be offered after the communion service; therefore, it is not clear if the conversions happened during the actual rite. However, the Lord's supper was certainly the focus of the service and provided the context for the manifested grace.

The question as to whether the Lord's supper ever functioned as a converting ordinance within any of the merging holiness bodies receives greater clarity upon examination of eucharistic practice in New England. The church in Franklin, New Hampshire, reported the following account: "Last Thursday night one soul sought and found the Lord and another one on Sunday morning *during the administration of the Lord's Supper*, when

---

complying with "church polity." Therefore, pastors and churches that primarily envision the eucharist as an ordinance, and are only complying with church polity, administer the eucharist only when necessary to fulfill the demands of church law. As a result, the performance of the sacrament is often minimized. In contrast, "*a sacramental vision*" seeks, even hungers for, the sacrament for its therapeutic and "empowering" qualities and sees it as central to the life of the church. Those guided by such a vision seek to make the celebration of the eucharist a robust and meaningful ritual event. Although the eucharist is both ordinance and sacrament Peterson argues that one of these postures, either viewing the eucharist as an ordinance or perceiving it as a sacrament, becomes dominant and "guides the performance." Campbell, "Means of Grace," in Abraham and Kirby, *Oxford Handbook*, 280–81; Peterson, "Post-Wesleyan Ecclesiology," 17–20; Staples, *Outward Sign*, 85–118; Dunning, *Grace, Faith, Holiness*, 542–4.

22. Peterson, "Post-Wesleyan Ecclesiology," 17–18.

23. "Sabbath," August 8, 7. Other articles depict equally rich worship that included weeping, experiences of "holy joy," and "the conscious presence of Jesus." Some individuals were converted, while others entirely sanctified. See "Sabbath," December 21, 4; "Notes and Personals," April 17, 3; "Notes and Personals," December 11, 6; "Sabbath," September 17, 3.

twenty-four souls amid shouts and tears received to their comfort the sacred emblems. Many souls were melted to tears of joy and penitential grief.
It was truly a season not soon to be forgotten."[24] Similar to the previous
description of the eucharist at Los Angeles, conversion in this account occurs in the context of the sacrament. However, the above account from New
Hampshire is more explicit and leaves little doubt that the converting grace
was bestowed in the sacrament itself. Both reports are characteristic of other
depictions of Nazarene celebrations of the Lord's supper.

Occasionally these descriptions of the eucharist were circumvented
with picturesque language. It served to illustrate robust encounters with the
Divine and expressed manifestations of the Spirit experienced by those participating in the sacrament. Although the depiction below does not speak of
conversions, the language expresses the atmosphere that often surrounded
eucharistic celebrations:

> We had the communion of the Lord's Supper for the first time in
> the Nazarene church in our city. Dr. [Bresee] you ought to have
> been there we had a "Pentecost," some shouted, some cried and
> some laughed for joy; we were truly sitting together in heavenly
> places. O hallelujah! How sweet is His presence here, what must
> it be when we shall see Him face to face? "And it doth not yet
> appear what we shall be, but we know that when He shall appear
> we shall be like Him, for we shall see Him as He is." O Hallelu-
> jah! Glorious anticipation![25]

Although the frequency of the Lord's supper never reached Wesley's
expectation for his spiritual heirs, the reports of Nazarene celebrations in
the East and West reflect a vibrant and rich experience of the eucharist in
the earliest days of the denomination, and there were instances when it
functioned as a converting ordinance. Occasionally some churches in the
South report on their observance of the Lord's supper in the *Pentecostal
Advocate* and *Holiness Evangel*; however, the accounts are fewer and they
typically lack the vibrant descriptions found in the *Nazarene Messenger* and
Beulah Christian.[26]

24. "Franklin," 8; italics mine.

25. Solberg, "Spokane," 10.

26. There were a few exceptions in the South; some of the accounts do speak of
the eucharist as being an "impressive" service, a "fine" service, or "one of the best I have
ever attended." One containing the richest language even stated that the Lord's supper
"awakened our love for Him who died for us." Suddarth, "Lord's Work," 7. Additionally
the *Pentecostal Advocate* contains depictions using vibrant language of eucharistic celebrations on the mission field and in General Assembly but typically not from Southern congregations. Despite these few exceptions the reports from the South generally

The reports of conversions occurring during the celebration of the Lord's supper are limited to the first-generation Nazarenes from the East and West. It is difficult, if not impossible, to tell how rapidly the vibrant celebrations of the Lord's supper began to disappear, but over time both eucharistic praxis and theology changed. The combination of the absence of a sacramental theology to guide them and the consequences of merging with holiness groups holding impoverished sacramental beliefs meant that the eucharist was devalued as the early generations died out. As Fitzgerald points out, most Nazarenes of today have little understanding of the depth of Wesley's eucharistic theology.[27] During the 1967 theology conference in Kansas City, Nazarene theologian Ross Price's summary reflects this departure from Wesley. It was a viewpoint not only expounded by Price but held by many in leadership:

> Wesley regards [the Lord's supper] as more than a confirming means of grace. With him it is a means of possible conversion or a converting means as well.
>
> We can agree with Wesley that none of us should feel himself worthy of or meriting God's grace, but we cannot agree that the taking of the sacrament is a converting, forgiving, or sanctifying rite. This is too Romish [sic] for us to acknowledge.[28]

Fitzgerald applauded Rob Staples, professor emeritus at Nazarene Theological Seminary, for his contribution of *Outward Sign and Inward Grace*, which presents a Wesleyan sacramental theology. Fitzgerald suggests that Staples's work "has caused a reconsideration of the views expressed by Ross Price, and a gradual acceptance of Wesley's views."[29] There is no doubt Staples's contributions have filled a much-needed void and have been a positive influence to a denomination that has distinguished itself by its Wesleyan roots. However, if the church continues to ignore an essential part of her ecclesial heritage, then she will experience the equivalent of sacramental

---

lacked the robust language found in the East and West. For accounts from the mission field and General Assembly, see "Holiness Church Annual Council," 6; Richards, "Missionary Bulletin," 10.

27. Fitzgerald, "Weaving Rope of Sand," 218.

28. Price, *Nazarene Manifesto*, 45–46. Originally Price's book was a paper presented at the Nazarene Theology Conference held in 1967. However, church leadership believed its content was important enough to be published for greater distribution among laity and clergy. The back cover of the book provides the following rationale for publication: "The Book Committee felt that [Nazarene Manifesto's] very significant message needed broad distribution. . . . It merits careful reading by every minister and thoughtful layman in the church."

29. Fitzgerald, "Weaving Rope of Sand," 219.

amnesia in both orthopraxy and orthodoxy. Furthermore, the problems created by years of devaluing the sacraments in both belief and practice will not find a quick remedy.

The Lord's Supper and the Reception of Members

One of the trends in the East, at least for some churches, was to receive members on the same Sunday that the Lord's supper was observed. This practice is noted by J. C. Bearse in his description of the John Wesley Church in Brooklyn:

> I began my pastorate with this church September 4th and have been hard at it ever since. . . . The Sunday services are well attended, nearly every seat in the main auditorium being filled in the evening. . . . There are seekers every Sabbath and they find the open fountain, praise the Lord! . . . There seems to be members received at every communion service, at least, so it has been since my coming.[30]

Although it is not stated explicitly, the tenor of this article suggests that the reception of members was scheduled to coincide with communion Sundays. Bearse indicates that members were received at every communion service since his arrival. Implied in his statement is the idea that communion Sunday was the customary time to receive members. In other words, because the rapid growth of the John Wesley Church and since communion Sunday was the allotted time to receive members, it became necessary to receive members at every Lord's supper in order to meet with the demands of the growing church. If this was the only evidence to support such a claim, then this position would be tenuous; however, other documents give credence to this argument.

There are reports from various churches in the East which are supportive of such a practice. Several accounts providing descriptions of eucharistic celebrations also indicate the number of members received. The reception of members frequently followed the sacrament as illustrated in this report: "At the communion service Jesus never seemed more precious. His spirit came upon us in melting power, and nine new members were received into the church."[31] The following account from Sag Harbor, New York, is even more revealing: "We expect to receive four souls on probation on next communion Sabbath, three of which are young men."[32] This pastor locates

30. Bearse, "John Wesley Church," 5.

31. "Beverly," 2.

32. "Sag Harbor," 8.

the next occasion for receiving probationary members by the communion schedule, rather than a specific date, or Sunday of the month.

A. B. Riggs also designates the timeframe for the reception of members by eucharist observance, rather than a specific date, Sunday of the month, or some other criteria: "Three joined on probation and two in full connection the last communion service."[33] All of this seems to evince a common practice in the East of receiving members on communion Sunday. There are some data indicating that in the West members were also received following the eucharist, but it is unclear if this was a normal and widespread practice. There is no indication from Nazarene periodicals that the Eastern pattern was followed in the South.[34] One possible explanation for why this practice is more evident in the East is because the Lord's supper was celebrated with greater regularity. The growing denomination meant there was an influx of new members for many churches. Reserving communion Sunday for the reception of members would not pose problems for the East. Since the Lord's supper was celebrated more often, many opportunities were available to receive members. The same may not be true for all the geographical regions of the denomination with a less robust eucharistic practice.

Ritual Forms

The freedom characteristic of other aspects of Nazarene worship also influenced sacramental practice. The sacraments are one of the few areas that the Church of the Nazarene has provided a ritual, but the rubrics are minimal. Additionally, due to the spontaneous preferences of the church, it is uncertain to what extent the written forms were followed. Fitzgerald states that unlike other aspects of worship that were free of written forms, the common practice of Nazarene clergy was to use the ritual in the *Manual* for the administration of the eucharist. He references an article by D. Shelby Corlett that stresses the sacred nature of the Lord's supper and encourages the use of the *Manual* ritual form, but Fitzgerald provides little support for the notion that pastors typically used the eucharistic rite in the *Manual*.[35]

33. Riggs, "Lowell," April 1900, 6. These are not isolated incidents, rather several churches report details of their sacramental services followed by the number of members received; see Lewis, "West Somerville," April 8, 8; Leach, "Keene," 3; Hosley, "Clintondale," 8.

34. The Grand Avenue Church was one of the churches in the West indicating that members were received following communion. "Grand Avenue Church," August 6, 8.

35. Fitzgerald, "Weaving Rope of Sand," 212–3.

There is little doubt that some pastors did use the *Manual* form; however, the problem with generalizing this assumption to all clergy is to ignore how deeply imbedded the desire for freedom in worship was in the Nazarene psyche. One contributor to the *Preacher's Magazine* advises pastors to memorize the rituals found in the *Manual*, rather than be tied to a written form. The article reasons that this would free the pastor by eliminating the distraction caused by *fumbling* through books and "last minute preparations."[36] Although the article encouraged memorization of the rite, in all likelihood, it simply reinforced the propensity for pastors to move away from written forms toward the spontaneity and freedom which Nazarenes have typically desired.

In response to Fitzgerald's assumption that Nazarene clergy commonly used the ritual forms printed in the *Manual* it is worthwhile to note that the *Manual* also required pastors to celebrate the sacrament a minimum of once quarterly. However, as Fitzgerald acknowledges and periodical articles indicate, not all pastors were complying with this stipulation.[37] The appearance of articles encouraging clergy to use the ritual in the *Manual* due to the eucharist's sacred nature does not mean they were following protocol. It is just as likely the articles were written to address deficiencies in practice rather than affirming the norm. There is even an indication that at least some clergy were celebrating the rite in a rather haphazard manner.[38] The great temptation for pastors who desired freedom over form was simply to offer the Lord's supper extempore, as is the case today where the use of the *Manual* or prayer book resources for celebrating the eucharist is limited to approximately half of all Nazarene clergy in the United States.[39]

Even though the Church of the Nazarene did retain written ritual forms for the sacraments, the reception of members, marriage, and funerals, most of them are rather meager rites. One would expect this to be the case, since the use of written forms was equated with the spiritual decay found in formalism. Prior to the merger with West, each of the churches from the Association of Pentecostal Churches in the East used its own rituals.

---

36. "Lord's Supper," 5.

37. Fitzgerald, "Weaving Rope of Sand," 211–2; "Observing the Sacrament," 3; Chapman," Question Box," March 25, 2; Chapman, "Question Box," January 3, 2.

38. The careless administration of both sacraments by pastors was on occasion illustrated in questions church members submitted to the *Herald of Holiness*; see Chapman, "Question Box," June 21, 13; Chapman, "Question Box," October 14, 13.

39. Fifty percent use the *Manual*, of that fifty percent 11 percent of clergy also use the *CRH*. Approximately two percent of Nazarene pastors use the *United Methodist Book of Worship*. Ellis, "Relationship Liturgical Practice," 407, 629.

One of the more robust eucharistic rites was that of First People's Church of Brooklyn, New York. It is important to note that the ritual is still impoverished and the language is closer to Zwingli than representative of Wesley's eucharistic theology.[40] Despite these limitations, it does contain modified elements found in Wesley's *Sunday Service*. This includes adapted portions of the following: the prayer of consecration, the prayer of humble access, the collect for purity interspersed with language akin to the *Kyrie eleison*, the *sanctus*, the *anamnesis*, and a rubric instructing the minister to end with extempore prayer. Although the ritual makes reference to Christ instituting the meal, the institution narrative is absent. The ritual for First People's Church and the ritual printed in the 1908 *Manual* of the Church of the Nazarene are shown in table 3.

Eucharistic Prayer Element	First People's Church Ritual
	Invitation
Prayer of Consecration Anamnesis (limited: focus is on past event without reference to present participation)	*Prayer as follows:* Almighty God, Father of our Lord Jesus Christ, Creator of all things and Judge of all men, who of thy tender mercy didst give thine only begotten Son Jesus Christ to suffer death upon the cross for our redemption; who made thereby the sacrifice of Himself once offered, a perfect and all-sufficient sacrifice for the sins of the whole world; and did institute and command us to continue, a perpetual memorial of his sufferings and death, until his coming again. O Lord, we are now at thy table to celebrate thy goodness shown in thy sacrificial death. Grant us grace that we may be enabled to partake of these emblems of thy most blessed body and blood in true faith.
Prayer of Humble Access	We do not presume to approach this sacrament, trusting in our own righteousness, but in thy manifold and great mercies. We are not worthy so much as to gather up the crumbs under thy table; for we from time to time have provoked thy wrath and indignation against us, by our manifold sins and transgressions, which we have committed by thought, word and deed, against thy Holy Majesty; but thou art the same God whose property it is to have mercy. Of thy great mercy thou hast promised forgiveness of sins to all them who, with hearty repentance and true faith, turn to thee.

40. Brent David Peterson, e-mail message to author, May 16, 2011.

Eucharistic Prayer Element	First People's Church Ritual
Collect for Purity with Kyrie Eleison language	Unto thee all our desires are known and from thee no secrets are hid; have mercy on us, most merciful Father, for thy Son, our Lord Jesus Christ's sake, cast all our transgressions behind thee into the sea of thy eternal forgetfulness. Cleanse thou the thoughts of our hearts by the inspiration of thy Holy Spirit more and more, that we may perfectly love thee, and worthily magnify thy holy name.
Sanctus	It becomes our duty, at all times and in all places, to give thanks unto thee, O Lord, Holy Father, Almighty God! Therefore we would, in concert with the angels and all the heavenly hosts, say: *(The congregation joining)*
	Holy, Holy, Holy, Lord God of Hosts, Heaven and earth are full of thy glory! Glory be to thee, O Lord Most High. Amen.
Prayer of Consecration (continues)	*(The Pastor continues):*
	Listen to our supplication, we humbly beseech thee, and grant us grace, that we receiving these thy gifts of bread and wine, according to the institution of thy Son, our Lord and Saviour Jesus Christ, in remembrance of his suffering and death, may be partakers of his most blessed body and blood, that our souls and bodies may be clean by the virtue of his death, and that he may evermore dwell in us and we in him.
Extempore Prayer	*The minister shall here receive the sacrament himself, and then administer to the others who are to partake. After all have partaken, the minister shall close with extempore prayer.*

Eucharistic Prayer Element	1908 Manual Ritual
	The administration of the Lord's supper shall be introduced by an appropriate sermon or a suitable address and the reading of 1 Cor. 11:23–39, Luke 22:14–20, or some other appropriate passage.
Invitation	*Let the minster give the following invitation:*
Anamnesis (limited: focus is on past event without reference to present participation)	The Lord Himself ordained this Holy Sacrament. He commanded His disciples to partake of the bread and wine, emblems of His broken body and shed blood. This is His table. The feast is for His disciples. Let all those who have with true repentance forsaken their sins, and have believed in Christ unto salvation, draw near and take these emblems, and, by faith, partake of the life of Jesus Christ, to your soul's comfort and joy. Let us remember that it is the memorial of the death and passion of our Lord, also a token of His coming again. Let us not forget that we are one, at one table with our Lord.
Prayer of Consecration Institution Narrative	*The minster, with the congregation kneeling, may offer prayer of confession and supplication, with the following prayer of consecration:* Almighty God, our Heavenly Father, who of Thy tender mercy didst give Thine only Son, Jesus Christ, to suffer death upon the cross for our redemption; hear us, O merciful Father, we most humbly beseech Thee, and grant that we, receiving these Thy creatures of bread and wine, according to Thy Son, our Saviour Jesus Christ's holy institution, in remembrance of His death and passion, may be made partakers of the benefits of His sacrificial death, who in the same night that He was betrayed, took bread, and when He had given thanks, He broke it and gave it to His disciples saying, Take, eat, this is my body, which is broken for you; do this in remembrance of me. Likewise, after supper He took the cup, and when He had given thanks, He gave it to them, saying, Drink ye all of this, for this is my blood of the New Testament, which is shed for you and for many, for the remission of sins; do this as oft as ye shall drink it, in remembrance of me. *Amen.* *Then may the minster, himself partaking, with the assistance of other ministers present, and when necessary of the Stewards, administer the Communion to the people kneeling.*
The Lord's Prayer Extempore Prayer	*(The Lord's Prayer with extempore prayer of thanksgiving.)*

Table 3. Rituals for the administration of the Lord's supper: First People's Church, Brooklyn, New York, and the 1908 *Manual*

Distribution of the Elements

A 1948 article detailing a prescribed method for "conducting"[41] communion suggests that when members of the congregation take their piece of
bread, it should be eaten "simulwtaneously [with] all the communicants,"[42]
and the individual communion cups should also be received together. The
purpose of this rubric was to increase "unity, harmony, and effectiveness."[43]
However, methods that incorporated the use of a common cup and loaf,
which are more efficaciously efficient at carrying such symbolic weight, if
ever used, never evolved as the normal practice for the vast portion of Nazarene congregations.[44]

Available evidence regarding the nature of the communion elements
points to the widespread use of pre-broken pieces of bread and individual
cups containing unfermented wine (i.e., grape juice).[45] Commonly referred
to as the "saloon method" by disapproving Methodists, Tucker indicates
that by the late nineteenth century this controversial method was used by
many Methodists. Those opposed to this technique were concerned that
individual cups posed a threat to one of the primary meanings of the Lord's
supper—unity and equality within the body of Christ. "Many Methodists
shared the sentiment of J.M. Buckley, . . . who described the individual cup
'as one of the most inconsistent and repugnant innovations ever foisted
upon any part of the Christian Church.'"[46]

Bangs states that Bresee's "communion ware consisted of a silver pitch-
er and chalice for the juice and a plate for the bread."[47] He does not indicate
if Bresee administered the eucharist through a common cup, intinction, individual cups, or used multiple methods. If Bresee did use a chalice, it seems
doubtful that techniques other than the use of the individual cups and pre-
broken pieces of bread ever became prevalent. Both the *Manual* and denominational periodicals discussing the rubrics of the Lord's supper are for

41. Strang, "Conducting the Communion Service," 15.

42. Ibid., 16.

43. Ibid.

44. This would include the use of a whole loaf and either drinking from a common chalice or receiving by intinction. Intinction appeared at the same time as did the
individual cups; both were offered as alternatives to drinking from a common cup, in
order to address the problem of communicable diseases. Tucker, *American Methodist
Worship*, 150–54.

45. Strang, "Conducting the Communion Service," 15–16; Hess, " Pastor in Communion," 42.

46. Tucker, *American Methodist Worship*, 152–3.

47. Bangs, *Phineas Bresee*, 236.

the most part silent on this issue. Chapman's instructions on conducting the eucharist illustrate the absence of discussion regarding preferences either for individual cups or a communion chalice: "I believe the sacrament of the Lord's Supper should be observed at regular set times—in connection with the regular services of the church. . . . The elements should be unleavened bread and sweet grape juice."[48] Notably absent from Chapman's remarks is any discussion on the distribution of the elements, such as whether to use individual cups, a chalice, or if both were acceptable. Details are given restricting the tokens of Christ's body and blood to unleavened bread and "sweet grape juice,"[49] but distribution appears to be a nonissue. Silence on the topic may be an indication that even if a chalice was used by Bresee or others, the practice of serving with individual cups was standardized by this time.

Like the holiness movement in general, the Church of the Nazarene was deeply connected to the temperance movement. The use of alcohol was prohibited in any context, including the eucharist. Following the pattern of the holiness movement, the earliest *Manual* of the church restricted the Lord's supper to unfermented wine, but it did not limit the type of bread. A mandate requiring the exclusive use of unleavened bread first appeared with the 1928 edition of the *Manual*[50] and remained until 2005. These restrictions, however, were tucked away in the Special Rules section of the *Manual*, which meant they could easily be overlooked.[51] A conspicuous rubric in bold font was added at the end of the ritual for the Lord's supper in the 1997 *Manual* restating the mandate found in the Special Rules, which limited the eucharistic elements to unfermented wine and unleavened bread. This perhaps was an indication that at least some of the restrictions on the elements were not being followed.[52]

---

48. Chapman, "Question Box," January 24, 2.

49. Ibid.

50. *Manual Nazarene* (1928), 33.

51. The "Special Rules" section was originally labeled "Special Advices" and is currently referred to as "The Covenant of Christian Conduct." Through the 1972 *Manual* the restriction on elements was placed under the subheading "Temperance and Prohibition," but this subheading disappeared with the 1976 edition.

52. This rubric was the only bold font to appear in the entire ritual section of the 1997 *Manual*, other than the ritual headings at the top of the page. This is further indication that either clergy were unaware of the mandate or they were ignoring it. It is unclear if this was a worldwide issue or restricted to isolated regions of the world and if the problem was related to either elements; or one in particular. When the restriction on unleavened bread was removed the rubric for unfermented wine remained in the ritual in bold font.

Chapman states that the mandate limiting the Lord's supper to the specified emblems was because leaven symbolized sin: "Our Lord's body did not 'see corruption'. The use of leaven was forbidden in feasts of the Jews because its presence always destroyed the full value of the type. Fermented wine, likewise, is a poor type of the blood of Jesus."[53] This regulation, however, did not stop clergy from using "ordinary baker's bread [and] common soda crackers."[54] Chapman chides those who used leavened bread as being lazy, thoughtless, and careless in their celebration of the Lord's supper.[55]

Structure of the Lord's Supper

Paradoxically, even while marginalizing the eucharist by minimizing the requirement to a quarterly celebration, denominational leadership encouraged clergy to approach it with planning and preparation. Chapman provides the following guidance:

> The time of day is not especially important, but in the regular services of the church the Sunday morning service is . . . I think usually the best time. . . . In the service itself, the sacraments should be the center. The hymns should be selected in keeping with the central purpose, the sermon should be pointedly directed to the central theme, and at the close of the actual celebration the meeting should be closed with earnest prayer and fervent benediction. To crowd the sacrament into a full program of some sort is, according to my judgment, a mistake from every consideration. And with proper preparation and right spirit Communion Sunday can be made the most blessed of the quarter.[56]

Bresee's most common practice was to administer the Lord's supper during the Sunday afternoon service; however, Chapman argues for a Sunday morning observance. He also instructs clergy to structure the entire service around it. Most believed that the sermon was to be derived from one of the institution narratives or other passage addressing the Lord's supper. The basic thought was that the length of the sermon should be significantly reduced, therefore instead of a sermon the pastor should provide a

---

53. Chapman, "Question Box," January 6, 13.

54. Ibid.

55. Ibid.; Chapman, "Question Box," February 12, 12.

56. Chapman, "Question Box," January 24, 2.

"communion meditation."[57] One contributor to *The Preacher's Magazine* suggested ten minutes as the appropriate length for a communion meditation. The hymns, Scripture readings, prayers, responsive readings (if used), and entire observance were to be "Calvary-centered."[58] The desired atmosphere was one of solemnity, rather than celebration.[59]

Although all this preparation was intended to make the service both *meaningful and sacred,* it had an adverse effect by further serving to move the eucharist outside of the communal life of the church. Special alterations to the service were made in both content and time allocations in order to provide room for this occasional addition to the Nazarene liturgy. The sermon and other components of worship were reduced and restructured to fit the demands of communion Sunday. Rather than being a central part of a balanced liturgy, the eucharist was almost an intrusion on worship and administered out of obligation rather than desire. The Lord's supper was no longer valued for its therapeutic qualities in healing the sin-sick soul when approached in faith. Therefore, Peterson suggests that instead of being central to the life of the church, as Wesley intended, the Lord's supper was marginalized and disconnected from the church's work and mission.[60]

Concluding Observations

There were other changes to the ritual further obstructing it as a means of grace. Even though the *Manual* still provided the rubric indicating a posture of kneeling for those who were able, John Riley, the President of Northwest Nazarene College, provided an alternative. He suggested that while kneeling at the altar was preferred, a viable option for larger congregations was to serve the congregation in the pews. He based this suggestion upon the eucharistic practice of the 1952 General Assembly.[61] The decision was obviously for practical reasons; however, for those choosing to follow this practice, it changed the congregation's response in the eucharist from an active to a passive state. Instead of going forward to receive the elements and kneel, they remained seated in their pew and waited for the bread and wine

57. Strang, "Conducting Communion," 15.

58. Riley, " Church's One Continuing Sacrament," 14.

59. Ibid., 12–13; Strang, "Conducting the Communion Service," 15.

60. Peterson, "Post-Wesleyan Ecclesiology," 17–20.

61. Riley, "Church's One Continuing Sacrament," 14. Riley was not alone in making this suggestion. It was believed that larger congregations needed to implement this strategy to move people through communion in a reasonable amount of time; see Hess, "Pastor in Communion," 42–43.

to be passed. Riley's pragmatic suggestion proved prophetic; the rubric for kneeling would be removed from the ritual for the Lord's supper within less than twenty years.

Ironically, many of those voices who argued that Communion should be approached with care and thoughtfulness probably did not realize the negative implications of some of the revisions made to both the ritual and the Article on the Lord's supper. One example is the removal of language from the 1928 *Manual* encouraging individuals "to partake of the privileges of this sacrament, as often as we may be providentially permitted."[62] Revisions like this and other practical changes such as the loss of the eucharistic hymns of the Wesleys are responsible for moving the Lord's supper to the fringe of belief and praxis.

Some of the damage inflicted on the Lord's supper occurred in more recent years. Rubrics for the eucharistic rite in the 1908 *Manual* instructed the minister to have the people kneel and provided the option for the pastor to pray a prayer of confession and supplication in addition to the prayer of consecration which was included in the ritual. The 1972 *Manual* not only removed all rubrics for kneeling, but it also eliminated the instruction to include the Lord's Prayer prior to the concluding extempore prayer. Before this revision, the Lord's Prayer had been a part of the Nazarene eucharistic rite since the church's inception. Unfortunately, the removal of the Lord's Prayer has unintentionally led to the further devaluation of Nazarene sacramental practice by distancing it from not only the historic rites of the early church, but also those followed by the Wesleys.[63]

Overall the balance between Word and Table found in Wesley's liturgical theology as well as that of the ancient church is absent from many Nazarene liturgies. The celebration of the Lord's supper was more of an intrusion on the normal worship pattern than a vital part of it. The overemphasis on the proclamation of the Word created an overly subjective atmosphere where attention was focused upon human initiative, rather than upon God's grace. This in turn fueled the individualism prevalent in contemporary culture by overemphasizing personal decision to the neglect of corporate responsibility.

62. *Manual Nazarene* (1908), 31.

63. While it is true that not all eucharistic rites of the ancient church contain the Lord's Prayer, many of them do. The problem with the Nazarene rite is not simply the removal of the prayer, but that the content of the prescribed ritual was already anemic. Therefore, the removal of the Lord's Prayer was not only a move away from written forms, but a significant reduction to the rite's meager theological composition. For more information on prayers of the early church, see Jasper and Cuming, *Prayers of the Eucharist*.

A robust sacramental theology and praxis reminds persons of who they are in Christ and therefore aids in countering the secular philosophies and systems of belief that invade the church, thus threatening our identity. The sacraments are essential because they "underscore the *objectivity* of our faith—what God has done for us prior to and apart from our own doings";[64] without them we are doomed to be inwardly focused upon self. Any church that minimizes the importance of the eucharist in thought and praxis will suffer the consequences. It is unfortunate that many of Wesley's heirs emphasized the preaching of the Word at the expense of the eucharist. It became the primary means of "sustaining and sanctifying grace."[65] Although the value of the Scripture preached and read is of utmost importance in Wesley's theology and praxis Borgen insists that this "is still a falsification"[66] of Wesley.

> Wesley's rich and balanced views on the relative worth and position of the various means of grace are reduced, and the balance destroyed. The ensuing result can only be regretted: the theologically impoverished heirs of Wesley, without realizing the consequences, open up the roads to a future revivalism in danger of shallowness; to conceptions of holiness that have lost the Wesleyan anchorage in the eternal wonder of Christ's atonement; and to a pragmatic activism where the motivating force is materialistic and subjectivistic rather than flowing from lives filled with the love of God, and, as a consequence, of all men.[67]

The church's ability to recover its identity within the rich and vibrant Wesleyan tradition from which it came, hinges upon its willingness and capability of reclaiming a vibrant sacramentalism.

Baptism

Baptism posed one of the foremost threats to unity among the merging bodies that eventually united to form the Church of the Nazarene. All groups emphasized the importance of baptism, but they had opposing views in both baptismal theology and praxis. As discussed previously it was only through significant concessions and by instituting policies of tolerance that the mergers became a reality. However, these differences were tenacious and continually the topic of questions and discussions in denominational publications.

---

64. Staples, *Outward Sign*, 38–39.

65. Borgen, *John Wesley on Sacraments*, 16.

66. Ibid.

67. Ibid.

The Demise of Infant Baptism

Over time these contrasting views impacted and changed baptismal practice within the church. One of the most obvious developments appears in the practice of infant baptism. Some of the merging bodies opposed infant baptism, but in order to facilitate the union they agreed to allow the practice if parents of young children requested it.[68] Bradley Estep has demonstrated in his work that infant baptism has been virtually replaced by the emerging practice of infant dedication.[69] Although it is not easily assessed, it is generally thought that currently most pastors dedicate infants, rather than baptize them.

This transition in baptismal practice from the early days of the denomination reflects what Martin Marty termed as the "baptistification"[70] of the church. The influx of individuals into the holiness movement who were migrating from ecclesial backgrounds holding a lower view of the sacraments diminished "the importance placed on the sacraments in general and of infant baptism in particular."[71] Personal decision and belief were overemphasized at the expense of divine initiative. The primary function of baptism was no longer upon God's activity but rather upon human response. Eventually, this resulted in the practice of infant baptism waning over time in favor of infant dedication.[72] Since Nazarenes increasingly believed that

68. One of those who opposed infant baptism was H. G. Trumbauer of the Holiness Christian Church. Concessions were made both by Trumbauer and Bresee in order to facilitate the uniting of these bodies. Trumbauer agreed to unite with a denomination that permitted infant baptism, and Bresee removed the words "for the remission of sins unto salvation" from the statement of faith on baptism. The removal of this phrase was no doubt to appease those who feared any inference that baptism was *ex opere operato* (i.e., grace is conveyed to the recipient "by the work performed"). However, it also proved to be a further departure from Wesley by denying the possibility of baptismal regeneration for both infants who were unable to oppose God's grace and from baptismal candidates that were truly repentant and seeking the grace of God. Trumbauer, Horace G. Trumbauer Diary, 14; Staples, *Outward Sign*, 192–3.

69. Estep, "Nazarene Baptismal Theology," 1–195.

70. Marty, "Baptistification Takes Over," 33–36.

71. Staples, *Outward Sign*, 161. Staples points out that among those with a lower view of the sacraments were "Quakers who did not practice the sacraments at all, and persons with various Anabaptist backgrounds." Some of them served in high positions of leadership, such as Edgar. P. Ellyson, a former member of the Society of Friends, who served for a time as a general superintendent in the Church of the Nazarene.

72. Some scholars competently argue that the relatively new practice of infant dedication found in evangelical denominations lacks scriptural precedence and was developed as an inept substitute for infant baptism. The rite is often so closely aligned to baptism that congregations are often left confused. This occurs when pastors use water in the rite or when the wording for the ritual is similar to the rite of baptism. Stookey suggests a more appropriate option to infant dedication: "A more acceptable alternative

the chief purpose of baptism is to serve as one's testimony to a personal religious experience, parents wanted to leave the decision of baptism to their
children once they had matured and could choose for themselves. Thus,
this movement towards believer's baptism not only reduced the occurrence
of infant baptisms, but also served to devalue the sacrament by focusing on
human response, rather than primarily envisioning baptism as a means of
grace in which God is the one who acts on our behalf.

Writing nearly twenty-five years ago, Stan Ingersol indicates that the
denomination's overemphasis on believer baptism and departure from the
practice of infant baptism demonstrates that the Church of the Nazarene
was losing an important part of its Wesleyan identity. He asserts that when
the church came into existence, it exhibited a character that was both
"Methodistic and baptistic, yet not completely one or the other,"[73] but it
was in danger of losing its Wesleyan dimension:

> While mainline Methodism now reflects the full pluralism of
> American culture, the Church of the Nazarene has come to
> reflect much of the pluralism found within American evan-
> gelicalism-much of it based on patterns of thought antitheti-
> cal to Wesleyan ideas of scripture, salvation, and the means of
> grace. This tendency has influenced Nazarenes to accent ever
> more strongly the believers' church side of their tradition at the
> expense of the Wesleyan side. . . . the point is nowhere better
> illustrated than in the case of current baptismal practice, where
> the trend increasingly is toward the exclusive practice of believ-
> ers' baptism, and increasingly by immersion. This is one of the
> strongest evidences (but by no means the only one) that Naza-
> renes are developing a Baptist soul and character at the expense
> of their own, and losing that creative and meaningful tension
> that characterized early Nazarene faith and practice.[74]

Ingersol's analysis is an accurate reflection of the current state of the church.
It is well documented that the doctrine of Christian perfection adopted by

---

liturgical form centers upon thanksgiving for the birth or adoption of a child." While
there is precedence in the New Testament for rites of thanksgiving, there is "no New
Testament basis for a service of the dedication of infants." If a pastor chooses to use a
thanksgiving rite, Stookey indicates that great care should be taken not to confuse the
rite with infant baptism. It does not have the same status as the sacrament. Care should
be taken that it is not conducted at the baptismal font, and the ritual wording should
not be similar to that of the rite of baptism. Otherwise it leads to confusion. For further
discussion on these issues, see Stookey, *Baptism*, 65–67.

73. Ingersol, "Christian Baptism Early Nazarenes," 174.

74. Ibid.

the holiness movement was a modified version of Wesley's theology.[75] Also evident is that Nazarene liturgical practice was vastly different from Wesley's model. However, even the distinctive aspects of Wesleyan theology and the remaining traces of his praxis evident in Nazarene worship in the beginning days have since either been forgotten or abandoned by most congregations. Due to the loss of revivalism the liturgy is no longer distinctive, instead it often reflects the pluralism of American evangelicalism. Worship has therefore become incapable of shaping and reinforcing a distinctive Wesleyan identity. This is revealed in virtually all aspects of worship, but perhaps it is most obvious in the sacraments.

Characteristics of the Baptismal Practice

The picturesque language commonly associated with eucharistic practice in the East and West also characterized some of the descriptions of baptismal services in the years prior to and shortly following the mergers. Baptisms were at times celebrated within the context of the Sunday morning liturgy, at other times on Sunday afternoon, and on occasion even in the middle of the week.[76] If candidates wanted to be immersed and the local church did not have the facilities, the baptism was held in the baptistery of a nearby church or outdoors near a body of water.[77] Some accounts provide details such as the number of people present at the service, the location of the service, and the spiritual climate. Many of the available reports from the early days of the denomination furnishing such data suggest that baptisms were often teeming with congregants. The following account from Dennisport, Massachusetts, describes a populous and quite vibrant baptismal service at the ocean:

> Last Sunday was a most glorious day with us, church full, some people coming from Eastham nineteen miles away, some from Orleans, Chatham, Brewster, and other towns and cities. . . . Hallelujah! In the afternoon we had a most impressive baptismal

75. See Staples, *Outward Sign*, 153–4; 202–4; Quanstrom, *Century of Holiness Theology*, 171–4.

76. J. C. Bearse reported in 1895 that he baptized three candidates by immersion on a Tuesday at his church in Malden, Massachusetts. H. F. Reynolds indicated that Bresee baptized two by immersion at a Sunday school gathering held on a Thursday. The *Nazarene Messenger* carried a report of baptisms at a Thursday night meeting. Bearse, "Notes from Malden," 2; Reynolds, "Overland Letters," 2; "Notes and Personals," January 8, 1902, 3.

77. This would often occur in the church of another denomination that would allow the Nazarene Church to use their facilities.

service at the sea shore, when three candidates confessed their faith in the glorious doctrines of the atonement in the presence of hundreds of spectators. The spirit was present in power, and conviction rested on many.[78]

The above report is not alone in describing well-attended services in which the Spirit moved within the context of the baptismal rite. An account from Manchester, New Hampshire, describes a woman who, while observing the service, first experienced conviction and then conversion while baptism was being administered:

> In the afternoon we had a baptismal service in the Swedish Baptist Church where we baptized by immersion 14 candidates, after preaching a sermon from Heb. 12:14, to an audience that filled the main floor and gallery, and fully fifty people packed in the aisles and vestibule. A Catholic woman came forward to be prayed for before we could get out of the tank of water, so had the privilege of pointing her to the Saviour from our position in the baptismal waters; she said she did not know how to pray, but urged to do her best, she repeated the Lord's prayer amidst tears and said Jesus saved her and immediately went home to get her husband also.[79]

The *Nazarene Messenger* reported on a Sunday morning service in which infants were being baptized. The baptisms were followed by the celebration of the Lord's supper. The church in Troy, Ohio, was in the midst of revival meetings with two evangelists present, D. A. Hill of Columbus, Ohio, and D. F. Brooks of New York. Brooks was a holiness evangelist from the Methodist Episcopal Church. The account describes an experientially rich service where both baptism and the eucharist were at the center:

> Sunday morning we had arranged for the baptismal service and we went according to our church Manual. Bro. Brooks was to preach after the baptismal ceremony. But the Holy Ghost fell upon the preacher and people as Dr. Brooks was administering the rite of baptism to the infants, and he was so filled with the power of God he could hardly proceed; and Bro. Hill was blessed and the saints were weeping and shouting and God was there in mighty power. After the baptismal service we had the communion of the Lord's Supper. This was also a time of shouting, a time of power and glory. It was at this time Bro. Brooks said he had heard from Heaven and would obey. He announced

78. Domina, "Dennisport," 13.
79. Schurman, "Manchester," 8.

he would join the Pentecostal Church of the Nazarene at the evening service. . . .

Bros. Hill and Brooks say they never saw such a day for a continuous power from morning till night, and it was the most blessed communion service of their lives.[80]

Like the previous accounts this report indicates that on occasion baptismal services were experientially robust events. People sensed the moving of the Spirit and at times conversions occurred within the context of the service. The narrative from Troy, Ohio, also indicates that the Lord's supper followed baptism. The practice of baptism coinciding with eucharist is noted in other parts of the country, but it occurs with much greater frequency in the East.[81] Although impossible to ascertain for certain, it is conceivable that the practice in the East of celebrating both sacraments together was not based upon an intentional theological decision for eucharist to follow baptism nor does it appear to be a consistent practice. Rather it was likely the result of the eucharist being celebrated with greater regularity in the East. The greater frequency at which the Lord's supper was celebrated meant there was a greater probability that baptism would coincide with the communion schedule.[82]

Areas of Contention

As previously noted the pluralism surrounding baptismal theology and praxis tolerated by the Church of the Nazarene was necessary because of the very diverse and sometimes dogmatic views held by the merging bodies. Three of the issues that repeatedly surfaced in denominational periodicals

80. Ward, "Correspondence," 4.

81. The *Pentecostal Advocate* in the South reports both sacraments being served during an evening service in a Holiness Church of Christ congregation in Pilot Point, Texas. The service also included ordinations. An article in the *Nazarene Messenger* reported that the Grand Avenue Church held a Sunday morning service where baptism and the Lord's supper were administered and new members were received. However, eucharist following baptism appears to be a rare occurrence rather than a regular and intentional practice. Suddarth, "Lord's Work," 7; "Grand Avenue Church," February 18, 8.

82. This assumption is not conclusive, but based upon the small portion of the numerous articles describing baptism that indicate it was followed with the celebration of the eucharist. The vast majority of reports only speak of the sacrament of baptism. It is, however, possible that both sacraments did coincide on other occasions, and that contributors to the periodicals were simply silent on the issue of the Lord's supper. Articles describing services where both sacraments were administered occasionally appeared in the *Beulah Christian*. For examples of these, see Riggs, "From Lowell," 6; Lewis, "Syracuse," 8; Manning, "Brandon," 14; Lewis, "West Somerville," 8.

were that of *baptismal mode, infant baptism,* and the *Trinitarian formula.* At least two of these areas of contention were among the factors contributing to the unorthodox and all too frequent practice of rebaptism that has characterized the church from the beginning.[83]

Addressing those in attendance at the 1911 General Assembly where he was elected as a general superintendent, E. F. Walker alluded to the division caused by disagreements over baptism:

> The sacrament about which there is most discussion is the sacrament of baptism. There is much division on this subject. I don't know how you regard baptism, but whatever your conception of its import may be, or whatever mode you may prefer, I say to you that if you are not sanctified you have not realized upon your sprinkling, or your pouring, or your immersion.[84]

Several of the merging bodies, like the Church of the Nazarene under the leadership of Bresee, had already accepted sprinkling, pouring, and immersion as viable options. However, as the holiness streams began to unite in the early part of the twentieth century, a process which came to culmination with the 1908 General Assembly in Chicago, compromises were necessary since some groups had significant differences of opinion on the issue of baptismal mode.

This process of compromise is exemplified in the union between two of the groups that eventually joined the Nazarenes. The New Testament Church of Christ had originally insisted that pouring was the only viable baptismal mode. This was the unwavering view of their deceased founder Robert Lee Harris. His widow, Mary Lee Cagle, strongly "defended pouring

---

83. Correspondence in denominational periodicals reveals that rebaptism was permitted by the denomination in certain situations, such as if an adult baptized as an infant desired believer baptism. Although people were strongly discouraged from seeking to be baptized again because they no longer found their first mode of baptism acceptable, it is likely that people were being rebaptized for this reason, since this was a major area of debate. Another indicator that people were probably being rebaptized because they were seeking a different mode rests in the fact that church leadership finds it necessary to continually publish articles insisting that mode does not matter. Although questions concerning the Trinitarian formula are not as frequent as issues of mode there are some who even inquired about the differences between being baptized in the name of the Father, Son, and Holy Spirit as opposed to being baptized in the name of Jesus. For examples of the dialog printed in the *Herald of Holiness* concerning these areas of dispute, see Chapman, "Question Box," April 26, 13; White, "Question Box," September 11, 20; White, "Question Box," May 16, 9; Chapman, "Question Box," July 27, 11; Chapman, "Question Box," March 19, 4.

84. "Sacrament of Baptism," 3.

as the [only] scriptural mode"[85] for baptism. However, this perspective softened over time. Eventually concessions were made so that union with the Independent Holiness Church was possible. The Independent Holiness Church accepted all modes as viable and was even known to receive unbaptized Christians as members. The groups finally agreed that while baptism was required for membership, mode was relinquished to the conscience of the one being baptized.[86]

Some of the merging bodies preferred immersion but, likewise, relinquished their position to allow any mode depending on the wishes of those receiving the sacrament. People were still passionate about their preferred mode, despite the concessions agreed to by the leadership of the various holiness bodies, which made union possible. This resulted in questions, debate, and sometimes division within the denomination, to which E. F. Walker was referring in his address to the 1911 General Assembly. Debate over these issues continued to appear for several years in denominational periodicals. The typical response by the ecclesial hierarchy to such questions is exemplified in a response by Chapman when asked about immersion. He does not stop with providing the standard answer to such questions but shares his own feelings on the matter:

> The Manual of the Church of the Nazarene, in common with the practices of other Christian denominations, permits the applicant to decide the question of the mode of baptism for himself; and in case a method is selected that the pastor considers unscriptural, he may make provisions for some other minister to administer the ordinance. I was baptized by immersion and really prefer that mode, but I would be sorry to hear that our ministers had thought it necessary to spend much time in their public or private ministrations on the subject of the mode of water baptism. . . . I do not think a real, full-fledged, broad minded Nazarene preacher should postpone a baptismal service because the mode selected by the applicant is not in agreement with his own preference.[87]

Confusion and controversy surrounding the issue of the mode of baptism continued for several years. One woman who considered sprinkling and pouring to be unbiblical states that the practice of sprinkling babies caused

85. Ingersol, "Christian Baptism Early Nazarenes," 167.

86. Ibid.

87. Chapman, "Questions Answered," February 7, 3. The *Herald of Holiness* frequently received various questions concerning baptismal mode; see Chapman, "Question Box," August 7, 8; White, "Question Box," May 29, 11; White, "Question Box," November 14, 11.

her so much grief that she was unable to "even look while such a service"[88] was being conducted. Stephen White, who served as editor of the *Herald of Holiness* beginning in 1948, noted the resiliency of tension over baptismal practices in an editorial on baptism:

> Quite a few people write in about water baptism. This is a subject that I am interested in, but I must confess that I have been baffled by the letters. I have found to my surprise that almost all those who are interested in water baptism are concerned about its mode. They are sure that the Bible teaches only one mode of water baptism, and that is what they believe in.[89]

White's comments several years into the church's history demonstrate the tenacity and longevity of the problem.

Concern over baptismal mode was one of the causes motivating some to seek rebaptism with a method they deemed more appropriate. A story appeared in both the *Beulah Christian* and the *Nazarene Messenger* detailing one such event:

> Several of the brethren who had been sprinkled were under conviction to be immersed, and they were waiting for light from God. Brother Angell, Principal of the Pentecostal College Institute, was among this number. He, with his wife, was standing on the shore of the lake, when suddenly he threw his overcoat off, and passing it with his hat to his wife, he stepped up to Brother Fuller and announced his desire to be baptized. . . . [He] had made no preparation for such an occasion. . . . He went in, pocket-book and all.[90]

Several others, still dressed in their Sunday attire, were rebaptized along with him.

J. B. Chapman believed there was insufficient scriptural support in the New Testament to legitimize rebaptism because one desired a different mode, "Those who claim that it is right to iterate baptism on account of a question of mode or some peculiar tenet in the Christian faith will certainly have to produce evidence from other sources than that of the New Testament."[91] Chapman also supposed that there was no justification to rebaptize a backslidden Christian who had returned to God. When asked

88. Chapman, "Question Box," July 27, 11.

89. White, "Water Baptism," 13.

90. Reynolds, "Grand Revival," 7; Reynolds, "North Scituate," 13.

91. Chapman, "Questions Answered," December 14, 2.

about this practice he simply answered, "No, not under any circumstances."[92] Despite these objections, he did consider it valid, even necessary, to practice rebaptism in certain situations. A former Roman Catholic sent a letter to the *Herald of Holiness* with the following question, "I was a Roman Catholic. [I] have never been baptized since becoming a Protestant. Do you think I should be baptized again?"[93] Chapman provided the following response,

> In Roman Catholic countries, like Latin America, some Protes-
> tant missions leave it for the individual to decide whether he will
> be baptized in his new faith. But my own observation is that the
> change from Catholic to Protestant in such cases is not consid-
> ered very radical either by the convert or his friends, and since we
> do not gain anything by compromise, I believe a Roman Catholic
> who becomes really converted should be baptized and unite with
> a Protestant denomination. This is for his own protection and for
> the sake of his witness to the power of the gospel.[94]

Chapman's answer reveals what he openly declares in other places. The purpose of baptism is to serve primarily as a testimony of one's personal experience of God. However, one cannot help but wonder why Chapman would instruct a backslidden Christian to forego seeking rebaptism, while he would recommend it to a former Catholic. He states his counsel is for "protection and for the sake of . . . witness";[95] however, it seems more likely his advice is further indication of the animosity towards formal churches that was inherent to Nazarene thought.[96]

Chapman's recommendation for rebaptism was not restricted to former Catholics, but was also an option for adults who were baptized as infants. Responding to a question on baptism in a 1938 issue of the *Herald of Holiness,* Chapman argues, "There is no requirement that one baptized in infancy should be subsequently baptized as an adult, but there is nothing

92. Chapman, "Questions Answered," January 16, 3. Later Chapman added a correction in his column by indicating he had unintentionally omitted a word from his
statement. He revised it to say, "No not under any *ordinary* circumstances." See Chapman, "Questions Answered," January 30.

93. Chapman, "Question Box," April 21, 14.

94. Ibid.

95. Ibid.

96. Chapman's belief that those coming from formal churches required rebaptism
is exemplified further in a question that was submitted to the *Herald of Holiness*, "Is
it necessary for a person who has been baptized and a member of another church to
be re-baptized upon becoming a member of the Church of the Nazarene." Chapman's
replied, "Not if the person comes from an evangelical church." Chapman, "Questions
Answered," September 1, 15.

to prohibit it."[97] He also acknowledges, in the same column, that there was no uniformity in Nazarene practice concerning the matter of rebaptizing adults who were baptized in infancy. When asked a few months later if it was acceptable for an adult who was baptized as an infant to be rebaptized, he gives a similar reply:

> If one who has been baptized as an infant is satisfied with this when he comes to years, then I believe that is sufficient, and that no one should bother him about it. If he is not satisfied and wants to be baptized as an adult, then I believe no one should forbid water—let him be baptized. And let him be baptized by sprinkling, by pouring or by immersion, and let no man judge him in this matter.[98]

Although Chapman's statement is limited to infants, its appeal to one's conscience has similarities to the article on baptism found in the *Manual* prior to the 1907 and 1908 mergers. The statement of faith on baptism, in the 1906 *Manual*, indicates that one may be rebaptized if the candidate's conscience allowed for it: "Whenever a person through conscientious scruples becomes desirous of again receiving the ordinance of baptism, it may be administered."[99] However, this declaration was removed from the 1907 *Manual* at the Chicago Assembly. This is the same assembly that united the Church of the Nazarene and the Association of Pentecostal Churches of America. Although the *Manual* never again contained a statement authorizing rebaptism, the practice remains common to the sacramental praxis of the church.[100]

97. Chapman, "Question Box," August 13, 10.

98. Chapman, "Question Box," December 23, 13.

99. *Manual Nazarene* (1906), 23.

100. Estep states that after the 1907 merger the church initially deemed rebaptism "inappropriate" and even prohibited the practice. However, the evidence validating this assertion is wanting. Estep supports his claim by referencing correspondence in the *Herald of Holiness* where rebaptism is discouraged. His primary support is a response Chapman makes to a subscriber who made the following inquiry, "Were the Ephesian disciples baptized with water, and why were they re-baptized by Paul?" Chapman's reply lacks clarity to say the least. However, it does not appear that Chapman is prohibiting rebaptism entirely. He begins by stating that Paul's action was not rebaptism since according to Chapman the Ephesians "had not been baptized in the Christian faith" in the first place. Then he changes the direction of his discussion to focus specifically upon the issue of baptismal mode and the use of grammar, deemed inappropriate by some (i.e., using the Trinitarian formula rather than baptizing in the name of Jesus) as grounds for rebaptism. Denominational periodicals reveal that both of these issues were areas of contention among Nazarenes. He does not prohibit rebaptism, but argues that the New Testament does not provide support for those desiring rebaptism because of an inappropriate mode or because Trinitarian grammar was used in their baptism.

Paradoxically, both the 1906 *Manual* and Chapman's recommendations are quite foreign to the traditional baptismal practice of the church throughout the ages. Stookey reminds us that the church universal has invariably rejected the practice of rebaptism: "Even when the rite has been repeated, it has been because in the judgment of those who administered the water for the second time, the first administration was not a true baptism; thus, the later event was understood as the first baptism."[101] Water was administered a second time only if it was believed the original rite was invalid, but even this was approached cautiously. Someone baptized by heretics did not necessarily invalidate its efficacy.[102] Augustine indicated that "the sacraments are not dependent upon the minister."[103] He reaches this conclusion

---

Estep also provides another piece of support claiming Chapman initially rejected rebaptism. He references a 1924 article where Chapman was asked if a backslider should seek rebaptism. Estep indicates Chapman's response as, "No, not under any circumstances." However, in a later issue Chapman corrects this statement to read, "No, not under any *ordinary* circumstances." Chapman's effort in this correction would seem to provide room for extenuating circumstances that would permit rebaptism. This argument is strengthened when Chapman's practice of discouraging rebaptism because of reasons he deems unacceptable is seen elsewhere, while he permits the practice in other circumstances. Instances of discouraging and encouraging rebaptism, depending on the situation, do occur a few years apart. Therefore, it is possible Chapman's position changed during the lapse, but this seems unlikely and there is no evidence to indicate that it did. History demonstrates that Chapman did not forbid rebaptism in all situations. The basic Nazarene position seems to be that issues such as baptismal mode and Trinitarian grammar were insufficient reasons for rebaptism; however, there were certain situations where rebaptism was valid, even encouraged. It is true, as Estep indicates, that the statement in the *Manual* sanctioning rebaptism was omitted and J.B. Chapman discouraged rebaptism in certain scenarios (while encouraging it in others), but there does not seem to be a ban levied against the practice. It is just as likely the *Manual* statement sanctioning rebaptism was removed to appease some of the merging bodies. This is not the same as banning the practice. If there was an actual prohibition against rebaptism it is logical that it would have appeared in the *Manual*. If there was an undocumented prohibition it was short lived. Estep, "Baptismal Theology and Practice," 29–31; Chapman, "Questions Answered," December 14, 2; Chapman, "Questions Answered," January 16, 3; Chapman, "Questions Answered," September 1, 15; Chapman, "Question Box," April 21, 14; Chapman, "Questions Answered," January 30, 2; Chapman, "Question Box," August 13, 10.

101. Stookey, *Baptism*, 49–50.

102. According to K. W. Noakes, "A controversy had arisen between the north African Church and Rome over the treatment of those who had been baptized by heretics but who now wanted to join the Catholic Church. . . . The Roman practice was to receive schismatics and heretics into communion by hand-laying alone, whereas Cyprian followed the established north African traditions of requiring that heretics and schismatics should be initiated fully." Noakes, "Initiation," in Jones, Wainwright, Yarnold, and Bradshaw, *Study of Liturgy*, 123–4.

103. Stookey, *Baptism*, 50.

because baptism finds its validity in God's action, rather than being primarily a human enterprise. "Baptism is God's firm and steadfast covenant promise,"[104] which cannot with integrity be initiated again. Although human response is an important part of any covenant, the primary focus is upon God's initiative.[105]

Stookey suggests that the act of rebaptism is tantamount to blasphemy because, in effect, the rebaptizer has invalidated the initial baptism. Rebaptism is a ritual act that denies the credibility of God's promise and sacramental gift to us.[106] Writing in 1943, Nazarene theologian H. Orton Wiley also warns that baptism is unrepeatable, since it is a rite of initiation. "It establishes a permanent covenant and is not therefore to be repeated."[107]

The absurdity of rebaptism in the mind of the early church thinkers is exemplified in Theodore of Mopsuestia's fourth-century baptismal homily:

> When the potter has made a vase, he can reshape it in water, as long as it retains the plastic quality of clay and has not yet come into contact with the fire; but once it has been baked there is no longer any way of reshaping it. So it is with us now: since we are by nature mortal, we need to undergo this renewal by baptism; but once we have been formed afresh by baptism and received the grace of the Holy Spirit, who will harden us more than any fire, we cannot undergo a second renewal or look to a second baptism, just as we can only hope for a single resurrection, since Christ our Lord also, as St. Paul said, 'being raised from the dead will never die again; death no longer has dominion over him.[108]

Theodore argued that baptism is as steadfast and unrepeatable as the resurrection of Christ from the dead. What must be remembered is that the enduring quality characteristic of both the resurrection and God's act in baptism is found solely in his divine nature and trustworthiness and not in human enterprise. While human beings may fail, sin, and therefore fall short of the baptismal covenant, God does not. Even the Anabaptists, who were considered unorthodox in their baptismal practices, denied accusations that they were rebaptizers because rebaptism was considered impossible. Instead they argued that infant baptism was not a legitimate baptism; therefore, their action was not a repeat but the first authentic baptism.[109]

104. Ibid., 51.

105. Ibid., 50–51.

106. Ibid.

107. Wiley, *Christian Theology*, 3:174.

108. Yarnold, *Awe-Inspiring Rites*, 188.

109. Stookey, *Baptism*, 50–51.

Dissonance in Baptismal Theology and Praxis

When the Church of the Nazarene's practice is contrasted to the baptismal theology of the historic church, the problem with Nazarene orthopraxy emerges.[110] Rebaptism was omitted from the doctrinal statement after 1906; however, the practice has continued in congregations, been legitimized in denominational periodicals, and was even encouraged by clergy since the beginning. Unlike the Anabaptists who denied the validity of infant baptism, the Church of the Nazarene has always and continues to sanction this practice in the *Manual*. Even though infant baptism has declined in Nazarene congregations and the general tendency is for clergy to prefer dedication, it is still considered valid by the denomination.[111] However, the Church of the Nazarene has *de facto* abrogated infant baptism by encouraging adults to be rebaptized as believers. This theological dissonance and unorthodox practice can in part be attributed to the absence of a liturgical theology and adequate sacramentalism to guide the church. Furthermore, when denominational leaders labeled sacramental practice and theology as one of the nonessentials so that the union might proceed, it encouraged a pluralism that has not only undermined sacramental theology but has contributed to negligence in practice.

Rob Staples in speaking of the effect of the American holiness movement on Wesleyan theology and practice provides clarity in understanding the consequences of the Nazarene mergers. His observations and visual imagery clarify the implications of the concessions that were made to facilitate the union between the various holiness streams:

> The headwaters of Wesleyanism lie in the Evangelical Revival in
> 18th-century England, which sprang largely from the preach-
> ing of John and Charles Wesley. The vitality and viewpoint of
> that revival is what I call classical Wesleyanism. The American

110. Gayle Felton states that "since 1786 Methodist church law had made no provision for rebaptism, but questions on the subject continued to surface." Confusion and misunderstandings over the issue have plagued American Methodism nearly since the beginning. It is interesting to note that the controversies concerning the practice of rebaptism within Methodism were under debate during the latter part of the nineteenth century when many of the early Nazarenes were departing Methodism. Like the Church of the Nazarene, rebaptism was still practiced within Methodism in the late twentieth century. A 1986 survey indicated that 45 percent of Methodist ministers were willing to rebaptize individuals when requested to do so. For further details on rebaptism within Methodism, see Felton, *Gift of Water*, 9–10, 89–91, 117–9.

111. Bradley Estep argues the gradual decline of infant baptism and the increase of dedications in his work on Nazarene baptismal theology and practice. Estep, "Baptismal Theology and Practice," 1–224.

holiness movement of the 19th century grew out of and was an attempt to renew the thrusts of that 18th-century movement. In other words, 18th-century Methodist preaching and teaching was the source and the mainstream. Later like-minded movements simply flowed into that stream, caught up by the current of revivalism and the call to "spread scriptural holiness over these lands." As they did so, they brought with them some unique features that were peculiar to their own time and place in history. In some cases the tributaries differed in content from the mainstream. . . . In many cases, I am persuaded that the tributaries flowing into the mainstream, although enriching it with some new elements, did not always help to purify the stream as a whole. Sometimes they polluted it instead, or . . . at least added elements that, in some respects, served to muddy the waters. . . . As for the sacraments, I believe that the Anabaptist currents that flowed into the Wesleyan stream through the holiness movement served to water down the Wesleyan doctrine of baptism . . . and to diminish the significance placed on the Lord's Supper by the Wesleys.[112]

It is important to note that those Nazarenes who descended from a Methodist heritage were still working with a diluted form of Wesley's doctrine and praxis. It was not classical Wesleyanism. The Wesleyan theology and practice which they knew had already undergone some of the changes Staples describes. The American Methodists had abandoned Wesley's *Sunday Service* a century earlier in favor of more spontaneous and subjective forms of worship. The American revivalistic movement also contributed significantly to the changes that were taking place. While the Nazarene descendants of the Methodist tradition had a great appreciation for the sacraments, they failed to work out a substantial sacramental theology. The fundamental importance of the practices that Wesley found central to his *via salutis* was not a part of their theological understanding. Consequentially they did not fully realize the implications of merging with groups whose sacramental heritage was not as rich. Therefore, the resulting merger with these quite diverse holiness streams, including those alien to a robust Wesleyan sacramental heritage, has certainly accentuated the problem that Staples defines.

112. Staples, *Outward Sign*, 15–16.

Baptism and Initiation into the Church

Uncertainty over the sacrament of baptism, which has historically affected the Church of the Nazarene in both theology and practice, is amplified when one questions the function of baptism. Universally speaking, the sacrament of baptism has served as the *rite of initiation* into the church. Wiley referred to baptism as both a sign and seal of the covenant of grace: "On God's part, the seal is the visible assurance of faithfulness to His covenant—a perpetual ceremony to which His people may ever appeal. On man's part, the seal is that act by which he binds himself as a party in the covenant, and pledges himself to faithfulness in all things; and it is also the sign of a completed transaction—the ratification of a final agreement."[113] Staples explains the meaning of this initiation further:

> In the New Testament, Christian baptism always carries the meaning of initiation into Christian faith and life. Wesley calls it "the initiatory sacrament, which enters us into covenant with God." As such, it has five interrelated but distinguishable meanings: (1) It is the mark of our inclusion in the new covenant that Christ established. (2) It is the symbol of our identification with the death of Christ. (3) It is the symbol of our participation in the resurrected life of Christ. (4) It is the symbol of our reception of the Holy Spirit, which is the Spirit of Christ. (5) It is the action through which we are made part of Christ's Body, the Church.[114]

Key to understanding the five meanings Staples lists above is realizing that God is the primary actor in baptism. He is the one who both marks us and initiates the covenant. Staples offers the following reminder: "baptism is primarily the sign of *grace* and only secondarily the sign of our *faith*."[115]

The primal importance of water baptism for Christian disciples finds it roots in the New Testament. K. W. Noakes points out that Paul expected Christians to undergo baptism. "Paul assumes that to become a Christian one is baptized; the 'once-for-all-ness' of baptism is a basic presupposition

113. Wiley, *Christian Theology*, 3:176. The article on baptism in the 1908 *Manual* declared that baptism was "a seal of the New Testament." However, that language was changed from "seal" to "symbol" in the 1915 *Manual*. The baptismal ritual for infants has retained the "seal" language since 1908, but "seal" was not added to the ritual for adult baptism until 1968. *Manual Nazarene (1908)*, 30; *Manual Nazarene (1915)*, 21; *Manual Nazarene (1968)*, 307.

114. Staples, *Outward Sign*, 122–60. Staples provides a full explanation of each of these meanings, which as he suggests are interrelated but have "instructive theological nuances . . . that can easily be missed if one does not consider them separately."

115. Ibid., 144.

of Paul's thought . . . Baptism is the frontier between two worlds, between two entirely different modes of life, or, rather, between death and life. Faith and baptism are inextricably linked . . . "[116] Noakes reemphasizes for us not only the impossibility of rebaptism in Paul's thought but also the essential nature of baptism for initiation into the church. Although it is the gift of the Spirit that makes one Christian, both repentance and "baptism in water"[117] are necessary elements in Christian initiation.

Examination of doctrinal statements and practices suggest that baptism does not function in this full capacity for Nazarenes. The article on baptism in the *Manual* is rather enigmatic. Absent is any mention that the sacrament functions as entrance into the church. Rather it states that baptism is "a sacrament signifying acceptance of the benefits of the atonement of Jesus Christ . . . and declarative of . . . faith in Jesus Christ."[118] Nowhere does it mention God's action in sacrament nor does it reveal baptism's ecclesial purpose. The focus primarily points to the individual's subjective experience of God and testimony thereof.

These issues become evident when the negligence in past and current baptismal practice is analyzed. Denominational leaders encouraged Nazarenes to be baptized, but the church's periodicals denote that their urging was not always heeded. The phenomenon of unbaptized church members is not entirely uncommon. This trend is exemplified in various questions submitted to the *Herald of Holiness* that appeared throughout a period spanning several years. For example, one layperson asked, "Our church takes in members without saying anything about baptizing them. Are not Nazarenes supposed to be baptized with water?"[119] Chapman responds by pointing out the pastor's responsibility in ensuring prospective members had been baptized. If there were those who were unbaptized it was the responsibility of the clergy to baptize them prior to receiving them into membership. Another inquired, "Can one join the Church of the Nazarene without water baptism . . . ?"[120] Chapman's answer reveals more than mere oversight: "It is expected that people who unite with the Church of the Nazarene shall have some water by some mode, though I understand some from the Friends church who have scruples against water baptism have been received into

---

116. Noakes, "Initiation," in Jones, Wainwright, Yarnold, and Bradshaw, *Study of Liturgy*, 113–4.

117. Ibid., 116.

118. *Manual Nazarene (2009)*, 35–36.

119. "Question Box," July 1, 13.

120. "Questions Answered," December 13, 2.

our church without being baptized."[121] Chapman's response is indicative not only of the neglect of baptismal practice, but the confusion that exists within the church over the significance of the sacrament. Although he expects Nazarenes to be baptized, he is aware of at least one instance where former Quakers were permitted to join the church and to ignore baptism because of their beliefs. It is doubtful that Nazarene leaders would have demonstrated the same tolerance in areas of theology and practice they considered essential.

When questioned if a church member could refuse baptism and still be compliant with Church of the Nazarene doctrine, Chapman replied, "Baptism with water is one of the sixteen tenets in the doctrinal statement of our church, and all full fledged Nazarenes believe in and practice water baptism."[122] Another individual spoke of pastoral neglect of the sacrament: "Why do so many pastors fail to preach on baptism at all and take in members without baptism in any form?"[123] Chapman simply states that pastors who are "remiss in [such] matters of duty are deserving of reproof."[124] Elsewhere he indicates that pastors should preach more than they do on water baptism and that it should be administered with greater "zeal and faith."[125] However, his justification for this advice reveals a one-sided sacramental understanding:

> No matter what the few may say, Christian baptism has a tremendous meaning to the big majority of people, and those who baptize have a special place in the affections of those whom they baptize. If I had a church I would have a baptistery in it and I would make baptism a prominent feature of my program, and in this I would be following the example of the primitive church.[126]

Chapman does appeal to early church practice as one of his reasons for justifying his personal preferences for baptismal practice; however, his motivation is heavily influenced by what he perceives as baptism's personal and emotive qualities as well as the potential experience it can generate in the lives of the congregation. Chapman does not mention God's initiative in baptism. While experience is important, the essence, validity, and potency of the sacrament rest upon more substantial tenets that are grounded not in

121. Ibid.

122. Chapman, "Questions and Answers," December 9, 2.

123. Chapman, "Question Box," August 19, 12.

124. Ibid.

125. Chapman, "Question Box," April 6, 11.

126. Ibid.

human response, but in the divine movement of God who has chosen to act in the sacrament on our behalf.

Approximately two decades earlier Chapman had stated that "baptism with water is an ordinance of the New Testament Church. It is the Scriptural method of making public confession of separation from the world and of devotement to Christ. It is the badge of membership in the visible church."[127] When questioned about the possibility of baptism cleansing one from sin, Chapman referred to those who make such assumptions as "putting the shadow for the substance."[128] Elsewhere when asked if water baptism replaced circumcision, he states, "Practically it did . . . [circumcision was] superseded by baptism which served the same purpose as an external ordinance of designating membership in the spiritual kingdom. Of course the real anti-type of circumcision is holiness of heart."[129] Missing from these descriptions is any mention of God's graceful work in the sacrament. Baptism for Chapman is foremost a sign of an individual's personal testimony to the work God has already accomplished in the heart, rather than primarily serving as both a sign and means of God's grace.

Many of Wesley's heirs in the holiness movement never completely grasped the full purpose of the sacraments in his *via salutis*. Referencing the effects of American revivalism on sacramental theology and practice, Dunning states, "The emphasis on dramatic, emotion-laden, will-oriented experience that resulted in a marked and sudden transformation has resulted in a depreciation of the sacraments."[130] Wesley does not specifically mention baptism as a means of grace since it was not repeatable; however, as Staples explains, he did believe grace was conveyed in the sacrament:

> Wesley's enumeration of means of grace . . . consists of those things that promote the subsequent ongoing development of the holy life. When he urges his listeners and readers to make use of the ordained means of grace, he speaks to adults, most of whom have been baptized. Nevertheless in his treatments of baptism, it is clear that he believes grace is conveyed through the sacrament also, when it is accompanied by faith, and thus it may properly be called a means of grace. Baptism is a "means of grace, perpetually, obligatory on all Christians."[131]

[handwritten marginal note: Baptism is a "Mean of Grace"]

127. Chapman, "Questions Answered," August 29, 2.

128. Chapman, "Questions Answered," October 6, 14.

129. Chapman, "Questions Answered," May 17, 3.

130. Dunning, *Grace, Faith, Holiness*, 549.

131. Staples, *Outward Sign*, 98–99.

During the late 1940s Stephen White, then editor of the *Herald of Holiness*, indicates that receiving unbaptized individuals into church membership was a frequent practice: "I think that we as a church do not give baptism the place that we should. I am informed that there are many who have been received into our churches who have not been baptized. This ought not so to be."[132] White also argues that the primary purpose in both infant and adult baptism "is to recognize the fact that the child [or adult] is a member of the Kingdom."[133] Although he refers to it as a means of grace, he does not specify or elaborate how God acts in the sacrament; rather his discussion focuses upon baptism as a public testimony of membership in the kingdom.

J. Kenneth Grider, then professor at Nazarene Theological Seminary, states in a 1969 article on baptism that it was *seldom* administered by clergy. He also suggested possible reasons for baptismal neglect; among them he posits the following observation: "Our very liberality on the mode and the time might contribute to the liberality of taking it or leaving it, whatever the mode or the time. We do not baptize more than we do, perhaps, because we rightly attach much more importance to the destiny-changing new birth than to either of the sacraments."[134]

Today confusion over the significance of baptism remains. Rebaptism is frequently practiced and encouraged by many Nazarene clergy.[135] Staples observes that sacramental practice, and especially baptism, is "meaningless and irrelevant"[136] for Christians in the Wesleyan/holiness tradition. Even though the church has from its beginning strongly encouraged both clergy and laity to be baptized prior to membership in the church, it is not a denominationally enforced obligation. The current *Manual* indicates that members must declare "their experience of salvation, their belief in our doctrines, and their willingness to submit to our government."[137] Baptism is not listed as one of the requirements for membership.[138]

It is encouraging that attempts at moving sacramental theology and practice toward a more Wesleyan and orthodox position are ongoing,

132. White, "Question Box," May 16, 9.

133. Ibid.

134. Grider, "Baptism," 12.

135. A 2006 survey indicated that 65 percent of Nazarene clergy encourage those baptized as infants to be rebaptized as adults. Seventeen percent believe baptized Catholics should be rebaptized before joining the Church of the Nazarene. Ellis, "Relationship Liturgical Practice," 630.

136. Staples, *Outward Sign*, 119.

137. *Manual Nazarene* (2013), 41.

138. Approximately 82 percent of Nazarene clergy receive individuals into membership who were never baptized. See, Ellis, "Relationship Liturgical Practice," 630.

however such changes will not come easily. One attempt occurred at the 2005 General Assembly of the Church of the Nazarene. The assembly had before it a resolution that would have made baptism mandatory, however the delegation voted "to not require Christian baptism for membership."[139] Disregard for baptism is not limited to new Christians or church members. It is found even among members of the clergy. As noted previously it is not only possible, but there are actual instances of pastors who were never baptized in water prior to their ordination.[140]

[handwritten marginal note: Do not Agree! Baptism]

139. *Visitor's Edition* (2005), JUD-817, 1; *Visitor's Edition* (2009), JUD-803, 5. The failed resolution if passed would have changed the wording of paragraph 29 in the 2009 *Manual* to read as follows (the words in italics were the proposed additions and/ or changes to the existing statement): "The membership of a local church shall consist of all who have been organized as a church by those authorized so to do and who have been publicly received by those having proper authority, after having declared their experience of salvation, *and consenting to Christian baptism and the declaration of* their *personal* belief in our doctrines, and *a* willingness to submit to our government." During the 2009 General Assembly in Orlando, Florida, resolution JUD-803 was presented to the General Assembly. JUD-803 if adopted would have made baptism a requirement for church membership. One of the members of the *Special Judicial Legislative Committee*, responsible for evaluating this legislation prior to the vote by the Assembly delegates, recommended that due to its significance for the denomination that it be referred for further evaluation. The delegates to the Assembly responded by assigning the resolution to the Board of General Superintendents for further study. Currently, the denomination's positon remains the same; there is still no baptismal requirement for church membership (See, paragraph 23 in *Manual Nazarene (*2013*)*, 40–41.

140. Supporting arguments for resolution JUD-803 presented at the 2009 General Assembly, which if passed would make baptism a requirement for membership, indicated the following: "It has even been the case that elders have been ordained in the Church of the Nazarene, having been charged to 'administer the sacraments,' who had not yet been baptized." Other support is evinced by a personal letter from a colleague who notes his own experience: "I was converted in a small Nazarene church when I was a freshman in high school in 1978. I went on to MidAmerica Nazarene University, graduating with a degree in biblical Literature in 1985. In response to a call to ministry, I continued my studies at Asbury Theological Seminary, graduating in 1989. From there I went to Canada, where I graduated in 1996 from the Toronto School of Theology with a Th.D. in Homiletics. While in Canada, I served as an Associate Pastor in two congregations. Upon returning to the States, I took an assignment as the Pastor of a Church of the Nazarene in Potomac, Illinois. During my tenure there, I was ordained an Elder in the Church of the Nazarene in 1998. All of this occurred without a baptism! In 2000, I moved to Boise, ID, to become pastor of Epworth-in-the-Foothills Chapel. By that time, my own theological and personal journey had convinced me of the necessity of undergoing baptism. So I was baptized at Epworth in June of 2000. *Visitor's Edition* (2009), JUD-803, 5; Brook Thelander, e-mail message to author, May 22, 2011.

Concluding Observations

Even though baptism was consistently urged upon Nazarenes, the sacrament did not hold the same place of prominence as did the emphasis on those doctrines considered vital. Substantial latitude was granted for Nazarenes to hold differences of opinion in baptismal practice that were far more than inconsequential issues. This becomes evident in an article in which Chapman was asked about Nazarene beliefs related to baptismal mode and the rebaptizing of adults previously baptized in infancy. He provided a rather verbose response expounding at length on his usual answers to such inquiries. What is significant is that Chapman's remarks reveal the rather low status baptismal praxis holds for him when compared to other doctrines of the church:

> Now the Church of the Nazarene . . . does hold . . . that water baptism is not a saving ordinance, but is an outward sign of the inner covenant of grace, and this position places it among those who make liberal interpretations of modes and times. . . . Its central thesis of doctrine is the Wesleyan interpretation of sanctification as a work of grace wrought in the hearts of believers subsequent to regeneration. Its central force is the possession of this experience in the hearts of its members . . . and it believes these things may be done by people without regard to their peculiar views on the question of water baptism. But it does believe in water baptism. It believes that all its members should be baptized with some water in some manner and at some time. But within this scope it leaves it to the individual to choose for himself as he believes the Scriptures to teach and as his own conscience requires. The ministers of the Church of the Nazarene have the same freedom in matters of baptism that laymen have, so far as the matter of their own baptism is concerned. But our ministers are prohibited from arguing on the subject, and when serving as pastors they are required to baptize candidates by the mode the candidate prefers or to arrange for such baptism at the hand of some other minister. Our plan is to urge everyone to get soundly converted, definitely sanctified, to be baptized after a manner that will settle the matter for themselves entirely, and then to give themselves without stint to the service of Jesus Christ to the very end of the day of life—and heaven after that.[141]

---

141. Chapman, "Question Box," August 13, 10; italics mine.

At least for Chapman the pluralism the Church of the Nazarene allowed in baptismal practice carried with it the requirement that pastors were to be silent of their own preferences. This seems to be part of the same approach to baptism that can be traced back to the mergers. The various holiness streams consisted of such diverse and sometimes passionate opinions on baptism that union was possible only through toleration and silence of one's personal beliefs of anything not considered essential to the propagation of entire sanctification. Choice of mode may be immaterial; however, irregular practices such as rebaptism, membership without baptism, and failure to recognize baptism primarily as a sign of God's grace are not. Chapman and other Nazarene leaders did not revere the sacraments in the same esteem as John Wesley. Therefore, baptism was in effect relegated to a less essential status, and matters such as mode and, in certain situations, the issue of rebaptism were left to the conscience of the individual.

Chapter 6

Occasional Services

Foot Washing

There is no evidence indicating to what extent, if any, foot washing was practiced in the Church of the Nazarene. Foot washing is rarely mentioned apart from occasional inquiries submitted to the *Herald of Holiness* concerning its meaning and significance for the contemporary church. Those inquiring generally wanted to know if there was biblical support to justify the practice. Some even asked why the Church of the Nazarene did not observe it as a sacrament: "How do you explain the fact that foot-washing is not observed as a sacrament?"[1] Chapman responded by first arguing it lacked historical support, since the groups practicing foot washing were limited. Then he added,

> Jesus washed His disciples' feet as an act and symbol of humble service, and commended such service to His disciples after Him. But this act on the part of our Lord never had such far-reaching symbolic meaning as baptism and the Lord's Supper as is evident from both the Scriptures and the understanding of God's people all down through the Christian centuries.[2]

Elsewhere Chapman reaffirmed his conviction that it was not Christ's intent to establish the literal washing of feet as an ordinance, rather he was pointing to the expectation of disciples to serve others.[3]

1. Chapman, "Question Box," October 22, 7.

2. Ibid.

3. Chapman, "Question Box," September 30, 13. Also, see Chapman, "Questions Answered," May 16, 3; Chapman, "Question Box," March 4, 7.

The Special Services of Methodism

Earlier it was noted that some of the holiness streams descending from Methodist traditions retained the fervency and frequency of the sacramental practices, that they knew, from their Wesleyan roots. This is especially true of the merging bodies from the West and East Coasts. However, also documented was the decline of these sacramental practices, which occurred after the initial years of the church when the leadership was passed to later generations. This trend is also evident in some of the special services of Methodism that found their way into early Nazarene practice.

Tucker points out that the special services celebrated by the Methodists "developed independently from the prayer book tradition."[4] They were never intended to replace the Sunday liturgy, yet they were an indispensable part of Methodist identity. Some of these "great festivals"[5] were retained by many of the Nazarene descendants of Methodism because of their evangelistic appeal and emphasis on inward religion. These worship services included the love feasts, watch night, and covenant services. The most beloved and widely celebrated of these for both the church in the West and East was the love feast.

Love Feasts

Bangs indicates that Bresee first celebrated the love feast while serving as a Methodist pastor in Pasadena, California; it occurred with the Christmas Day love feast of 1887. This became an annual event, which followed Bresee when he founded the Church of the Nazarene in Los Angeles. The love feast on Christmas Day was unique in that it was more than a local event. Initially it had attracted members of the holiness movement from various congregations and denominations. The 1903 *Nazarene Messenger* stated that it was First Church's practice to send out invitations to the service. It also indicated that approximately five hundred individuals attended the event that year; in 1909 it was estimated that between six to seven hundred people were present.[6]

The first three Christmas love feasts were held in Pasadena, and then it was moved to Los Angeles area churches. The venue changed yearly until 1896 when it was permanently located at Los Angeles First Church of the Nazarene. The love feast began at promptly 9:30 a.m. and typically concluded

---

4. Tucker, *American Methodist Worship*, 60.

5. Ibid.

6. Bangs, *Phineas Bresee*, 152–3; "Christmas," 3; "Christmas Love Feast," December 30, 6.

around noon.[7] Descriptions indicated that they were experientially rich events as depicted in the following account: "A multitude gave witness to the precious blood of Jesus, and at times there were such outbursts of holy power that songs and shouts took the place of other forms of testimony."[8]

The Christmas love feast included the following elements: Scripture readings related to Christ's birth, prayer, songs, an offering, the sharing of bread and water, and as many testimonies as time permitted. Accounts indicate that in subsequent years Bresee would rehearse the history of the Christmas love feast he inaugurated in 1887. It was also customary to present to the congregation those who attended the initial love feast celebration in Pasadena. Bangs stated that in the latter years of the Christmas love feast it "became almost exclusively Nazarene and died out within a year or so of Bresee's death."[9]

During his pastorate at the Church of the Nazarene in Los Angeles, Bresee celebrated the love feast bi-monthly. It was an afternoon celebration that alternated monthly with a eucharistic service. The bi-monthly love feast celebrations were in addition to the Christmas event.[10] The content differed slightly from the Christmas love feasts, since the bi-monthly meetings were not tied to the celebration of Christmas and were local events. However, the basic structure was similar. The following report describes the format: "After songs and prayer and the reading of the Word, the bread and water was taken by a large company. Then came an hour of speaking one to another of the goodness of God; and the fires of holy triumph burned. Two came to the altar and were blest."[11]

Like the love feast celebrated on Christmas day, the bi-monthly feasts were often experientially vibrant events. On many occasions, there were individuals at the altar seeking conversion or sanctification:

> In the afternoon we had our bi-monthly love feast. This service
> was unusually helpful and blessed, and as one of the brethren

7. The exception to this schedule was when Christmas fell on Sunday. The 1904 *Nazarene Messenger* indicates that the Christmas love feast was moved to the afternoon and lasted two and one-half hours. "At the First Church," 3.

8. "Christmas Love Feast," December 11, 6. See also, "Chrismas Love-Feast," December 14, 8; "Christmas Love Feast," December 30, 6–7.

9. Bangs, *Phineas Bresee*, 224; Shepard, "Christmas Lovefeast," 6; "Christmas Day," 6; "Christmas," 3; "Christmas Love-Feast," December 28, 10; Pierce, "Christmas Lovefeast," 7; "Christmas Love Feast," December 30, 7.

10. The December 10, 1903, *Nazarene Messenger* indicated that a bi-monthly love feast was held on the first Sunday of that month at Los Angeles First Church. Another article in the same issue announced the upcoming Christmas love feast; both were held in December of that year. "Christmas Love Feast," December 10, 6; "Sabbath at First Church," December 10, 3.

11. "Victory Day," 4.

testified, reminded one of an old-fashioned camp-meeting. The house was more than three-fourths filled and the shouts of victory went up from all parts of the house as the glad testimonies to a full salvation rolled in. At times there were fully a score of persons standing on their feet awaiting their turn to testify. At the close of the service seven souls came to the altar seeking deliverance either from guilt or the inbeing of sin, and two were sanctified wholly in the congregation and came forward to declare the same.[12]

The value placed upon the love feast by Bresee is evinced in other ways it was used. Sometimes the bi-monthly love feast was celebrated on festive occasions, such as Easter or Pentecost. Occasionally it was added to other special days, such as Thanksgiving or the anniversary celebration of the Church of the Nazarene's organization.[13]

There were other congregations in the West that also celebrated the love feast. Among them were the Compton Avenue and the Spokane, Washington, churches that followed Bresee's model of holding a bi-monthly love feast. Some congregations even celebrated a Christmas love feast, no doubt influenced by the popularity of the one held at Los Angeles First, which was inaugurated by Bresee years earlier.[14]

Love feasts were also an integral part of many denominational events. When Bresee went to Chicago in August of 1904 to organize a church, a love feast was one of the scheduled events: "The meeting culminated yesterday—Sabbath, August 28th. An old-fashioned Lovefeast [sic] was held at 9 a.m., and as the people partook of the bread and water—tokens of love for each other—the fire of heavenly love burned in their hearts and the place was filled with glory."[15] Love feasts were also celebrated in camp meetings, district assemblies, and the general assembly.[16]

Scholars have noted that following Bresee's death the love feast was in decline. Apparently, the celebration of the love feast at general assembly was discontinued after 1919. The Christmas love feast at Los Angeles First also ceased to exist once Bresee was gone.[17] It is difficult to determine the

12. "Sabbath July 6th," 7.

13. "Notes and Personals," March 31, 3; "Victory Day," 4; "Thanksgiving at First Church," 8; "Anniversary Day," 3; "Notes and Personals," October 20, 3.

14. "Spokane," April 14, 5; "Compton Avenue Church," November 18, 8; "Spokane," January 21, 5; John W. Goodwin, "San Diego," January 2, 7.

15. Bresee, "Chicago," 6.

16. "San Francisco," 4; "Northwest District Assembly," 2; Goodwin, "Southern California," 8; "Great Union," 2.

17. Fitzgerald, "Weaving Rope of Sand," 213; Bangs, *Phineas Bresee,* 224.

speed at which love feasts faded or precisely when the practice disappeared completely. The regional periodicals which furnished reports about local congregations, including some information concerning their worship practices, were soon replaced with an official denomination-wide publication that came into existence in 1912.[18] One periodical could not publish the same quantity of local church reports as could three regional publications. Additionally, due to the expanding church, the amount of space the new periodical, *Herald of Holiness*, could commit to local church news was limited. Therefore, the increase in the number of churches in combination with the decline in reporting space meant that less information was available. It is likely that less space also meant that churches could not provide as much detail in their reports. There are indications that some congregations were still holding love feasts even as late as the 1940s.[19] However, it appears to have rapidly declined with the passing of the first generation of Nazarenes who cherished the practice. This would include Bresee, as well as leaders in the East where love feasts were also a prominent feature in camp meetings, district assemblies, and the celebrations of some local congregations.

Several camp meetings in the East celebrated the love feast with regularity. Normally they were held on a Sunday morning preceding worship. Among those camp meetings observing the love feast were Silver Lake and Leicester in Vermont; Douglas, Hebron, and Rock in Massachusetts; Willimantic and Quinnebaug [sic] in Connecticut; and Bailey in Rhode Island. The love feast was also observed at district assemblies in the East including: New England, Pittsburgh, and New York.[20]

Reports in the *Beulah Christian* indicated that several local congregations observed the love feast. One announcement from an 1890 issue stated that People's Evangelical Church in South Providence, Rhode Island, would observe the love feast on the first Sunday of every month at nine in the morning.[21] However, it is difficult to determine the regularity at which most churches in the East were celebrating the love feast. Descriptions of love feasts in the East also indicate that they were often affectively robust services, such as the following that took place during a revival in Cortland, New York: "The last day of the Sabbath . . . was the crowning day of the meeting. We began with a lovefeast [sic] at 9:30 a.m. and it ran up till 10:30 without

18. Smith, *Called Unto Holiness*, 264–5.

19. Sumner, "West Chester," 26.

20. Read, "Silver Lake," 2; "Leicester," 11; "Douglas Camp Meeting," 9; "Bailey Camp Meeting," 11; Williams, "Notes From Willimantic," 3; "Quinnebaug [sic] Camp Meeting," 2; "Camp Hebron," 8; Davis, "Rock Camp Meeting," 3; Pierce, "New England Assembly," 1; Cain, "Pittsburgh District Assembly," 2; Norberry, "New York District Assembly," 2.

21. "South Providence," 4.

a break, excepting the breaks made by the Holy Spirit. There was a wave of glory swept over the people which set some running, some shouting, and some crying, Hallelujah. It was glory."[22]

A unique feature of the love feast in the East is that in some instances it was celebrated in conjunction with the eucharist. The pastor of the Salem, Massachusetts, church provided the following account: "Last Sunday . . . was a great day for the few despised people in the witch city. God met us at our love-feast and communion in the morning."[23] Descriptions such as this one do not specify the order of the service in which both are celebrated; therefore, it is unclear if anything separates the two services or if they are blended together. However, some accounts do indicate that the love feast was separated from the Lord's supper by the sermon. The Utica Avenue Pentecostal Church of the Nazarene in Brooklyn, New York, reported that the *old-fashioned loved feast* would take place at 9:30, followed at 10:30 with "preaching and communion."[24] Celebration of both the love feast and eucharist was not limited to churches. William Howard Hoople, district superintendent of the New York District, stated that the district assembly would begin with "an old-fashioned love feast . . . followed by the Lord's Supper."[25]

The prominent role the love feast occupied in the corporate spirituality of congregations in the West and East, around the turn of the twentieth century, is not so easily discerned in the South. Reports depicting love feasts in the West and East are abundant in the *Nazarene Messenger* and *Beulah Christian*; however, accounts from the South appearing in the *Holiness Evangel* or *Pentecostal Advocate* are sparser. One article by C. B. Jernigan announcing the activities of the upcoming Oklahoma District Assembly does indicate that a love feast would be held on the Sunday morning of assembly prior to the preaching service. However, a later article describing the events of the assembly fails to mention the love feast. It references the Sunday morning sermon by the general superintendent by stating that it was a "feature of the most profound interest."[26] Any attempt to identify the author's reasons for mentioning the sermon while remaining silent on the love feast is difficult.

22. Cartey, "Cortland," 8.

23. McNeill, "Evangelistic Echoes," 14. Several churches in the East describe following the practice of celebrating both the love feast and communion; see Higgins, "Harvest Hallelujahs" 8; Schurman, "Lynn," 8; Davidson, "Bradford," 8.

24. Fletcher, "Harvest Hallelujahs," 8. A report on the Fitchburg, Massachusetts, church also indicated that the love feast was separated by the preaching service; see "Personals," 5.

25. Hoople, "New York District Assembly," 5.

26. Jernigan, "Oklahoma District Assembly Program," 5; "Oklahoma District Assembly," 8–9.

However, it is worth noting the contrast between the reports in the South from those in the West and East. Differences in the South are more than an issue of fewer reports. References to the love feast are more abundant in the West and East, but also it is significant that the reports describing these events often contain experientially vibrant language.[27] This phenomenon is comparable to reports describing eucharistic practice.

Although any mention of love feasts rarely appeared in Nazarene publications after the early years of the denomination, an article devoted to the topic was published in a 1961 issue of *The Preacher's Magazine*. It signified that at least one California pastor was employing the love feast on a regular basis in preparation for scheduled revival meetings. Apparently, this was a practice he had been following for some time:

> We are now in revival. God met with us in the very first opening service. How thrilled this pastor's heart, to see sinners stepping out of their own will to seek God at the altar! . . .
>
> What had we done? All the "groundwork" possible to clear the way for the Lord to come. . . . On Wednesday night before the revival a bread-breaking love feast was held for the people already in the church—a time of communion and witnessing that is produced only by such a service.
>
> Too often the revival is delayed until the members have restored fellowship. The barriers to clear channels have been removed. This is why I have used our bread-breaking service.
>
> As a young pastor I had read *A Prince in Israel*, the life story of Dr. Bresee, and of his "love feasts"—times when the Holy Spirit came in waves of glory. That was what I wanted. But I didn't know how to conduct such a service. So I wrote to an older pastor, asking for help, and then bravely announced that within two months we would have such a service. . . . God came upon us with great rejoicing and times of weeping among the people.
>
> . . . I have had these services in all my pastorates and I have witnessed that it seems to be the opening of refreshing showers,

27. It is important to note that not all accounts in the East and West use rich language; some simply mention that a love feast occurred, but the volume of reports and the number with experientially rich language are noticeably greater than reports from Southern churches. Additionally, there are accounts in the South that do indicate a vibrant spiritual encounter in celebrating the love feast, but these are infrequent. One such account comes from the Holiness College in Des Arc, Missouri: "On Sunday at 3:00 p.m. we held our annual college lovefeast [sic] in the chapel, and it was one of the oldtime lovefeasts [sic], where each one broke the other's bread, and how God blessed it! There were concessions made and tears shed as men embraced each other, and women did likewise, and waves of glory rolled." McBride, "Des Arc," 6.

an opportunity to restore fellowship, and times when God comes to prepare the way for revival.[28]

F. A. Brunson's article reveals several things. Although we do not know when he first started using the love feast, it appears to be several years prior to 1961, since he started as a *young pastor,* and has implemented the love feast in "all . . . [his] pastorates."[29] He also indicated that when he first started serving as a pastor he was unaware of the practice, which supports the notion that the love feast had fallen into disuse a few years before his ministry began. It was only by reading Bresee's biography that he learns of the practice.

Brunson does not reveal the exact content of the love feast celebrated in his congregation. Therefore, it is uncertain how closely his use of the feast represented the practice of the early Nazarenes. He describes it as a time of *communion and witnessing,* but provides few other details of what occurred in the service other than indicating that bread was shared between individuals in an attempt to mend broken relationships in the congregation. It is possible that this is all that was intended when he states that the love feast provided an opportunity for communion and witnessing—in other words it is doubtful the reference to communion refers to celebrating the Lord's supper in conjunction with the love feast. There is no indication it involved the same elements found in early Nazarene descriptions. It also seems apparent that Brunson did not use water in the celebration within his own congregation. His description of the practice he follows makes no mention of water being shared. The notion that water was absent in Brunson's observance is supported by a letter he received from H. Orton Wiley. Brunson quotes a portion of the letter where Wiley states that bread and water were used in earlier times, but "later it was more common to serve just the bread."[30]

The cessation of love feast observance was noted in an article printed in a 1946 issue of the *Herald of Holiness.* One subscriber inquired as to why the "old-fashioned love feasts"[31] had disappeared. Chapman first responded by questioning the scriptural support for the love feast and then indicated "its practice was never very wide-spread . . . [except within] early Methodist societies and in some other groups"[32] that testified to its *usefulness.* Evident in this question and response is not only the apparent absence of the practice by the late 1940s, but Chapman's own estimation of the love

28. Brunson, "Bread-breaking," 33–34.
29. Ibid., 34.
30. Ibid., 33–34.
31. Chapman, "Question Box," November 25, 13.
32. Ibid.

feast. Instead of encouraging the practice as he did for things he valued and believed were essential, he minimizes its importance.[33] This is clearly a departure from not only John Wesley, but also Bresee and many of the first-generation Nazarenes on both the West and East Coasts who found this Methodist tradition important to both corporate and personal piety.

Watch Night and Covenant Renewal Service

Although love feasts were substantially more prevalent in Nazarene practice, there are, during the early years, occasional references to the observance of watch night services in denominational periodicals. The same cannot be said for Wesley's covenant renewal service, since references to this practice are virtually non-extant. Tucker indicates that reports of covenant renewal services in American Methodism are also scarce and their appearance was "short-lived."[34] The absence of the covenant renewal service in American Methodism would likely account for the lack of references among Nazarene groups descending from Methodism.

The watch night service among Nazarenes was normally held on New Year's Eve. References to the watch night, for congregations in the West, quite often indicated that they began around eight o'clock in the evening and concluded sometime after midnight.[35] First Pentecostal Church of the Nazarene in Oakland, California, reported that their four-and-one-half-hour service was so filled with song, prayer, reading the word, and testimony that no time remained for "recess or coffee and doughnuts."[36] It was similar in fashion to Oakland's report from the previous year which stated:

> We had to resort to no extraordinary and outlandish methods
> to keep up the interest during the entire four hours. There were
> no dough-nuts and coffee nor cake nor anything to satisfy the
> physical man. We had bread to eat that many folks knew noth-
> ing of. . . . We sang and prayed and testified, and shouted a little,
> and rejoiced and praised God, and had a good time in general.[37]

Watch night served as an alternative to what was considered worldly celebrations of the incoming year; therefore, like other Nazarene services, it was

---

33. Ibid.

34. Tucker, *American Methodist Worship*, 69.

35. "Watch Night," January 7, 3; "Notes and Personals," January 8, 1903, 3; "Notes and Personals," January 8, 1902, 3; "Berkeley Notes," 10; Linaweaver, "Oakland," 4.

36. Linaweaver, "Oakland," 4.

37. Linaweaver, "Watch Night," 3–4.

evangelistic. Expectations were that the meeting would yield seekers at the altar experiencing conversion and entire sanctification. Reports regularly affirm that the watch night fulfilled this intended purpose.[38]

One 1902 article describing the watch night service at Los Angeles First indicated that more than an hour at the beginning of the meeting was spent in prayer. This was followed by a sermon by Nazarene evangelist C. W. Ruth, while testimonies occupied the last hour of the service. References to the 1903 watch night at Bresee's church stated that the hour of prayer was preceded with the congregation standing and singing a "hymn of praise."[39] Other years providing descriptions of the service indicate a similar structure with slight variations.[40]

Although there is no specific mention of Nazarene congregations ending watch night by observing a covenant renewal service per se, there are hints that Bresee alluded to some sort of covenant renewal. References sometimes indicate that he ended the service with the reading of Joshua's covenant renewal ceremony in Josh 24:21–28.[41] On one occasion he preceded the Joshua text by asking individuals "to kneel before the Lord and . . . hold personal communion with God while the old year passed."[42] Another account does not mention the Joshua passage, but states, "The congregation stood together in recognition of the holy covenant upon them, bowed in silent prayer and thus welcomed the New Year."[43]

Practices in the East differed somewhat from Breese's church in the West. Utica Avenue Pentecostal Church of the Nazarene, Brooklyn, New York, followed the New Year's Eve watch night service with an all-day meeting on New Year's Day. The Goshen Vermont Church observed both the love feast and the Lord's supper during watch night; the meeting lasted past four o'clock in the morning.[44] Some congregations in the South observed the eucharist in conjunction with the New Year's Eve watch. The following

---

38. "Watch Night," December 26, 6; "At the Tabernacle," January 4, 3; "Notes and Personals," January 8, 1902, 3; "Chicago," January 13, 4; Lanpher, "Lowell," 8; "Salem," 5; "Reports from the Field," February 1, 3; Fisher, "Through the Holidays," 2.

39. "Notes and Personals," January 8, 1903, 3.

40. "Notes and Personals," January 8, 1902, 3; "Notes and Personals," January 8, 1903, 3.

41. "Notes and Personals," January 8, 1903, 3.

42. "Watch Night," January 7, 3.

43. "Notes and Personals," January 8, 1902, 3.

44. "Brooklyn," January 1, 6; "Brooklyn," December 9, 14; Rickert, "Goshen," 15. Other congregations in the East and West also indicated a watch night service followed by an all-day meeting on New Year's, see "Spokane," December 21, 9; Bryant, "Cundy's Harbor," 8.

account from Cannon, Texas, describes a solemn, but emotional eucharistic observance during watch night:

> We had a watch night service Monday night and closed with the sacrament of the Lord's Supper. This part of the service was especially impressive. While dear Brother Shaw was helping administer the sacrament, God's power came on him in a marvelous way he could hardly proceed. And as the year 1906 passed into eternity we looked back down the ages through these emblems to our Saviour bleeding and dying on the cross for us, and then turned to look forward to his coming again to make up his jewels. The saints shouted and many sinners wept and trembled.[45]

Other than occasional description signifying that the watch night would include the eucharist or love feast, references in the East and South generally lack additional details that would reveal the exact content of the service. However, since its purpose in all geographical regions was evangelistic it is a reasonable assumption that the watch night contained those revivalistic elements Nazarenes found important in harvesting seekers at the altar.

Summary

The objective of preceding five chapters is to provide a thorough, yet concise, analysis of Wesley's liturgical praxis and thought and the history of liturgical practice within the Church of the Nazarene. Our exploration included an examination of those practices extant during the formative years following the birth of the denomination; insight into the divergent traditions and beliefs the merging bodies brought with them regarding the sacraments and the liturgy; an overview of the revisions and transformation of the Nazarene liturgy that occurred over time; and the ramifications of those changes for Wesleyan spirituality.

There is no question that the period during the early days of the denomination was spiritually robust with an abundance of transformation occurring in both the hearts and lives of the men and women who worshipped in the Church of the Nazarene. It is an atmosphere that many within the church long for once again. However, the revivalistic mechanism relied upon to instigate such change was limited, and in the vast expanse of church history, has not served as a conventional replacement for the

---

45. "From Cannon," 10. For another instance of the Lord's supper occurring during watch night, see Fisher, "Through the Holidays," 2.

doxological nature of corporate worship. Although, the Methodist movement in England was a revivalistic movement, revivalism served Wesley's
formative purposes in conjunction with the worship of the church and not
as a replacement to it. The adoption of the revival model for worship comes
long after John Wesley's leadership during the era of American revivalism.
Certainly, we live in an age when the church needs to emphasize spiritual
renewal through revival and other God-given means of grace. However,
evangelism or some other utilitarian purpose, no matter how important it
might be, is incapable of serving as a valid replacement to the sole purpose
of worship—doxology.

Chapter 7

Conclusion: An Earnest Appeal for the Cultivation of Doxology in Worship

Lessons from the Past

I have discovered, through conversations with clergy and laity alike, a desire among some Nazarenes to return to the "glory days of the past." A resident hunger exists within the church to revisit the era of revivalism when *holy fire fell* and transformation was a constant. Perhaps you are numbered among those who share such sentiments because of a God imbued desire for spiritual renewal within the Christian community. It is likely that those attracted to the revivalism of the past know it either by experience, through reading historical accounts, or in hearing the stories told by previous generations of men and women who experienced the touch of God's grace in mighty and redeeming ways. When clergy, on occasion, are dismayed over the absence of the commitment and sacrifice resident in the historical church there is an eagerness to recover the era when faith was passionate. Although the desire to be part of a vibrant church capable of transforming the world is shared by many Nazarene leaders, clergy, and laity—disagreement exists over the means and methods necessary to make such a spiritually vibrant church possible.

It is my suspicion that most long for the fervency and spiritual hunger found within our Nazarene forbears at the turn of the twentieth-century. Ironically, the revivalistic model of worship, still desired by some today, was a novelty in the mid-nineteenth century. This new paradigm posed a significant departure from a variety of liturgical patterns and rhythms previously focused upon doxology rather than evangelism. The methodology of John Wesley, which gave birth to the Methodist movement, including the use of revivals, did not replace the historic worship of the church; rather they were a supplement to it and occurred outside of corporate worship. This was Wesley's desire and expectation.

There is certainly an important place for services of revival and spiritual renewal occurring beyond the context of weekly worship. However, evangelism is not a valid replacement to doxological worship. It is noteworthy to remember that our generation forgets that our Nazarene pioneers also had an array of measures in addition to revivals and revivalistic worship to foster renewal. Included in this list were the beloved and well attended love feasts, Tuesday holiness meetings, class meetings, etc. However, the tool of revivalism found greater use and over time, the other measures changed and eventually were forgotten. Thus, it is the revivals and the revival model for worship that most still remember and many cherish. American revivalism's desire to redeem their world by co-opting a camp meeting liturgical model to assist in that purpose was certainly noble. It is unfortunate this was the preferred form of worship on the Lord's day, since the camp meeting model is an inadequate replacement to worship that is solely focused on the glorification of God.

Revivalism was the only heartfelt form of worship the early Nazarenes knew, therefore they readily adopted it as their own without a clear understanding of liturgical history. In their appraisal of the spiritual decay witnessed in the prayer book churches of their day, the leaders within the American holiness movement misdiagnosed the cause of the problem. Wesley witnessed similar problems in the Church of England, but instead of abandoning the worship of the church he instituted additional measures to provide balance and bring renewal. In contrast, Wesley believed the worship found in the *BCP* was vital in cultivating a robust spirituality in the Methodists.

The removal of doxology as the center of worship and restructuring worship for utilitarian purposes, even something as important as evangelism, unintentionally shifted the focus of worship off God and onto human need. Redirecting the heart of worship from the glorification of God to human need is at least one of the factors responsible for current identity problems and a catalyst for the uncertainty in worship today. The renewal of the church will require a different model of worship to compliment and support the various means of grace and spiritual disciplines that are key to Christian nurture.[1]

1. It is important to note that renewal will require more than a new model of worship. A robust theology and practice of worship is essential, but it is only one piece of the puzzle. Knight reminds us that Wesley's doctrine cannot be separated from the rich environment of worship, personal piety, and community that made the Wesleyan revival possible. See, Knight III, *Presence of God*, 2.

What Is at Stake in Christian Worship?

Since the turn of the millennium denominational leaders and scholars from the academy have not only recognized the existence of a problem, but have attempted to identify the possible cause(s) for the diminution of the Wesleyan doctrine of Christian perfection among both Nazarene clergy and laity. This dilemma is often referred to as a theological identity crisis, since the propagation and promotion of the doctrine once central to the denomination is significantly impaired.[2] Not surprisingly, this phenomenon has followed the path of revivalism, which started to wane in the mid to late 1960s. Anticipating the eventual demise of revivalism and fearing numerical decline, the Church of the Nazarene, like other holiness denominations, replaced the revival model of worship with the pragmatic methods and tactics offered by the church-growth movement.[3]

The absence of revivalism and its influence in the structure and composition of worship removed the primary and only substantial means for promoting the doctrine within the local church. Not only was the voice that promoted the Nazarene formulation of Christian perfection gone, but a vacuum was left in worship. Although not intentional, the doctrine of Christian perfection eventually ceased to be the main concern as it was replaced with finding ways to help the church grow.[4] Even though holiness was still a central concern of Nazarenes and the subject of its literature and denominational gatherings, the void left in worship, by the absence of revivalism, was filled with the means and methods of the church-growth movement, which lacked a competent theological understanding of the formative power of liturgy.

Nazarenes intended for worship to glorify God; however, the liturgy's primary purpose was not doxological but evangelistic. For the church to evangelize in worship, pragmatic methods aimed at increasing attendance were sought and implemented.[5] Like the condition resident in other churches "much of what passes for worship . . . [in Nazarene congregations] takes its cues and rules straight from consumer-oriented marketing strategies."[6] Today the focus of contemporary liturgies is often upon highly subjective and entertaining forms of worship that have the capacity to attract and retain the masses. However, the identity Nazarenes once found in the quest

2. Dunning, "Christian Perfection," 151, Drury et al., *Counterpoint*, 18; Bond, "This We Believe"; Gunter, "God."

3. Drury et al., *Counterpoint*, 22–23.

4. Ibid., 20, 108.

5. Staples, *Outward Sign*, 26–28.

6. Hoskins, "Wesleyan Liturgical Identity," 130.

for the pious life and the pursuit of inward holiness intrinsic to the tradition of John Wesley, or its modified version as exemplified by the American holiness movement, has been largely lost to contemporary Nazarenes.

This problem is more serious than the loss of distinction between the beliefs of Nazarenes and the beliefs of those from other denominations. *What is at stake is the loss of Christian identity*, which includes not only a severance from ties to classical Wesleyanism but also involves a severing from an identity rooted in Christian antiquity. In other words, the lines are not only blurred between denominations but also between the church and the philosophies and beliefs that permeate secular culture.[7] Even persons within the church are finding it increasingly difficult to know what it means to be distinctively Christian, that is, Christian as defined by Scripture and the historical Church.

The Body and Christian Formation?

The loss of identity threatening the church is a complex issue quite likely involving the convergence of several factors. However, one of the foremost contributors to this problem is the pragmatism that has guided the denomination's liturgical practice divorced from a substantial liturgical theology nestled in both historic Christianity and the thought and practice of John Wesley. The liturgy's place of primary importance in this equation is due to its normative and constitutive qualities. Christian worship provides not only the standard for how to live and act in the world, but through the words, signs, symbols, and gestures of ritual action it has the capacity to both shape and transform individuals and communities of faith; inscribing into one's very bones an identity that is distinctively Christian.[8]

Although the early Nazarenes adamantly rejected the rituals they found within the prayer book worship of their day, they adopted others. Worship was vibrant and filled with a new set of words, signs, symbols, and gestures that were borrowed from American revivalism and the camp meeting movement. This included ritual actions such as shouting, the altar call, the waving of handkerchiefs, marching, handshaking, and others. Early Nazarene worship was filled with active participation, vocal response, and bodily engagement. Today, most of those practices are relegated to the past. They are either minimal or non-extant. Faith is often internalized as a private experience with God. The accountability that once existed between individuals and the church, enabling individuals to grow and be nurtured in

7. Anderson, *Worship and Christian Identity*, vii; Staples, "Things Shakeable," 5.

8. Jennings, "On Ritual Knowledge," 112, 117; Anderson, *Worship and Christian Identity*, 34, 58, 174, 191.

the faith, is sought by few. Certainly, these characteristics are not descriptive of all in the church, however these problems are becoming more prevalent.

Concern over the privatization of faith adversely affecting the Christian formation of those who worship in Nazarene congregations is not merely idle speculation. A 2006 survey measuring the relationship between worship practice and spirituality in the Church of the Nazarene suggested that many believe their relationship with God is essentially a private matter. A major problem with overly subjective faith, is that faith is not merely *personal faith* but it becomes *private*. When faith is *private* the individual becomes accountable to no one, rather faith is egocentric.[9] No longer is the individual subject to the authority of the church's teaching. The eventual end of this path is relativism where a person creates one's own truth. In other words, "What is true for you is true for you and vice versa. Who am I (or who are you) to suggest otherwise?"

The fact that more than one-third of those surveyed believe their relationship to God stands apart from any official church teaching further exemplifies the seriousness of this problem. This is significant, since it represents a rather large group of individuals who apparently hold their own personal beliefs above church doctrine. Although the vast majority of those surveyed agree that regularly attending worship is necessary to their spiritual walk, it appears that for many the corporate body is secondary to personal faith. Over one-third think that it is possible to be Christian without regularly attending church. While most find church membership important, paradoxically, 38 percent believe that a person's choice to either join the church or not join the church has no bearing on a person's spiritual life. Consistent with this apparent trend toward privatized spirituality is data indicating over one-third of respondents believe their personal devotions are more important than corporate worship. In other words, what one does, as an individual is more highly valued and important than worshipping and engaging with the community of faith.

It is also alarming that less than one quarter believe that the church is an indispensable part of being saved and sanctified. This leaves the vast percentage unwilling to concede that the church is necessary for God's redemptive work in salvation or sanctification, which implies either a very low view of the church or a narrow understanding of the church's role in the *via salutis* (the way of salvation). Taken together these variables suggest that attitudes of individualism are widespread within Nazarene congregations and pose real concerns for Nazarene identity and spirituality.[10]

9. Anderson, *Worship and Christian Identity*, 205.

10. For more additional information and statistical data see, Ellis, "Relationship

As part of their quest for inward holiness, Nazarenes have always gravitated toward the freedom and spontaneity in worship that fosters subjective experiences of God. Uncertainty as to whether this proclivity toward freedom and spontaneity in worship would become problematic caused denominational leaders like J. B. Chapman concern. Chapman, along with others in leadership, encouraged pastors to temper the freedom and spontaneity in worship by bringing more order into the Nazarene liturgy.[11] Although revivalism waned and was replaced by the church-growth movement, the desire for freedom in worship remains.

In recent years spirituality has become internalized even further in the absence of ritualization and with the ubiquity of subjective forms of worship. The prevalence of gospel songs, contemporary music, and repetitive choruses, many of which are theologically bankrupt and filled with highly subjective content, is a major force in fueling this problem. However, it is also reinforced by impoverished sacramental practice and the rubrics which accompany them. Those sacramental rites intended to foster corporate identity and build relationships within the body are often restructured in ways that facilitate individualism rather than cultivate unity. This spirit of individualism is also a repercussion of the very things which are absent from Nazarene liturgies, namely those objective means that offer a corrective voice to chronic individualism. Among these missing elements are the creeds, the Wesleyan hymns, written prayers, responsive readings, and the public reading of abundant portions of Scripture. Furthermore, strong sentiments toward individualism are at least partly the result of deficient liturgies which fail to offer a corrective voice to culture. Ironically, in some instances impaired liturgies can fortify some of the very philosophies that are alien to Christian faith.

Alien philosophies are a threat to those inside and outside of the church. In his *Cultural Liturgies* project James Smith reminds us that we do not exist in a vacuum rather every day Christians and non-Christians alike encounter life transforming practices. Practices located within what he terms *cultural liturgies*. Smith has expanded the normal understanding of "liturgy" (e.g. worship practices within the church) to include those entities containing a set of practices that form and shape one's identity whether they be religious or secular.[12] Smith cautions us that cultural liturgies are found within such unsuspected and welcomed places as the shopping mall,

---

Liturgical Practice," 505, 581–4, 670.

11. "Forms of Worship," 6; "Use of the Hymn," 6; Chapman, "Program of Worship," 1–2.

12. Smith, Desiring the Kingdom, 25.

sports arena, on Facebook, and when using a Smartphone. Cultural liturgies communicate a variety of philosophies, which are often in conflict with the values of the Kingdom of God including consumerism, nationalism, and materialism. Smith argues that liturgical practices, both secular and sacred, "shape and constitute our identities by forming our most fundamental desires and most basic attunement to the world." Liturgies orient us toward our hearts desire—direct us to what we love. "What we desire or love ultimately is a vision of what we hope for, what we think the good life looks like."[13]

Arguing from a philosophical perspective Smith indicates that we are "'liturgical animals,' creatures who *can't not* worship and who are fundamentally formed by worship practices."[14] However, simply naming an activity of the church *worship* does not necessarily mean that it will form individuals in ways that instill Kingdom values; even if that is our intended goal. The church must be knowledgeable and intentional about its formation. That is, the church must understand what values its practices are instilling. Concern over the verbal content of worship (e.g. the words used) is not enough. Worship is more than the words that we say or the sermon preached. Rather, much of the formation that occurs in worship is nonverbal and works gradually over time without an awareness transformation is occurring. Smith insists that for worship to bring authentic transformation more is required than simply providing information. Our habits and dispositions are in dire need of reformation. Worship that is going to work at these deeper levels "requires formative measures that are fundamentally aesthetic and imaginative.[15] We need to be moved not merely convinced."[16] This means that what occurs with our bodies is as important as what we think with our minds if we are going to be formed into the image of Christ.

Social anthropologists and theorists in ritual studies have long emphasized the existence of powerful means for the transmission of knowledge other than verbal communication. Mary Douglas insists upon the indispensable value of ritual, and the symbols contained there within, for the enabling of societies to communicate meaning. She maintains that sentiments

---

13. Ibid., 27.

14. Smith, Imagining the Kingdom, 3; italics mine.

15. Smith expands the meaning of *aesthetics* beyond the contemporary and more limited understanding of the term often used simply in reference to art and beauty. When Smith employs *aesthetics* he intends the original Greek understanding which refers to knowledge gained through the senses. Imagination, for Smith, refers to the way in which "we construe our world on a precognitive level" that occurs primarily through the senses "because it is so closely tied to the body." See, Smith, Imagining the Kingdom, 16–17, 116.

16. Smith, Imaging the Kingdom, 166.

of antiritualism and the resulting loss of ritual and symbols in both contemporary society and the church is one of the most serious problems of this age. Ritual action contains both communicative and transformative qualities for communities; with its loss a society's connection to the past is severed. That which is true of secular society is also true of the community of faith. A society cannot continue to reject ritual and endure.[17]

Anderson also reminds us that the expressive, normative, and constitutive power of ritual and ritualization as practiced within the context of worship is "the central means by which the church shapes the faith, character, and consciousness of its members."[18] Through continual engagement in Christian worship over time, the practices in which we engage are habituated. That is to say, they get into our bones and penetrate into the very fabric of our being shaping us "spiritually, cognitively, and above all physically."[19] This concept of habituated bodily knowing is foreign to most evangelical liturgies where the spoken word is the primary means of communicating meaning. However, as Anderson states, "what we know in our bodies is more powerful than what we know in words."[20] We should be as concerned with orthopraxy, that is, with doing things correctly, as we are about orthodoxy or believing the right things. Liturgical theologians remind us there is a reciprocal relationship between what a community of faith does in the liturgy and what it believes. This is exemplified in the Latin tag *lex orandi, lex credendi* or the law of prayer establishes the law of belief. Wainwright further clarifies it is equally true that what a community believes also affects what occurs in its worship.[21]

Other theologians have pointed out that this maxim should be lengthened to include *lex orandi, lex credendi, lex vivendi*.[22] Not only is there an interdependent relationship between prayer and belief, but also one exists between what occurs in worship and "living the moral, spiritual life."[23] A church's liturgy not only affects the beliefs of her members but also their ethical behavior. One's true worship and love for God is manifested in one's relationship with others.[24]

---

17. Douglas, *Purity and Danger*, 79; Douglas, *Natural Symbols*, 1–4, 7, 22, 52, 53.

18. Anderson, *Worship and Christian Identity*, 4.

19. Anderson, "Liturgical Catechesis," 353.

20. Ibid., 355. For further reading on the importance and power of the body in knowing, see Connerton, *How Societies Remember*, 72–104.

21. Wainwright, *Doxology*, 218.

22. Saliers, *Worship As Theology*, 187; Irwin, *Context and Text*, 55–56.

23. Irwin, *Context and Text*, 55.

24. Saliers, *Worship As Theology*, 186–7.

It is due to the formative power of the liturgy that a church's worship must be evaluated critically through the lenses of the social sciences, philosophy, ritual studies, and liturgical theology. One must remember, "worship is not primarily man's initiative, but God's redeeming act in Christ through His Spirit."[25] However, much contemporary worship has degenerated from doxology into highly subjective forms that focus more upon man's worship of God rather than actually worshipping God. Although there is not one pattern of worship that should be followed by all congregations in all ages, there are timeless components of the liturgy that are universally essential to authentic Christian worship.[26] Identifying those essentials and creating patterns of worship that are culturally relevant and truly doxological, as opposed to overly subjective or even egocentric liturgies, is the daunting, but crucial task of liturgical theology.

Wesley's Middle Way

Throughout his life John Wesley continually endeavored to bring balance between the two extremes of formalism and enthusiasm in both his personal pursuit of inward holiness as well as within his work among the Methodists. It is this *via media* (i.e., the middle way) defining much of Wesley's thought and practice that is also evident in his liturgical concerns. Although Wesley criticized the formalism that often-characterized Anglicans and their worship, he had high regard for the *BCP*.[27] Despite his great admiration for the *BCP* and realizing the shape of American Methodist Worship differed significantly from the Church of England, he had no qualms about modifying the *BCP* in creating the *Sunday Service*. He did so to make the prayer book more suitable for the American context.[28] Furthermore, drawing upon the "Anglican triad of Scripture, Christian tradition, and reason" as a foundation, Wesley granted even greater liberty to the American Methodists on the condition that they used both Scripture and the primitive church as their sources for "liturgical praxis."[29]

In British Methodism, the society meetings were no substitute for the Sunday liturgy.[30] Wesley expected Methodists to attend the worship services

25. Wainwright, *Doxology*, 242.

26. Johnson, "Can We Avoid Relativism," 154–5.

27. Wesley, *John Wesley's Sunday Service*, 2.

28. Tucker, *American Methodist Worship*, 5–8.

29. Wesley, "Letter of September 10, 1784," in *John Wesley's Sunday Service*, iii; Tucker, *American Methodist Worship*, 4.

30. Wesley, "Annual Minutes 1766," in *Works (BE)*, 10:325–6.

in their own church.[31] The Methodist society meetings were not intended to replace Anglican worship, but to fortify it by nurturing the Methodists' inward experience of God to combat the dangers of formalism. Worship, however, was necessary to address the parallel problem of enthusiasm. The various means of grace found within the context of prayer book worship provide a resolution to enthusiasm by reminding us of the true nature of God found within Scripture. Those means include the public reading of Scripture, the Lord's supper, and the prayers found within the BCP.[32]

Although Wesley deemed all the instituted means found within the context of the BCP liturgy vital to Christian faith, it was his robust eucharistic practice, as well as its central role in his writing, teaching, and preaching, that placed the Lord's supper at the forefront of the Wesleyan movement. The eucharist for Wesley was both a confirming and converting ordinance. He believed that it served as a means to communicate God's preventing, justifying, and sanctifying grace.[33]

Maddox points out that Wesley's ardent desire for the Methodists to attend parish worship was inspired more by "soteriological than ecclesiastical concerns."[34] The instituted means of grace that were evident within the context of the BCP liturgy, Scripture, prayer, and the eucharist, were as essential to Christian formation as those means that were a part of the Methodist societies. The inclusion of additional aspects of the BCP liturgy into Methodist society meetings occurred only after Wesley realized that his attempt to convince Methodists to faithfully attend the worship of their local churches was dwindling. The value he placed upon the traditional Anglican liturgy is further evinced in Wesley's choice to retain and modify the BCP for the Americans rather than replace it.[35] The revisions Wesley made to the BCP in the *Sunday Service*, as well as his adoption of other services, such as the covenant service, love feasts, and the watch night, also reveal Wesley's belief that while there are certain components essential to the liturgy, worship also needs to be adapted to the cultural and social context of the congregants.[36]

It is of essence to remember that Wesley's distinctive doctrines were not formed, shaped, and propagated in the lives of his people in isolation; rather a thoughtful and intentional liturgy was among those forces that

---

31. Sanders, "An Appraisal Wesley's Sacramentalism," 64; Taves, *Fits*, 64; Hildebrandt, Beckerlegge, and Dale, "Introduction," in *Works (BE)*, 7:57.

32. Knight III, *Presence of God*, 47.

33. Borgen, *Wesley on Sacraments*, 119.

34. Maddox, *Responsible Grace*, 206.

35. Ibid.

36. Tucker, *American Methodist Worship*, 4–8.

reinforced Methodist identity. Although Wesley was in pursuit of an experiential religion, which differed significantly from the lifelessness evident
in much of the Anglicanism of his day, he did not perceive inward religion
in conflict with a structured liturgy, as did the members of the American
holiness-movement. Rob Staples states that, for Wesley,

> both spirit and structure were important, and they were not
> mutually exclusive. Structure was not opposed to spirit but was
> its very conduit. Forms of worship, ordered services, the Book
> of Common Prayer, hymns that directed the soul to God, an-
> cient creeds, written prayers, and the like were the very channels
> through which God could send His convicting, regenerating,
> sanctifying Spirit. They were "means of grace." Foremost among
> the structures were the sacraments.[37]

The fear and avoidance of ritual by the early pioneers of the Church of
the Nazarene have unintentionally resulted in detrimental consequences for
the spirituality and the identity of their ecclesial heirs. Their failure to realize
the essential nature of rituals and symbols in communicating meaning has
in effect further severed the church from its connection to Christian antiquity and classical Wesleyanism. Eventually those groups that abandon ritual
lose their distinctive qualities. This is evinced by the more recent dilemma
of Nazarenes finding it difficult to distinguish their particular beliefs and
practices from those of other evangelical denominations, even if on paper
those groups are quite doctrinally distinct.[38] Unfortunately, the recovery
and acceptance of those rituals may prove quite difficult. Adults who were
never exposed to a symbolic liturgical tradition in their childhood may find
it challenging to accept such symbols as meaningful.[39]

---

37. Staples, *Outward Sign*, 288.

38. Douglas argues that symbols are absolutely necessary to communicate meaning, to express values, and they are "the main instruments of thought." Without ritual
and a "coherent symbolic system" societies cannot continue to exist. Douglas, *Natural
Symbols*, 22, 40, 52, 53.

39. Pratt believed that in order for religious symbolism to become powerful in an
individual's experience they must be exposed to it in childhood. Although adults not
experiencing robust ritual symbols in childhood may in time find rituals meaningful
it will never have the same power in their life or reach the same level of meaning as
one who was immersed in ritual symbolism in the early years of life. He also states that
the opposite is true. An adult immersed in ritual symbolism as child, but then later
rejects it, will "to some degree" continue to be under their influence in often "subtle and
unrecognized ways." Wulff, *Psychology of Religion*, 514–5.

A Guiding Rule

Although the issue of Nazarenes losing their theological identity is troubling enough, the problem of anti-ritualism goes even deeper than the inability of individuals to distinguish their church from other denominations. This is because ritualization, within the context of the liturgy, is a vital mechanism enabling persons to learn "what it means to be Christian."[40] Engaging in ritual is not meaningless but "one way of many ways in which human beings construe and construct their world."[41] It is through the liturgy that individuals learn not only to think differently, but to act differently by providing a different pattern on which to model one's life.[42] Therefore, without the presence of a robust liturgy to both shape and transform individuals into the image of Christ and to serve as a voice critiquing culture, thus countering the assault upon the church by secular philosophies, one's Christian identity is at risk.

The early Nazarenes, who adopted Wesley's theology apart from its rich sacramental and liturgical context, did so without realizing the relationship between practice and belief or what is commonly referred to as *lex orandi est lex credendi*, the rule of prayer is the rule of belief.[43] Although voices like Former General Superintendent William Greathouse have warned Nazarenes as to the dangers of the overly subjective trends in current worship practices,[44] most within the denomination are either unaware of the problem or are uncertain how to address it. Foremost among the obstacles the church will need to overcome as it works to nurture meaningful and vibrant worship is to reverse the minimal importance the denomination has traditionally given to liturgical theology.

The reductionism found in the current approach to worship is evinced in several areas, beginning with the absence of any liturgical or thoroughgoing sacramental theology to guide worship practice. Additionally, the revivalism that temporarily served to give the liturgy its shape and uniformity is now defunct. Therefore, worship decisions are quite often made on pragmatic grounds in attempts to increase attendance or appease personal desires, rather than thinking through the theological implications of those choices. Another clue is revealed when examining the academic requirements for ordination candidates or prospective clergy, for which the study of liturgy is minimal

40. Anderson, *Worship and Identity*, 80.

41. Jennings, "On Ritual Knowledge," 112.

42. Ibid., 117; Anderson, *Worship and Identity*, 81.

43. Muller, *Dictionary Latin and Greek*, 175.

44. Greathouse, "Present Crisis in Worship."

at best.[45] Ultimately this lack of attention given toward addressing liturgical problems has served only to amplify the current crisis in worship.

Characteristics of a robust and sound liturgical praxis, in the classical Wesleyan tradition, will not readily begin to appear in Nazarene congregations until the church is more aggressive in giving credence to *lex orandi est lex credendi*. First, however, the Church of the Nazarene will need to overcome its phobia of the prayer book that Wesley believed essential and important to the pursuit of inward religion for the Methodists. My intent here is not a plea for the full, uncritical recovery of Wesley's *Sunday Service* in its present form or that of the Anglican prayer book or any tradition for that matter. Rather it is to stress the urgency of incorporating into contextually sensitive liturgies what Gordon Lathrop refers to as the essentials of Christian worship.[46] It is hoped that this historical and critical analysis of Nazarene worship will serve as a catalyst within the denomination to not only appreciate the fervent spirituality of our Nazarene forbears, but also instill a willingness to critique current practice and facilitate suggestions for moving toward an orthopraxy that is capable of nurturing an identity that is not only Wesleyan, but faithful to the whole of Christian tradition.

Due to the formative nature of worship it is without question that any approach to corporate worship should be cautious and planned with deliberate intention. This involves giving serious consideration to the way the practices in which Nazarene's engage weekly shape those who worship in our churches. Although history demonstrates that one uniform pattern in which all Christians should worship does not exist, church tradition is ignored only at great peril. History does provide insight into the enduring practices of the church that have nurtured Christians since antiquity, as well as revealing practices detrimental to both individual and corporate

---

45. The Church of the Nazarene provides guidelines to its academic institutions so that the courses which are developed will meet the denomination's educational requirements placed upon clergy. Ministers are not eligible for ordination until they have fulfilled these requirements. The guidelines for the denomination's ministerial course of study are stated in terms of desired outcomes. Outcomes are listed for each educational area the church deems essential for ministry including: biblical literature; theology; the doctrine of holiness; church history; Nazarene history and polity; management, leadership, finance and church administration; etc. Courses are then designed to meet these desired outcomes. The majority of these areas have multiple outcomes listed. The outcome for worship is singular and states, "Ability to envision, order, and participate in contextualized theologically grounded worship and to develop and lead appropriate services for special occasions (i.e., wedding, funeral, baptism, and Lord's Supper." The statement is expectedly vague and brief because the church has not established a thoroughgoing liturgical theology to express the meaning of "theologically grounded worship." *Course of Study*, April, 2004.

46. Lathrop, *Holy Things*.

spirituality. New patterns and innovations in worship require conscious and careful evaluation utilizing the tools available to us through various disciplines including liturgical theology and the social sciences.

Perhaps it would be most fitting to conclude this discussion with guidance provided to us by John Wesley in his sermon *Catholic Spirit*. "I dare not therefore presume to impose my mode of worship on any other. I believe it is truly primitive and apostolical. But my belief is no rule for another. . . . My only question at present is this, 'Is thine heart right, as my heart is with thy heart? . . . Is thy heart right with God? . . . Is thy heart right toward thy neighbor? . . . if thou lovest God and all mankind, I ask no more . . . "[47]

---

47. Wesley, "Catholic Spirit," in *Works* (BE), 2:86–90. For a complete understanding of Wesley's definition of what it means for one's heart to be right with God and neighbor read this sermon in its entirety.

Bibliography

Adams, John D. "A Mourners' Bench or." *The Preacher's Magazine* 43, no. 6 (June 1968) 10–11.

Anderson, E. Byron. "Liturgical Catechesis: Congregational Practice as Formation." *Religious Education* 92 (Summer 1997) 349–62.

———. "Worship and Belief: Liturgical Practice as a Contextual Theology." *Worship* 75, no. 5 (Spring 2001) 432–52.

———. *Worship and Christian Identity: Practicing Ourselves.* Collegeville: Liturgical, 2003.

"Anniversary Day." *Nazarene Messenger*, October 22, 1903, 3.

Asbury, Francis. *The Letters.* Vol. 3. 3 vols. The Journal and Letters of Francis Asbury, Edited by Elmer T. Clark, J. Manning Potts and Jacob S. Payton. Nashville: Abingdon, 1958.

"At the First Church, Los Angeles." *Nazarene Messenger*, December 29, 1904, 3.

"At the Tabernacle." *Nazarene Messenger*, April 12, 1906, 8.

"At the Tabernacle." *Nazarene Messenger*, January 4, 1906, 3.

"At the Tabernacle." *Nazarene Messenger*, July 25, 1907, 8.

"At the Tabernacle." *Nazarene Messenger*, March 26, 1908, 8.

"At the Tabernacle." *Nazarene Messenger*, November 22, 1906, 8.

"At the Tabernacle." *Nazarene Messenger*, October 8, 1908, 8.

"At the Tabernacle: Los Angeles." *Nazarene Messenger*, February 7, 1907, 8.

"Bailey Camp Meeting." *Beulah Christian*, June 23, 1906, 11.

Baker, Frank. *John Wesley and the Church of England.* London: Epworth, 2000.

Bangs, Carl. *Phineas F. Bresee: His Life in Methodism, The Holiness Movement, and the Church of the Nazarene.* Kansas City: Beacon Hill, 1995.

———. "A Spiritual Vocabulary." *Herald of Holiness*, March 14, 1949, 7.

Barber, Grant. "The Spiritual Significance of Lent." *Herald of Holiness*, March 8, 1933, 8–9.

Barbieur, Carrie. "Old-Time Singing." *Herald of Holiness*, March 3, 1920, 13.

Bassett, Paul. "Church of the Nazarene." In *The Renewal of Sunday Worship*, edited by Robert E. Webber, 37–40. Peabody, MA: Hendrickson Publishers, 1993.

Bearse, J. C. "John Wesley Church, Brooklyn." *Nazarene Messenger*, October 28, 1909, 5.

———. "Notes from Malden, Mass." *Beulah Christian,* October 1895, 2.

Benson, Louis FitzGerald. *The English Hymn: Its Development and Use in Worship*. New York: Hodder & Stoughton, 1915.

Benson, Mrs. J. T. "The Home: Fasting and Lent." *Herald of Holiness*, August 18, 1920, 8.

"Berkeley Notes." *Nazarene Messenger*, January 7, 1904, 10.

"Beverly, Mass." *Beulah Christian*, May 6, 1911, 2.

"Bible School Notes." *The Holiness Evangel*, February 1, 1907, 7.

Bond, Jim. "This We Believe." In *US/Canada Theology Conference Church of the Nazarene*. Kansas City, MO: N.p., 2004.

Borgen, Ole E. *John Wesley on the Sacraments: A Theological Study*. Grand Rapids, MI: Francis Asbury, 1985.

Bradshaw, Paul F. "Difficulties in Doing Liturgical Theology." *Pacifica* 11 (June 1998) 181–94.

Bresee, Phineas F. "Chicago, Ill." *Nazarene Messenger*, September 8, 1904, 6.

———. "Further Suggestions to Preachers." *Herald of Holiness*, September 4, 1912, 5.

———. "The Lamb Amid the Blood-Washed." *Nazarene Messenger*, March 6, 1902, 1–2, 7.

Brokhoff, John R. "Make the Advent Season Count." *The Preacher's Magazine* 56, no. 2 (December–February 1980–81) 30.

"Brooklyn." *Beulah Christian*, August 1902, 8.

"Brooklyn, N. Y." *Beulah Christian*, December 9, 1905, 14.

"Brooklyn, N. Y." *Beulah Christian*, January 1, 1910, 6.

Brown, H. D. "The Scripture Lesson." *Herald of Holiness*, September 3, 1938, 12, 18.

Brown, H. N. "All-Day Meetings in Brooklyn." *Beulah Chrisitan*, January 1902, 8.

Brunson, F. A. "The Bread-breaking Love Feast." *The Preacher's Magazine* 36, no. 9 (September 1961) 33–34.

Bryant, A. K. "Cundy's Harbor, Me." *Beulah Christian*, January 9, 1909, 8.

Bulletin: First Church of the Nazarene Los Angeles. April 19, 1936. Lenexa, KS: Nazarene Archives.

Bulletin: First Church of the Nazarene Los Angeles. August 8, 1943. Lenexa, KS: Nazarene Archives.

Bulletin: First Pentecostal Church of the Nazarene Los Angeles. December 13, 1914. Lenexa, KS: Nazarene Archives.

Bulletin: Kansas City First. March 7, 1971. file 2262-04. Lenexa, KS: Bulletin Collections, Nazarene Archives.

Busic, David, and Jeren Rowell. "Preacher to Preacher." *Preacher's Magazine* (Lent-Easter 2002) 1.

Byron, Lloyd B. "Preaching." *The Preacher's Magazine* 6, no. 6 (June 1931) 15–16.

Cain, C. N. "Pittsburgh District Assembly." *Beulah Christian*, June 6, 1908, 2.

"Camp Hebron Closing Camp for 1909." *Beulah Christian*, September 4, 1909, 8.

Campbell, Ted A. "John Wesley and the Asian Roots of Christianity." *The Asia Journal of Theology* 8, no. 2 (October 1994) 281–94.

———. "Means of Grace and Forms of Piety." In *The Oxford Handbook of Methodist Studies*, edited by William J. Abraham and James E. Kirby, 280–91. New York: Oxford University Press, 2009.

———. *The Religion of the Heart: A Study of European Religious Life in the Seventeenth and Eighteenth Centuries*. Columbia: University of South Carolina Press, 1991.

Carey, F. S. "Harvest Hallelujahs: Morrisville, Vt." *Beulah Christian*, September 26, 1908, 8.

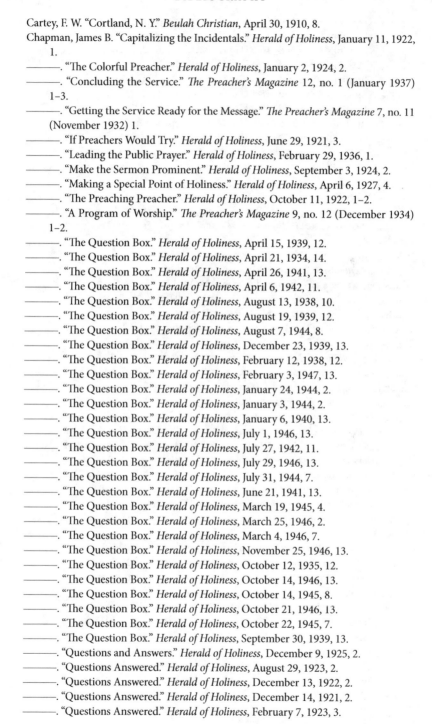

Cartey, F. W. "Cortland, N. Y." *Beulah Christian*, April 30, 1910, 8.

Chapman, James B. "Capitalizing the Incidentals." *Herald of Holiness*, January 11, 1922, 1.

———. "The Colorful Preacher." *Herald of Holiness*, January 2, 1924, 2.

———. "Concluding the Service." *The Preacher's Magazine* 12, no. 1 (January 1937) 1–3.

———. "Getting the Service Ready for the Message." *The Preacher's Magazine* 7, no. 11 (November 1932) 1.

———. "If Preachers Would Try." *Herald of Holiness*, June 29, 1921, 3.

———. "Leading the Public Prayer." *Herald of Holiness*, February 29, 1936, 1.

———. "Make the Sermon Prominent." *Herald of Holiness*, September 3, 1924, 2.

———. "Making a Special Point of Holiness." *Herald of Holiness*, April 6, 1927, 4.

———. "The Preaching Preacher." *Herald of Holiness*, October 11, 1922, 1–2.

———. "A Program of Worship." *The Preacher's Magazine* 9, no. 12 (December 1934) 1–2.

———. "The Question Box." *Herald of Holiness*, April 15, 1939, 12.

———. "The Question Box." *Herald of Holiness*, April 21, 1934, 14.

———. "The Question Box." *Herald of Holiness*, April 26, 1941, 13.

———. "The Question Box." *Herald of Holiness*, April 6, 1942, 11.

———. "The Question Box." *Herald of Holiness*, August 13, 1938, 10.

———. "The Question Box." *Herald of Holiness*, August 19, 1939, 12.

———. "The Question Box." *Herald of Holiness*, August 7, 1944, 8.

———. "The Question Box." *Herald of Holiness*, December 23, 1939, 13.

———. "The Question Box." *Herald of Holiness*, February 12, 1938, 12.

———. "The Question Box." *Herald of Holiness*, February 3, 1947, 13.

———. "The Question Box." *Herald of Holiness*, January 24, 1944, 2.

———. "The Question Box." *Herald of Holiness*, January 3, 1944, 2.

———. "The Question Box." *Herald of Holiness*, January 6, 1940, 13.

———. "The Question Box." *Herald of Holiness*, July 1, 1946, 13.

———. "The Question Box." *Herald of Holiness*, July 27, 1942, 11.

———. "The Question Box." *Herald of Holiness*, July 29, 1946, 13.

———. "The Question Box." *Herald of Holiness*, July 31, 1944, 7.

———. "The Question Box." *Herald of Holiness*, June 21, 1941, 13.

———. "The Question Box." *Herald of Holiness*, March 19, 1945, 4.

———. "The Question Box." *Herald of Holiness*, March 25, 1946, 2.

———. "The Question Box." *Herald of Holiness*, March 4, 1946, 7.

———. "The Question Box." *Herald of Holiness*, November 25, 1946, 13.

———. "The Question Box." *Herald of Holiness*, October 12, 1935, 12.

———. "The Question Box." *Herald of Holiness*, October 14, 1946, 13.

———. "The Question Box." *Herald of Holiness*, October 14, 1945, 8.

———. "The Question Box." *Herald of Holiness*, October 21, 1946, 13.

———. "The Question Box." *Herald of Holiness*, October 22, 1945, 7.

———. "The Question Box." *Herald of Holiness*, September 30, 1939, 13.

———. "Questions and Answers." *Herald of Holiness*, December 9, 1925, 2.

———. "Questions Answered." *Herald of Holiness*, August 29, 1923, 2.

———. "Questions Answered." *Herald of Holiness*, December 13, 1922, 2.

———. "Questions Answered." *Herald of Holiness*, December 14, 1921, 2.

———. "Questions Answered." *Herald of Holiness*, February 7, 1923, 3.

———. "Questions Answered." *Herald of Holiness*, January 16, 1924, 3.

———. "Questions Answered." *Herald of Holiness*, January 30, 1924, 2.

———. "Questions Answered." *Herald of Holiness*, March 18, 1925, 6.

———. "Questions Answered." *Herald of Holiness*, May 16, 1923, 3.

———. "Questions Answered." *Herald of Holiness*, May 17, 1922, 3.

———. "Questions Answered." *Herald of Holiness*, May 31, 1922, 3.

———. "Questions Answered." *Herald of Holiness*, October 6, 1926, 14.

———. "Questions Answered." *Herald of Holiness*, September 1, 1926, 15.

———. "We May Sing the Victor's Song." *Herald of Holiness*, February 4, 1925, 1–2.

———. "We Must Preach Doctrine." *Herald of Holiness*, February 29, 1928, 4.

———. "A Well Planned Worship Service." *The Preacher's Magazine* 14, no. 6 (June 1939) 2–3.

———. "What of the Church Year." *The Preacher's Magazine* 3, no. 1 (January 1928) 2.

———. "Why the Long Sermon." *Herald of Holiness*, June 18, 1919, 7.

———. "The Word Must Be Preached in Power." *Herald of Holiness*, November 8, 1922, 1.

"Chicago, Ill." *Nazarene Messenger*, January 13, 1910, 4.

"Chicago." *Pentecostal Advocate*, December 23, 1909, 16.

"Christmas." *Nazarene Messenger*, December 31, 1903, 3.

"Christmas Day." *Nazarene Messenger*, January 2, 1902, 6.

"Christmas Love Feast." *Nazarene Messenger*, December 10, 1903, 6.

"Christmas Love Feast." *Nazarene Messenger*, December 11, 1902, 6.

"Christmas Love Feast." *Nazarene Messenger*, December 30, 1909, 7.

"Christmas Love-Feast." *Nazarene Messenger*, December 14, 1905, 8.

"Christmas Love-Feast." *Nazarene Messenger*, December 28, 1905, 10.

"Church Dedication." *Pentecostal Advocate*, June 24, 1909, 7.

Church Manual: First Peoples' Church of Brooklyn, New York. Brooklyn, NY, 1906.

Ciprico, H. H. B. "Church Music." *Herald of Holiness*, January 28, 1920, 7.

Clark, J. C. D. "The Eighteenth-Century Context." In *The Oxford Handbook of Methodist Studies*, edited by William J. Abraham and James E. Kirby, 3–29. New York: Oxford University Press, 2009.

Collins, J. S. "Reports from the Field: Fair View." *The Holiness Evangel*, March 1, 1907, 3.

"Compton Avenue Church." *Nazarene Messenger*, December 23, 1909, 8.

"Compton Avenue Church." *Nazarene Messenger*, November 18, 1909, 8.

Connerton, Paul. *How Societies Remember.* Cambridge: Cambridge University Press, 1989.

Corlett, D. Shelby. "The Lenten Season." *Herald of Holiness*, March 15, 1941, 2–3.

———. "Notes and Comments." *Herald of Holiness*, October 14, 1939, 4.

———. "Pastoral Prayers." *Herald of Holiness*, October 26, 1940, 4.

———. "Pentecost Sunday." *Herald of Holiness*, May 4, 1940, 4.

———. "Preaching Holiness." *Herald of Holiness*, November 25, 1939, 2–3.

———. "Public Reading of the Bible." *Herald of Holiness*, July 31, 1937, 3.

———. "Spiritual Demonstration." *Herald of Holiness*, September 21, 1935, 4.

Cornell, C. E. "Long-Winded Preachers." *Herald of Holiness*, September 25, 1912, 5.

———. "Nazarenes and Shouting." *Herald of Holiness*, January 24, 1934, 8.

———. "Nazarenes and Shouting." *Herald of Holiness*, March 10, 1926, 7.

———. "Preaching Without Results." *Nazarene Messenger*, June 11, 1908, 2.

———. "Shouting Not the Fashion in the Churches." *Herald of Holiness*, October 31, 1923, 3.

———. "Shouting." *Herald of Holiness*, April 23, 1913, 6.

Course of Study Evaluation Worksheet: College or University Program. Kansas City, MO: Nazarene, 2004.

Cowan, H. G. "Shouting or Rejoicing." *Herald of Holiness*, January 21, 1925, 6.

Cowles, C. S. "Advent Sermon: The Astonishing Christmas Miracle." *The Preacher's Magazine* 65, no. 2 (December–February 1989–90) 42–44.

Cunningham, Floyd, ed. *Our Watchword & Song*. Kansas City, MO: Beacon Hill, 2009.

Dalton, Tom. "From Correspondents: Lowell, Mass." *Beulah Christian*, August 12, 1905, 15.

Davey, Randall E. "Worship and Preaching Helps." *The Preacher's Magazine* 68, no. 2 (December–February 1992–93) 54–80.

Davidson, James M. "Bradford, Pa." *Beulah Christian*, March 4, 1911, 8.

Davies, Rupert E., ed. *The Methodist Societies: History, Nature, and Design*. Vol. 9, The Works of John Wesley. Nashville: Abingdon, 1989.

Davis, C. Howard. "Experience Profession." *Beulah Christian*, September 15, 1904, 4.

———. "Rock Camp Meeting." *Beulah Christian*, August 1893, 3.

Dawn, Marva J. *Reaching Out without Dumbing Down: A Theology of Worship for the Turn-of-the-Century Culture*. Grand Rapids, MI: W.B. Eerdmans, 1995.

Day, E. L. "Church Music: Its Use and Abuse." *Herald of Holiness*, December 26, 1928, 7–8.

"Decoration Day." *Nazarene Messenger*, May 31, 1900, 5.

Dieter, Melvin. *The Holiness Revival of the Nineteenth Century*. Studies in Evangelicalism. Edited by Kenneth E. Rowe and Donald W. Dayton. Metuchen, NJ: Scarecrow, 1980.

Dodge, Kenneth L. "The Evangelistic Invitation and the Altar Service." *The Preacher's Magazine* 43, no. 6 (June 1968) 11ff.

Domina, F.W. "Dennisport, Mass." *Beulah Christian*, June 22, 1907, 13.

———. "Harvest Hallelujahs: Dennisport, Mass." *Beulah Christian*, November 14, 1908, 8.

"Douglas Camp Meeting." *Beulah Christian*, September 29, 1906, 9.

Douglas, Mary. *Natural Symbols*. New York: Routledge Classics, 2008.

———. *Purity and Danger*. New York: Routledge Classics, 2010.

Dray, John R. P. "Church and Chapel in a Cornish Mining Parish: 1743 to the Death of John Wesley." *Evangel* 26 (Summer 2008) 48–61.

Drury, Keith, Richard S. Taylor, Kenneth J. Collins, and Wallace Thornton Jr. *Counterpoint: Dialogue with Drury on the Holiness Movement*. Salem, OH: Schmul, 2005.

Du Bois, Lauriston J. "Prayer and Worship." *The Preacher's Magazine* 36, no. 6 (June 1961) 5–7, 28.

———. "The Scriptures in Worship." *The Preacher's Magazine* 36, no. 5 (May 1961) 2–4.

Dunn, Thos. J. "First Church, Los Angeles." *Nazarene Messenger*, February 25, 1909, 8.

Dunning, H. Ray. "Christian Perfection: Toward a New Paradigm." *Wesleyan Theological Journal* 33, no. 1 (Spring 1998) 151.

———. *Grace, Faith, and Holiness: A Wesleyan Systematic Theology*. Kansas City, MO: Beacon Hill, 1988.

Ellis, Dirk R. "The Relationship Between Liturgical Practice and Spirituality in the Church of the Nazarene with Special Reference to John Wesley's Doctrine of Christian Perfection." PhD diss., Andrews University, 2012.

Estep, Bradley K. "Baptismal Theology and Practice in the Church of the Nazarene: A Preservation of Plurality." PhD diss., Union Theological Seminary, 2000.

"Fanaticism." *Nazarene Messenger*, January 17, 1907, 6–7.

"Fanaticism and Humbugs." *Nazarene Messenger*, June 27, 1907, 6–7.

Felton, Gayle Carlton. *The Gift of Water: The Practice and Theology of Baptism Among Methodists in America*. Nashville: Abingdon, 1992.

"Fifty-Seven Minutes." *Herald of Holiness*, August 5, 1946, 13.

Finch, Oscar J. "The Church in Worship." *Herald of Holiness*, August 12, 1946, 7–8.

Fisher, William E. "Through the Holidays with Him." *Pentecostal Advocate*, January 16, 1908, 2.

Fitzgerald, James Nelson. "Weaving a Rope of Sand: The Separation of the Proclamation of the Word and the Celebration of the Eucharist in the Church of the Nazarene." PhD diss., Vanderbilt University, 1999.

Fletcher, Joseph. "Harvest Hallelujahs: Brooklyn, N. Y." *Beulah Christian*, March 21, 1908, 8.

"Forms of Worship." *Nazarene Messenger*, February 11, 1909, 6.

"Fourth of July." *Nazarene Messenger*, July 5, 1900, 6.

"The Fourth of July." *Nazarene Messenger*, July 11, 1901, 6–7.

"The Fourth of July." *Nazarene Messenger*, June 27, 1907, 8.

"Franklin, N. H." *Beulah Christian*, June 11, 1910, 8.

"From Cannon, Tex." *Pentecostal Advocate*, January 10, 1907, 10.

"Fruitless Ministry." *Beulah Christian*, July 10, 1909, 6.

Gallaway, Craig B. "The Presence of Christ with the Worshipping Community: A Study in the Hymns of John and Charles Wesley." PhD diss., Candler School of Theology, 1988.

Girvin, E. A. "Seven Characteristics of Our Church." *Nazarene Messenger*, October 22, 1903, 7.

———. *Phineas F. Bresee: A Prince in Israel*. Kansas City: Nazarene, 1982.

González, Justo L. *The Reformation to the Present Day*. The Story of Christianity. San Francisco: Harper & Row, 1984.

"The Good Old Hymns." *Nazarene Messenger*, October 24, 1901, 7.

Goodwin, John W. "Plain Words to Preachers." *The Preacher's Magazine* 12, no. 3 (March 1937) 25–27.

———. "San Diego, Cal." *Nazarene Messenger*, January 2, 1908, 7.

———. "Southern California District Camp-Meeting." *Nazarene Messenger*, September 2, 1909, 8.

Gould, J. Glenn. "Music and the Church Service." *Herald of Holiness*, January 23, 1929, 7–9.

"Grand Avenue Church." *Nazarene Messenger*, April 9, 1908, 8.

"Grand Avenue Church." *Nazarene Messenger*, August 6, 1908, 8.

"Grand Avenue Church." *Nazarene Messenger*, February 18, 1909, 8.

"The Great Union General Assembly." *Nazarene Messenger*, October 22, 1908, 2.

Greathouse, William. "The Present Crisis in Nazarene Worship." Lenexa, KS: Nazarene Archives, 1989.

Green, Carl C. "The Pastoral Prayer." *The Preacher's Magazine* 71, no. 4 (June–August 1996) 16–17.

Grider, J. Kenneth. "Baptism: The Doctrine and Its Practice." *The Nazarene Preacher* 44, no. 3 (March 1969) 12–14.

———. "Spirit-Baptism the Means of Sanctification: A Response to the Lyon View." *Wesleyan Theological Journal* 14, no. 2 (Fall 1979) 31–50.

Grimes, Ronald L. "Ronald L. Grimes: Modes of Ritual Sensibility." In *Foundations in Ritual Studies: A Reader for Students of Christian Worship*, edited by Paul Bradshaw and John Melloh, 131–65. Grand Rapids, MI: Baker Academic, 2007.

Gunter, Nina. *God—What in the World Are You Doing?* MP3 Recording. Kansas City, MO: Nazarene, 2007.

Hay, John Jr. "Introduction." *The Preacher's Magazine* 69, no. 4 (June–August 1994) 54.

Haynes, B. F. "Doctrinal Preaching." *Herald of Holiness*, December 4, 1912, 3.

———. "Great Hymns for Holiness." *Herald of Holiness*, October 20, 1915, 2.

———. "Helpful Suggestions for Young Preachers." *Herald of Holiness*, July 12, 1922, 3.

———. "Missing an Opportunity." *Herald of Holiness*, December 23, 1914, 4.

———. "The Proper Length of a Sermon." *Herald of Holiness*, June 19, 1912, 3.

Heitzenrater, Richard P. *Wesley and the People Called Methodists*. Nashville: Abingdon, 1995.

Hess, Weaver W. "The Pastor in the Communion Service." *The Preacher's Magazine* 18, no. 3 (May–June 1943) 41–3.

Higgins, A. H. "Harvest Hallelujahs: Peabody, Mass." *Beulah Christian*, April 18, 1908, 8.

Hills, A. M. "Pastoral Theology: Public Prayer." *The Preacher's Magazine* 3, no. 9 (September 1928) 7–10.

Hohenstein, Charles R. "*Lex Orandi, Lex Credendi*: Cautionary Notes." *Wesleyan Theological Journal* 32, no. 2 (Fall 1997) 140–57.

"Holiness Church Annual Council and General Assembly Nazarene Church." *Pentecostal Advocate*, October 29, 1908, 6.

Hoople, William Howard. "New York District Assembly." *Beulah Christian*, May 6, 1911, 5.

Hoskins, Steven T. "The Wesleyan/Holiness Movement in Search of Liturgical Identity." *Wesleyan Theological Journal* 32, no. 2 (Fall 1997) 121–39.

Hosley, H. B. "Clintondale, N. Y." *Beulah Christian,* June 1900, 8.

Huff, Will H. "The Altar Service." *The Preacher's Magazine* 38, no. 3 (March 1963) 3–4.

"Hyde Park, N. Y." *Beulah Christian,* April 1899, 4.

"In This Issue." *The Preacher's Magazine* 60, no. 2 (December–February 1984–85) 1.

Ingersol, Stanley. "Christian Baptism and the Early Nazarenes: The Sources That Shaped a Pluralistic Baptismal Tradition." *Wesleyan Theological Journal* 27 (1992) 161–80.

"Installation at Malden, Mass." *Beulah Christian*, May 8, 1909, 6.

Irwin, Kevin W. *Context and Text: Method in Liturgical Theology*. Collegeville, MN: Liturgical, 1994.

Jacob, W. M. *Lay People and Religion in the Early Eighteenth Century*. New York: Cambridge University Press, 1996.

Jasper, Ronald C. D., and G. J. Cuming. *Prayers of the Eucharist: Early and Reformed*. Collegeville, MN: Liturgical, 1990.

Jennings, Theodore. "On Ritual Knowledge." *The Journal of Religion* 62, no. 2 (April 1982) 111–27.

Jernigan, C. B. "Oklahoma District Assembly Program." *Pentecostal Advocate,* November 3, 1910, 5.

Johnson, Maxwell E. "Can We Avoid Relativism in Worship? Liturgical Norms in the Light of Contemporary Liturgical Scholarship." *Worship* 74, no. 2 (March 2000) 135–55.

"July 4th 1902." *Nazarene Messenger,* July 10, 1902, 4.

"July 4th 1902." *Nazarene Messenger,* July 3, 1902, 6.

Kavanagh, Aidan. *On Liturgical Theology.* Collegeville, MN: Liturgical, 1992.

Keck, Leander E. *The Church Confident.* Nashville: Abingdon, 1993.

Kiefer, R. J. "Lenten Retirement." *Herald of Holiness,* February 14, 1934, 8.

Knapp, Jeffery H. "Throwing the Baby Out with the Font Water: The Development of Baptismal Practice in the Church of the Nazarene." *Worship* 76, no. 3 (May 2002) 225–44.

Knight III, Henry H. *The Presence of God in the Christian Life: John Wesley and the Means of Grace.* Pietist and Wesleyan Studies. Metuchen, NJ: Scarecrow, 1992.

Lanpher, C. P. "Lowell, Mass." *Beulah Christian,* January 9, 1909, 8.

Larson, Darrell. "When We All Get to Heaven: The Ecumenical Influence of the American Gospel Song." *Restoration Quarterly* 36, no. 3 (January 1994) 154–72.

Lathrop, Gordon W. *Holy Things: A Liturgical Theology.* Minneapolis: Fortress, 1993.

Leach, John H. "Keene, N. H." *Beulah Christian,* May 1894, 3.

Lehman, F. M. "Shouting." *Herald of Holiness,* August 30, 1916, 7.

"Leicester, Vt., Camp Meeting." *Beulah Christian,* June 9, 1906, 11.

Leth, Carl M. "In Spirit and in Truth: The Search for True Worship." *The Preacher's Magazine* 70, no. 3 (March–May 1995) 12–13.

Lewis, A. R. "West Somerville, Mass." *Beulah Christian,* April 8, 1911, 8.

———. "West Somerville, Mass." *Beulah Christian,* August 1901, 8.

Lewis, Burt W. "Syracuse, N. Y." *Beulah Christian,* August 14, 1909, 8.

Lillenas, Haldor. "The Literature of Hymnology." *Herald of Holiness,* November 15, 1941, 7–8.

Linaweaver, P. G. "Oakland, Cal." *Nazarene Messenger,* January 9, 1908, 4.

———. "Watch Night Around the Bay." *Nazarene Messenger,* January 10, 1907, 3–4.

"Lincoln Place, Pa." *Beulah Christian,* July 8, 1905, 14.

Lint, Richard A. "The Altar and How to Use It." *The Preacher's Magazine* 70, no. 3 (March–May 1995) 10–11.

London, A. S. "Music and Education." *Pentecostal Advocate,* September 29, 1910, 2.

"The Lord's Supper." *The Preacher's Magazine* 23, no. 4 (July–August 1948) 5.

"Los Angeles." *Nazarene Messenger,* August 3, 1899, 4.

Maddox, Randy L. *Responsible Grace: John Wesley's Practical Theology.* Nashville, TN: Kingswood, 1994.

"Maintaining the Form and Spirit of Reverence." *Herald of Holiness,* August 27, 1924, 1–2.

Manning, C. S. "Brandon, Vt." *Beulah Christian,* December 16, 1905, 14.

Manual: Church of the Nazarene [1968]. Kansas City, MO: Nazarene, 1968.

Manual: Church of the Nazarene [1972]. Kansas City, MO: Nazarene, 1972.

Manual: Church of the Nazarene [1997–2001]. Kansas City, MO: Nazarene, 1997.

Manual: Church of the Nazarene [2005–2009]. Kansas City, MO: Nazarene, 2005.

Manual: Church of the Nazarene [2009–2013]. Kansas City, MO: Nazarene, 2009.

Manual: Church of the Nazarene [2013–2017]. Kansas City, MO: Nazarene, 2013.

Manual Holiness Church of Christ. Pilot Point, TX: The Holiness Evangel, 1907.

Manual of the Church of the Nazarene [1906]. Los Angeles: Nazarene, 1906.

Manual of the First Pentecostal Church of Lynn, Mass. Providence, RI: Pentecostal Printing Co., 1898.

Manual of the History, Doctrine, Government, and Ritual of the Church of the Nazarene [1928]. Kansas City, MO: Nazarene, 1928.

Manual of the History, Doctrine, Government, and Ritual of the Pentecostal Church of the Nazarene [1915]. Kansas City, MO: Nazarene, 1915.

Manual of the Pentecostal Church of the Nazarene [1907]. Los Angeles: Nazarene, 1907.

Manual of the Pentecostal Church of the Nazarene [1908]. Los Angeles: Nazarene, 1908.

Marsh, L. W. "Method of Divine Worship." *Herald of Holiness,* September 17, 1913, 6–7.

———. "Release the Accelerator, Please." *Herald of Holiness,* February 7, 1923, 9.

Marthaler, Berard. *The Creed: The Apostolic Faith in Contemporary Theology.* Mystic, CT: Twenty-Third Publications, 1993.

Marty, Martin E. "Baptistification Takes Over." *Christianity Today,* September 2, 1983, 33–36.

McBride, J. B. "Des Arc, Mo., Holiness College." *Pentecostal Advocate,* June 17, 1909, 6.

McCall, Charles R. "The Heritage of Lent." *The Preacher's Magazine* 61, no. 3 (March–May 1986) 4–6.

McGraw, James. "The Seasonal Sermon." *The Preacher's Magazine* 52, no. 11 (November 1977) 1–2.

McNeill, Alexander J. "Evangelistic Echoes: Salem, Mass." *Beulah Christian,* October 20, 1906, 14.

Messer, E. D. "Some Present Day Nazarene Leaders." *The Preacher's Magazine* 8, no. 10 (October 1933) 12–13.

Middendorf, Jesse C. *The Church Rituals Handbook.* Kansas City, MO: Beacon Hill, 1997.

Milligan, Herbert F. "Harvest Hallelujahs: Cliftondale, Mass." *Beulah Christian,* April 4, 1908, 8.

"Mission Church." *Beulah Christian,* May 1892, 4.

Mitchell, Nathan D. "Nathan D. Mitchell: New Directions in Ritual Research." In *Foundations in Ritual Studies,* edited by Paul Bradshaw and John Melloh, 103–30. Grand Rapids, MI: Baker Academic, 2007.

Morgan, Bernice. "Shouting Christians." *Herald of Holiness,* January 12, 1948, 8.

Morgan, S. L., Sr., "Our Poor Public Prayers." *The Preacher's Magazine* 34, no. 5 (May 1959) 34–35.

Muller, Richard A. *Dictionary of Latin and Greek Theological Terms: Drawn Principally from Protestant Scholastic Theology.* Grand Rapids, Mich.: Baker Book House, 1985.

Mund, Fred A. *Keep the Music Ringing: A Short History of the Hymnody of the Church of the Nazarene.* Kansas City, MO: Nazarene, 1979.

"My Complaints About Worship Services." *The Preacher's Magazine* 55, no. 3 (March–May 1980) 10–11, 55.

Neill, Stephen. *Anglicanism.* 4th ed. New York: Oxford University Press, 1977.

Noakes, K. W. "Initiation: From New Testament Times Until St. Cyprian." In *The Study of Liturgy,* edited by Cheslyn Jones, Geoffrey Wainwright, Edward Yarnold SJ and Paul Bradshaw, 112–27. New York: Oxford University Press, 1992.

Norberry, John. "New York District Assembly." *Beulah Christian,* May 20, 1911, 2.

————. "Portsmouth, R. I., Campgrounds." *Beulah Christian*, August 19, 1911, 5.
"Northwest District Assembly." *Nazarene Messenger*, June 25, 1908, 2.
"Notes and Personals." *Nazarene Messenger*, December 11, 1902, 6.
"Notes and Personals." *Nazarene Messenger*, December 4, 1902, 3.
"Notes and Personals." *Nazarene Messenger*, January 8, 1902, 3.
"Notes and Personals." *Nazarene Messenger*, January 8, 1903, 3.
"Notes and Personals." *Nazarene Messenger*, March 31, 1904, 3.
"Notes and Personals: First Church, Los Angeles." *Nazarene Messenger*, April 17, 1902, 3.
"Notes and Personals: Los Angeles, Cal." *Nazarene Messenger*, October 20, 1904, 3.
"Observing the Sacrament of the Lord's Supper." *Herald of Holiness*, January 19, 1927, 3.
"The Oklahoma District Assembly." *Pentecostal Advocate*, November 24, 1910, 8.
Oliver, J. W. "The Sermon." *Herald of Holiness*, December 15, 1915, 6.
"Organize." *Nazarene Messenger*, July 11, 1907, 6–7.
"The Quinnebaug Camp Meeting." *Beulah Christian*, November 1897, 2.
Outler, Albert Cook, ed. *John Wesley*, A Library of Protestant Thought. New York: Oxford University Press, 1964.
Paul, Mary Rearick. "Worship and Preaching Helps." *The Preacher's Magazine* 69, no. 3 (March–May 1994) 54.
Peel, J. E. "Peoria, Ill." *Nazarene Messenger*, April 23, 1908, 4.
"Personals." *Beulah Christian*, January 11, 1908, 5.
Peterson, Brent David. *Created to Worship: God's Invitation to Become Fully Human.* Kansas City, MO: Beacon Hill, 2012.
————. "A Post-Wesleyan Eucharistic Ecclesiology: The Renewal of the Church as the Body of Christ to Be Doxologically Broken and Spilled Out for the World." PhD diss., Garrett-Evangelical Theological Seminary, 2009.
Pierce, D. Rand. "Farewell at Lynn." *Beulah Christian*, January 19, 1905, 7.
————. "A Great Day." *Beulah Christian*, January 5, 1905, 4.
————. "New England Assembly." *Beulah Christian*, May 21, 1910, 1.
Pierce, Robert. "The Christmas Lovefeast." *Nazarene Messenger*, December 27, 1906, 7.
————. "Some Suggestions on Peaching." *Nazarene Messenger*, July 18, 1907, 6–7.
Plummer, Alfred. *The Church of England in the Eighteenth Century.* London: Methuen & Co., 1910.
Price, Ross E. *Nazarene Manifesto.* Kansas City, MO: Nazarene, 1968.
Purkiser, W. T. *Called Unto Holiness: The Second Twenty-Five Years,* 1933–58. Vol. 2. Kansas City, MO: Nazarene, 1983.
Quanstrom, Mark R. *A Century of Holiness Theology: The Doctrine of Entire Sanctification in the Church of the Nazarene: 1905 to 2004.* Kansas City, MO: Beacon Hill, 2004.
"The Question Box." *Herald of Holiness*, February 6, 1952, 17.
Rack, Henry D. *Reasonable Enthusiast: John Wesley and the Rise of Methodism.* 2nd ed. Nashville: Abingdon, 2002.
Rattenbury, J. Ernest. *The Eucharistic Hymns of John and Charles Wesley.* Akron, OH: OSL Publications, 1996.
Read, Mrs. J. E. "Silver Lake, Vermont, Campmeeting." *Beulah Christian*, July 10, 1909, 2.
Reed, Louis A. "The History and Significance of the Lord's Supper." *The Preacher's Magazine* 23, no. 4 (July–August 1948) 10–12.

Reid, Isaiah. "The Altar Service." *The Preacher's Magazine* 38, no. 5 (May 1963) 10–11, 21.

"Reports from the Field." *The Holiness Evangel*, December 9, 1908, 3.

"Reports from the Field." *The Holiness Evangel*, February 1, 1908, 3.

"Revivals." *Beulah Christian*, January 1895, 4.

Reynolds, Hiram F. "Overland Letters: Annual Outing." *Beulah Christian*, August 8, 1908, 2.

Reynolds, Marshall T. "A Grand Revival." *Beulah Christian*, December 5, 1908, 7.

———. "North Scituate, R. I." *Nazarene Messenger*, December 17, 1908, 13.

Richards, Henrietta. "Missionary Bulletin: Mexico." *Pentecostal Advocate*, May 12, 1910, 10.

Rickert, H. H. "Goshen, Vt." *Beulah Christian*, January 19, 1905, 15.

Riggs, A. B. "From Lowell, Mass." *Beulah Christian*, February 26, 1910, 6.

———. "Lowell, Mass." *Beulah Christian*, April 1900, 6.

———. "Lowell, Mass." *Beulah Christian*, January 22, 1910, 6.

Riley, John. "The Church's One Continuing Sacrament." *The Preacher's Magazine* 29, no. 2 (February 1954) 12–14, 17.

Rothenbusch, Esther. "Is Not This the Land of Beulah? The Search for the Holy Spirit in American Gospel Hymns." *Review and Expositor* 94, no. 1 (Winter 1997) 53–77.

Routley, Erik. *The Musical Wesleys: Studies in Church Music.* London: Jenkins, 1968.

Ruth, C. W. "The Altar Service." *The Preacher's Magazine* 38, no. 1 (January 1963) 7–8, 37.

———. "Concert Praying, or United Praying." *Herald of Holiness*, July 27, 1932, 5–6.

Ruth, Lester. *Early Methodist Life and Spirituality: A Reader.* Nashville: Kingswood, 2005.

———. *A Little Heaven Below: Worship at Early Methodist Quarterly Meetings.* Nashville: Kingswood, 2000.

———. "Liturgical Revolutions." In *The Oxford Handbook of Methodist Studies*, edited by William J. Abraham and James E. Kirby, 313–31. New York: Oxford University Press, 2009.

———. "Reconsidering the Emergence of the Second Great Awakening and Camp Meetings Among Early Methodists." *Worship* 75, no. 1 (July 2001) 334–55.

"Sabbath." *Nazarene Messenger*, August 8, 1901, 7.

"Sabbath." *Nazarene Messenger*, December 21, 1899, 4.

"The Sabbath." *Nazarene Messenger*, September 17, 1903, 3.

"The Sabbath." *Nazarene Messenger*, September 6, 1900, 4.

"Sabbath at First Church." *Nazarene Messenger*, December 10, 1903, 3.

"Sabbath at First Church." *Nazarene Messenger*, July 7, 1904, 3.

"Sabbath at First Church." *Nazarene Messenger*, May 11, 1905, 10.

"Sabbath at First Church." *Nazarene Messenger*, October 9, 1902, 3.

"Sabbath, July 6th." *Nazarene Messenger*, July 10, 1902, 7.

"Sabbath Services." *Nazarene Messenger*, October 12, 1899, 4.

"Sacrament of Baptism." *Beulah Christian*, October 21, 1911, 3.

"Sacramental Service." *Nazarene Messenger*, May 3, 1900, 5.

"Sag Harbor, N. Y." *Beulah Christian*, November 7, 1908, 8.

"Salem, Mass." *Beulah Christian*, January 22, 1910, 5.

Saliers, Don E. "Seasons of the Gospel: An Overview of the Liturgical Year." *Reformed Liturgy & Music* 25, no. 1 (Winter 1991) 11–14.

————. *Worship as Theology: Foretaste of Glory Divine*. Nashville: Abingdon, 1994.

"San Francisco District Camp-Meeting." *Nazarene Messenger*, July 30, 1908, 4.

Sanders, Paul Samuel. "An Appraisal of John Wesley's Sacramentalism in the Evolution of Early American Methodism." ThD diss., Union Theological Seminary, 1954.

Schaefer, Mary M. "*Lex Orandi, Lex Credendi*: Faith, Doctrine and Theology in Dialogue." *Studies in Religion/Sciences Religieuses* 26, no. 4 (1997) 467–79.

"School Notes." *The Holiness Evangel*, December 16, 1906, 7.

Schurman, W. G. "Lynn, Mass." *Beulah Christian*, October 16, 1909, 8.

————. "Manchester, N. H." *Beulah Christian*, February 26, 1910, 8.

Scott, J. D. "Editorial: Experimental Religion." *The Holiness Evangel*, September 15, 1909, 4.

Searle, Mark. "Ritual." In *Foundations in Ritual Studies*, edited by Paul Bradshaw and John Melloh, 9–16. Grand Rapids: Baker Academic, 2007.

Shepard, W. E. "The Christmas Lovefeast." *Nazarene Messenger*, December 28, 1899, 6.

Shoemaker, Robert Brink. *The London Mob: Violence and Disorder in Eighteenth-Century England*. London: Hambledon and London, 2004.

"Short Sermons." *Nazarene Messenger*, December 14, 1905, 8.

"Shout!" *Beulah Christian*, May 4, 1907, 5–7.

"Singing in the Church Service." *Herald of Holiness*, November 10, 1915, 2.

Smith, James K. A., *Desiring the Kingdom: Worship, Worldview, and Cultural Formation*. Grand Rapids: Baker Academic, 2009.

————. *Imagining the Kingdom: How Worship Works*. Grand Rapids: Baker Academic, 2013.

Smith, Timothy Lawrence. "John Wesley's Religion in Thomas Jefferson's America." In *The 19th Century Holiness Movement*, edited by Melvin Dieter, 31–39. Kansas City: Beacon Hill, 1998.

————. *Called Unto Holiness: The Story of the Nazarenes*. Kansas City: Nazarene, 1962.

Solberg, Edw. "Spokane, Wash." *Nazarene Messenger*, February 13, 1902, 10.

"South Providence." *Beulah Christian*, October 1890, 4.

"Spokane, Wash." *Nazarene Messenger*, April 14, 1904, 5.

"Spokane, Wash." *Nazarene Messenger*, January 21, 1904, 5.

"Spokane, Washington." *Beulah Christian*, December 21, 1907, 9.

Staples, Rob L. *Outward Sign and Inward Grace: The Place of Sacraments in Wesleyan Spirituality*. Kansas City, MO: Beacon Hill, 1991.

————. "Things Shakeable and Things Unshakeable in Holiness Theology." In *Edwin Crawford Lecture*, 1–9. Nampa, ID: Northwest Nazarene University, 2007.

————. "What About Applause in Worship." *The Preacher's Magazine* 64, no. 3 (March–May 1989) 48–49, 57.

"Stockton, Cal." *Nazarene Messenger*, February 25, 1904, 10.

Stookey, Laurence Hull. *Baptism: Christ's Act in the Church*. Nashville: Abingdon, 1982.

————. *Calendar: Christ's Time for the Church*. Nashville: Abingdon, 1996.

Stowe, Eugene. "The Responsive Reading." *The Preacher's Magazine* 29, no. 7 (July 1954) 23.

Strang, C. B. "Conducting the Communion Service." *The Preacher's Magazine* 23, no. 4 (July–August 1948) 15–17.

Suddarth, Fannie E. "The Lord's Work at Pilot Point." *Pentecostal Advocate*, April 9, 1908, 7.

"Suggested Rules for Preachers." *Nazarene Messenger*, December 31, 1903, 6.

Sumner, Mary M. "West Chester, PA." *Herald of Holiness*, May 25, 1940, 26.

"Sunday, October 4th." *Beulah Christian*, October 24, 1908, 1.

"Sunday." *The Holiness Evangel*, March 24, 1909, 3.

Sykes, Stephen, John E. Booty, and Jonathan Knight. *The Study of Anglicanism*. rev. ed. London: SPCK/Fortress, 1998.

Taves, Ann. *Fits, Trances, & Visions: Experiencing Religion and Explaining Experience from Wesley to James*. Princeton, NJ: Princeton University Press, 1999.

"Texas Holiness University." *Pentecostal Advocate*, May 7, 1908, 5.

"Thanksgiving at First Church." *Nazarene Messenger*, November 18, 1909, 8.

Toler, Stan. "Worship and Preaching Helps." *The Preacher's Magazine* 68, no. 1 (September–November 1992) 58.

Trowbridge, L. B. "Why Do Holiness People Shout." *Herald of Holiness*, September 25, 1912, 5.

Trumbauer, Horace G. "Horace G. Trumbauer Diary [inserted pages]." In *H.G. Trumbauer Collection*. Lenexa, KS: Nazarene Archives, 1907.

Tucker, Karen B. Westerfield. *American Methodist Worship*. New York: Oxford University Press, 2001.

"Tuesday New Year's Meeting." *Nazarene Messenger*, January 3, 1901, 4–5.

Tyerman, Luke. *The Life and Times of the Rev. John Wesley, M.A., Founder of the Methodists*. Vol. 2. 2nd ed. London: Hodder and Stoughton, 1872.

"The Use of the Hymn." *Nazarene Messenger*, September 5, 1907, 6–7.

Van Dyken, Tamara J. "Singing the Gospel: Evangelical Hymnody, Popular Religion, and American Culture; 1870–1940." PhD diss., University of Notre Dame, 2008.

"Victory Day." *Nazarene Messenger*, May 9, 1901, 4.

Visitor's Edition: Delegate's Handbook: Twenty-Seventh General Assembly Church of the Nazarene. Kansas City, MO: Nazarene, 2009.

Visitor's Edition: Delegate's Handbook: Twenty-Sixth General Assembly Church of the Nazarene. Kansas City, MO: Nazarene, 2005.

Wace, Henry, and William C. Piercy, eds. *A Dictionary of Early Christian Biography*. Peabody, MA: Hendrickson Publishers, 1999.

Wade, William Nash. "A History of Public Worship in the Methodist Episcopal Church and Methodist Episcopal Church, South, From 1785 to 1905." PhD diss., Notre Dame, 1981.

Wainwright, Geoffrey. *Doxology: The Praise of God in Worship, Doctrine, and Life*. New York: Oxford University Press, 1980.

Waldie, Margaret. "Beverly, Mass." *Beulah Christian*, February 16, 1907, 15.

Walker, Williston. *A History of the Christian Church*. 3rd ed. New York: Charles Scribner's Sons, 1970.

Ward, George. "Correspondence: Troy, Ohio." *Nazarene Messenger*, November 4, 1909, 4.

"Watch Night." *Nazarene Messenger*, December 26, 1901, 6.

"Watch Night." *Nazarene Messenger*, January 7, 1904, 3.

Watson, Richard, and Thomas O. Summers. *The Life of the Rev. John Wesley: To Which Are Subjoined Observations on Southey's Life of Wesley*. Nashville: Smith & Lamar, Agents, for the Methodist Episcopal Church, South, 1912.

Webber, Robert E. *Worship Is a Verb: Eight Principles Transforming Worship*. 2nd ed. Peabody, MA: Hendrickson, 1996.

"Wesley and Singing." *Beulah Christian*, August 1893, 4.

Wesley, John. *The Appeals to Men of Reason and Religion and Certain Related Open Letters*. Vol. 11 of *The Works of John Wesley*. Edited by Gerald R. Cragg. Nashville: Abingdon, 1984.

———. *A Collection of Hymns for the Use of the People Called Methodists*. Vol. 7 of *The Works of John Wesley*. Edited by Franz Hildebrandt, Oliver A. Beckerlegge, and James Dale. Nashville: Abingdon, 1989.

———. *John Wesley's Sunday Service of the Methodists in North America*. Quarterly Review Reprint Series. Nashville: United Methodist, 1984.

———. *Journals and Diaries I, (1735–1738)*. Vol. 18 of *The Works of John Wesley*. Edited by Reginald W. Ward and Richard P. Heitzenrater. Nashville: Abingdon, 1988.

———. *Journals and Diaries II, (1738–1743)*. Vol. 19 of *The Works of John Wesley*. Edited by Reginald W. Ward and Richard P. Heitzenrater. Nashville: Abingdon, 1990.

———. *Journals and Diaries IV, (1755–1765)*. Vol. 21 of *The Works of John Wesley*. Edited by Reginald W. Ward and Richard P. Heitzenrater. Nashville: Abingdon, 1992.

———. *Journals and Diaries VI, (1776–1786)*. Vol. 23 of *The Works of John Wesley*. Edited by Reginald W. Ward and Richard P. Heitzenrater. Nashville: Abingdon, 1995.

———. *Journals and Diaries VII, (1787–1791)*. Vol. 24 of *The Works of John Wesley*. Edited by Reginald W. Ward and Richard P. Heitzenrater. Nashville: Abingdon, 2003.

———. *The Letters of the Rev. John Wesley, A.M., (1772–1780)*. Vol. 6., Edited by John Telford. London: Epworth, 1931.

———. *The Methodist Societies: History, Nature, and Design*. Vol. 9 of *The Works of John Wesley*. Edited by Rupert E. Davies. Nashville: Abingdon, 1989.

———. *The Methodist Societies: The Minutes of the Conference*. Vol. 10 of *The Works of John Wesley*. Edited by Henry D. Rack. Nashville: Abingdon, 2011.

———. *Sermons I, 1–33*. Vol. 1 of *The Works of John Wesley*. Edited by Albert Cook Outler. Nashville: Abingdon, 1984.

———. *Sermons II, 34–70*. Vol. 2 of *The Works of John Wesley*. Edited by Albert Cook Outler. Nashville: Abingdon, 1985.

———. *Sermons III, 71–114*. Vol. 3 of *The Works of John Wesley*. Edited by Albert Cook Outler. Nashville: Abingdon, 1986.

———. *Letters*, Vol. 13, of *The Works of John Wesley*. 3rd ed. Edited by Thomas Jackson. 1872. Reprint. Grand Rapids: Baker, 2007.

"West Somerville, Mass." *Beulah Christian*, November 26, 1910, 6.

"Where the Written Sermons Would Have Failed." *Herald of Holiness*, November 26, 1913, 4.

White, James F. "Introduction." In *John Wesley's Sunday Service of the Methodists in North America*, 9–21. Nashville: United Methodist, 1984.

———. *Introduction to Christian Worship*. 3rd ed. Nashville: Abingdon, 2000.

White, Stephen S. "The Question Box." *Herald of Holiness*, December 19, 1949, 9.

———. "The Question Box." *Herald of Holiness*, May 16, 1949, 9.

———. "The Question Box." *Herald of Holiness*, May 29, 1950, 11.

———. "The Question Box." *Herald of Holiness*, November 14, 1951, 11.

———. "The Question Box." *Herald of Holiness*, September 11, 1950, 20.

———. "Water Baptism." *Herald of Holiness*, February 5, 1951, 13.

Wilcox, Vernon L. "The Pastoral Prayer in the Worship Service." *The Preacher's Magazine* 55, no. 3 (March–May 1980) 14.

Wiley, H. Orton. *Christian Theology*. Vol. 3. 3 vols. Kansas City, MO: Beacon Hill, 1943.

———. "From Easter to Pentecost." *Herald of Holiness*, March 30, 1932, 2.

———. "Observing the Lenten Season." *Herald of Holiness*, March 8, 1933, 4.

———. "Protestants and Lenten Observance." *Herald of Holiness*, March 16, 1932, 2.

———. "Public Worship." *Herald of Holiness*, January 12, 1935, 2–3.

———. "Strongly, Constantly, Explicitly." *Herald of Holiness*, May 31, 1933, 3.

———. "The Value of Special Days." *Herald of Holiness*, September 24, 1930, 3.

Williams, R. M. "Notes from Willimantic Camp Ground." *Beulah Christian,* September 1891, 3.

Williams, R. T. "After Which." *Herald of Holiness*, November 10, 1934, 5.

Wiseman, Neil B., ed. *Two Men of Destiny: Second Generation Leaders in the Nazarene Movement*. Kansas City, MO: Beacon Hill, 1983.

Wordsworth, E. E. "The Pastoral Prayer." *The Preacher's Magazine* 32, no. 2 (February 1957) 23.

———. "Shouting." *Herald of Holiness*, January 11, 1933, 6.

———. "Singing with the Spirit." *Herald of Holiness*, September 4, 1937, 11–12.

Wulff, David M. *Psychology of Religion: Classic and Contemporary*. 2nd ed. New York: John Wiley & Sons, 1997.

Wynkoop, Mildred Bangs. "Rules for Public Prayer." *The Preacher's Magazine* 9, no. 11 (November 1934) 30.

Yarnold, Edward. *The Awe-Inspiring Rites of Initiation*. Collegeville, MN: Liturgical, 1994.

Young, Samuel. "Lengthen That Altar." *Herald of Holiness*, September 3, 1951, 1.

Index

Advent. *See* calendar.

Aldersgate, 20–21

altar call, 2, 4, 6, 8n30, 67, 78, 83, 89,
103, 107n71, 109, 116–24, 141,
150
decline of, 77
purpose of, 63
as ritual, 68n76, 202

American holiness movement, xiv–xv,
47–48, 56, 57n41, 64, 67, 69, 177,
200, 202, 209

American Methodist. *See* Methodist.

Anabaptist, 1, 144, 165n71, 176–78

anamnesis, 131, 156, 158

Anderson, E. Byron, xviii, xxi, 2–3, 6–7,
10–11, 202–3, 206, 210n40

Anglican, ix, xxi, 1, 12, 13n1, 14, 17–20,
24, 28, 30, 39–40, 46, 48, 50,
64–66, 72–73, 124, 207–8, 211

announcements, 2, 83, 85, 87–89, 110–
11, 116

Applause. *See* worship.

Apostles' Creed. *See* creeds.

Asbury, Francis, 24–25, 49–50

Association of Pentecostal Churches of
America, 57–59, 145, 155, 174

Augustine, Saint, xiv, 2–3, 122, 175

Baker, Frank, 15, 43

Bangs, Carl, 67–69, 74n89, 80–81, 93,
141–42, 147n13, 159, 188–90

baptism, x, xv, xvii, 5, 10, 18, 21, 51,
54, 58–64, 78, 79n97, 115, 123,
143–44, 164–87, 211n45
areas of contention, 59, 62, 63n60,
164, 165n68, 169–72
believer, 59, 64, 166, 173, 182–83
dissonance in theology and praxis of,
63, 144, 180–82, 185
of infants, 58–61, 165–68, 176–77
Lord's supper served, 169
Manual (1906) statement allowing
rebaptism, 59n50, 174
mode, 58–59, 61–62, 166–67, 171–72
neglect of, 144, 180–88
rebaptism of adults, 59, 60n50,
63n61, 170, 173–76, 183
rebaptism of former Roman
Catholics, 173
rebaptism of those baptized as
infants, 63n61, 170n83, 183
replacing circumcision, 182
Spirit baptism, 1, 122, 130, 138, 219
unbaptized ordained clergy, 63n62,
184n140

baptism and Christian initiation, 179–84

baptism and church membership, 180,
183–84

baptismal regeneration, 60, 165n68

Bassett, Paul, 76

Bearse, J. C., 153, 167n76

bodily knowing, 7, 10–11, 205n15, 206

Book of Common Prayer, ix, xiv, 5, 12,
    19n30, 24, 26–27, 30, 32, 46, 48,
    68, 73, 79, 200, 207–9
Book of Common Prayer/Anglican
    Liturgy, 12, 19, 24, 26–27, 30, 46,
    68, 73, 208
Borgen, Ole, 22–23, 31, 33–34, 44, 164
Bradshaw, Paul, 5
Bresee, Phineas, 44, 58–63, 67–74, 93,
    122, 126, 165n68, 188–96
    baptismal practice, 167n76, 170
    influence of, 80–81
    practice of the Lord's supper, 74n89,
        146–7, 150–51, 159–60
    prayer book worship, view of, 68–72,
        74, 86, 104n57
    worship praxis, 84–86, 96–98, 110,
        116n102, 118–19
British Methodist. See Methodist.
Brunson, F. A., 194
Busic, David, 112n85
Byron, Lloyd B., 122n131, 127n140

Cagle, Mary Lee, 170
calendar, 112n85, 122, 125–34
    Advent, 123–25
    Ash Wednesday, 130
    Baptism of the Lord, 123
    Christmas, 49, 84, 122–25, 127–29,
        132–34, 188–90
    civil, 112, 127–31
    commemorative days, 112, 125–28,
        131
    confusion of Advent with Christmas,
        132–34
    Easter, 122, 124–25, 127–30, 132, 190
    Father's Day, 127
    Fourth of July, 112, 125–8, 134
    holy days, 112, 123, 125–26, 128,
        130–31
    Holy Week, 130
    Lent, 124, 128–30, 132
    Memorial Day, 112, 126
    Mother's Day, 112, 122–23, 127,
        130–31
    national holidays, 125–28, 131
    New Year's, 122, 125–27, 195–96

Pentecost, 10, 123, 127, 130–32, 138,
    151, 190
Thanksgiving, 122–28, 133, 190
camp meetings, 54, 56, 67, 79, 98–99,
    138, 190–91, 200, 202
Campbell, Ted, 23, 36, 149n21
Carey, F. S., 136n167
cathedral (service/worship/church),
    70–72, 104, 124, 134
Catholic. See Roman Catholic.
Chapman, James B., 61, 116, 126, 128,
    140n186, 182, 185–86, 187, 194
    baptism and membership, 180–82
    baptismal mode, 62n55, 171–72,
        185–86
    creeds, 114
    freedom and order in worship,
        86–88, 110, 116, 204
    influence of, 80–82
    Lord's supper, 148–50, 155n38,
        160n48, 161
    perspective on music, 94–99, 101–2
    preaching thought and praxis, 116–22
    public prayer, 104–5
    rebaptism, 170n83, 172–74, 173n100
Christian antiquity. See primitive church.
Christian identity. See worship.
Christian perfection, xiii, 1, 6, 37, 48,
    52, 57, 60, 62–63, 67, 75, 94–95,
    116, 120, 122, 130, 138, 166, 186,
    196, 201
Christmas. See calendar.
Church of England, xiv, 14–21, 24, 27–
    30, 39, 46n168, 72–73, 200, 207
church-growth movement, 5, 65, 75, 103,
    128, 201, 204
class meetings, 56, 200
Coke, Thomas, 24–25, 49
commemorative days. See calendar.
communion. See Lord's supper.
Congregationalists, 14
consubstantiation, 42
contemporary music/worship, 4, 66n68,
    77, 94–103, 143, 201, 204, 207
conversion, 6, 34, 42, 54, 64, 67, 69, 75,
    93, 100, 116, 120n120, 151–52,
    168, 189, 196
Corlett, D. Shelby, 82, 129–31, 154

Cornell, C. E., 75n90, 139
covenant service, xv, 43–44, 195–96, 208
creeds, 69n78, 113–16, 122, 204, 209

Dalton, Tom, xiii, 72, 135n163
Davey, Randall E., 123
Dawn, Marva, 100–101
Deism, 17, 28
Disciples of Christ, 146
dissenter, 15, 28, 32, 39
Douglas, Mary, 8–9, 68n76, 205–6,
        209n38
doxology, 3, 5–6, 115, 198, 199–200, 207
Du Bois, Lauriston J., 106
Dunning, H. Ray, 182
The Duty of Constant Communion,
        19n30, 40, 148

Easter. *See* Calendar.
Eastern Christianity, 25
Enlightenment, 6–7, 17
enthusiasm, 29–32, 38, 55, 69, 72n83, 84,
        137, 207–8
entire sanctification. *See* Christian
        perfection.
essentials and nonessentials, 60–64, 139,
        177
Estep, Bradley K., 165, 174n100,
        177n111
eucharist. *See* Lord's supper.

fanaticism, 56, 70–74, 72n83, 85, 106,
        134, 137
Farther Appeal, A, 15, 32n98
Father's Day. *See* calendar.
Finch, Oscar J., 111n83
Fitzgerald, James Nelson, 62, 69, 77n94,
        146, 152, 154–55
foot washing, 187
formalism, 28–30, 38, 55, 57, 69, 71–73,
        85, 108, 119, 123–24, 128, 155,
        207–8
Fourth of July. *See* calendar.
free-church tradition, 4, 65, 68n76, 78–79
freedom in worship, *See also* spontaneity,
        14, 24–25, 46, 50–52, 55, 73, 83,
        86–88, 100, 107, 123–24, 133,
        137, 139, 146, 154–55, 204

General Assembly, 58, 93, 141, 151n26,
        162, 170–71, 184n139
Gould, J. Glenn, 97
Greathouse, William, xviii, 101–2, 210
Grider, J. Kenneth, 138n176, 183
Grimes, Ronald L., 11n49, 68n76

habit, 10, 118
habituation, 10–11
Haynes, B. F., 94n20, 117n105
Heitzenrater, Richard, 18, 20, 50
Hills, A. M., 61, 105
holidays. *See* calendar.
Holiness Christian Church, 58–60, 84,
        165n68
Holiness Church of Christ, 58n43,
        58n44, 146, 169n81
holiness streams, 44, 56–60, 62n59, 67,
        72, 134, 144, 146, 170, 177–78,
        186, 188
holy days. *See* calendar.
Holy Week. *See* calendar.
Hoople, William Howard, 59, 192
Hoskins, Steven T., 201n6
hymns. *See* music and Wesley, John.

Independence Day. *See* calendar.
Independent Holiness Church, 58n44,
        171
individualism and private faith, 3–4, 9,
        53, 55, 100, 102, 113, 116, 143,
        163, 202–4
Ingersol, Stanley, xviii, 60–62, 64, 166
Inskip, John, 56
Irwin, Kevin, 3, 206n22

Kavanagh, Aidan, 2
Knight III, Henry H., 23, 30, 31n93,
        32–39, 200n1
Kyrie eleison, 156–57

Lathrop, Gordon W., 108, 211
lectionary usage. *See* Scripture.
Lent. *See* calendar.
lex orandi, lex credendi, 2–5, 63, 115, 206,
        210–11
liberty in nonessentials. *See* essentials
        and nonessentials.

liturgical pragmatism, 6, 53, 55, 74–76, 131, 202
liturgical worship. *See* prayer book.
liturgy. *See* worship.
London, A. S., 93n17
Lord's supper, xv, 9–10, 14–17, 19, 21n45, 23, 27, 32, 39–43, 45, 50–57, 63, 69, 74, 78–79, 89, 105, 122, 141, 143, 144–64, 149, 168–69, 178, 187, 196–97, 208, 211
  administered spontaneously, 5, 63n61, 79, 155
  constant communion, 19n30, 40, 42, 50, 74, 145, 148
  as converting ordinance, 42, 44, 150–53, 208
  devaluing of, 39n139, 57, 63, 77, 89, 123, 144–45, 148–50, 152, 163–64, 178
  frequency of, 39n139, 50–51, 57, 69n78, 74, 143, 145–50
  individual cups, 159–60
  intinction, 159
  as means of grace, 22, 30, 39, 40–42, 45
  as memorial, 41, 57, 156, 158
  as ordinance, 21n45, 44, 149–50
  reception of new members coinciding with, 153–54
  rubrics and methods for celebration of, 32, 63, 105, 154–63
  served with baptism. *See* baptism, Lord's supper served.
  served with the love feast, 192, 194
  served in the pews, 162–63
  structure of the service, 146n12, 150, 157–8, 161–62
  therapeutic benefits, 42, 45, 149–50, 162
  vibrant experience of, 53, 67, 74, 151–52, 151n26, 168
love feast, xv, 23, 43–44, 53–54, 67, 74, 78, 147, 188–97, 200, 208

Maddox, Randy, 35, 39, 42–43, 46, 208
McBride, J. B., 193n27
McGraw, James, 127–28

means of grace, 7, 21–24, 28–46, 63, 68, 98, 109n77, 129, 149n21, 152, 162, 164, 166, 182–83, 198, 200, 208–9
Methodist, ix–xi, xiv, xviii, 12, 15–30, 32, 36–40, 43–58, 64, 68, 73–74, 80, 86, 95, 96, 98, 104, 109n77, 134–40, 142, 145, 159, 166, 168, 177n110, 178, 188–200, 207–9, 211
Methodist Book of Worship, The United, 5, 79, 155n39
Middendorf, Jesse C., 78n95
Mitchell, Nathan, 11
Moravians, 30, 43
Mother's Day. *See* calendar.
Mund, Fred A., 77n94, 100, 102
music, 2, 4, 6, 11, 65–66, 70, 73, 77, 83–84, 87, 89, 91–104, 109–10, 113, 116, 141–43, 204
  camp meeting hymns, 54
  concerns over music used in worship, 92–99
  gospel songs, 67, 76, 83, 87, 99, 101–2, 204
  hymns, 76–77, 83–88, 90–103, 115, 142, 161–63, 204, 209
  special music, 76, 89, 103

narcissism, 102, 116, 143
National Camp Meeting Association, 56
national holidays. *See* calendar.
Nazarene Publishing Company/House, 4n18, 64n65, 70, 77n94, 93, 99, 152n28, 193
New Testament Church of Christ, 58, 170
New Year's Day. *See* calendar.
Nicene Creed. *See* creeds.

Occasional Conformity Act, 16
offering, 2, 66n68, 83, 85, 87–90, 110–11, 116, 131, 189
ordinance, 17, 41, 44–45, 59–60, 147, 149–53, 171, 174, 182, 185, 187, 208
orthodoxy, 6, 17, 60n50, 153, 170, 176–77, 183, 206
orthopraxy, 6, 63, 153, 177, 206, 211

Outler, Albert, 19n30, 34, 40
Oxford University, 18, 20–21, 28

Palmer, Phoebe, 57n41
Paul, Mary Rearick, 123n132
Pentecostal Church of the Nazarene,
    57n39, 61, 93, 169, 192, 195–96,
Peterson, Brent, 64n65, 145, 149,
    150n21, 162
Pierce, D. Rand, 137
pragmatism. *See* liturgical pragmatism.
prayer book, ix, xiv, xvii, xxi–xxii, 4,
    6n25, 8, 11, 24–26, 30, 38, 46, 48,
    51, 55, 65, 66n68, 68–69, 71, 74,
    79, 155, 207, 211
    tradition, 44, 57, 68n76, 104n57,
        112–13, 130, 143, 188, 200
    worship, 70, 107, 112, 124, 130, 202,
        208
prayer, 31–32, 104–8
    concert praying, 106, 135
    extemporary, 4, 26, 32, 54, 67, 104–5
    formal. *See* prayer, written.
    Lord's Prayer, the, 52, 83, 86, 104–5,
        158, 163, 168
    pastoral, 4, 76, 88–89, 104, 106–7
    public, 27, 31, 86, 104–8
    united, 106, 150
    written, ix, 26, 32, 71, 76, 89, 104,
        105n62, 107, 204, 209
preaching service, xv, 51, 53, 83, 91–124,
    126, 192
preaching. *See* sermon and preaching.
preliminaries, 2, 6, 52, 78, 83, 88, 91, 109,
    111, 116
Presbyterian, 13–14, 52, 58, 104n57
Price, Ross E., 152
primitive church or Christian antiquity,
    xiv, 7, 10, 24–25, 43, 46, 55, 113,
    181, 202, 207, 209, 211–12
Prosper of Aquitaine, 2–3
Puritans, 14, 20, 30

Quakers, 14, 58, 144, 165n71, 181
quarterly meeting, 44, 53–54, 138

Rack, Henry, 18–19, 43, 49
Rattenbury, J. Ernest, 39
real presence, 42
Reed, Louis A., 145
Rees, Seth C., 62n59
religious experience, xiii, 1, 5, 7–10, 20–
    22, 30, 36–38, 41, 53n19, 54–55,
    72, 74, 77, 94–97, 99–100, 102–3,
    109–10, 115, 120, 131, 134–43,
    150–51, 166, 173, 180–83, 199,
    202, 204, 208
    bodily expression, 8, 67, 135–42
    language used to describe, 74, 114,
        134–8, 151, 167, 193
    shouting, 8n31, 67, 136–42, 139n84,
        168, 192, 202
revivalism,
    decline of, 6, 65, 75, 103, 107n71,
        121, 128, 167, 201, 204, 210
    influence of, 4, 52, 55–57, 62, 65,
        67–69, 79, 89, 98, 116, 164, 178,
        182, 199–200, 202, 210
revivalistic worship model. *See* worship.
Riggs, A. B., xiii, 135, 154, 169n82
ritual studies, xv, 66–67, 205, 207
ritual in the Church of the Nazarene,
    forms, 4–5, 65–66, 73–74, 78–79,
        104, 142, 150, 154–58, 160,
        162–63, 165n72, 179n113
    perspective, 68–71, 86, 104–5, 124,
        128, 142
    pastoral use of rituals in the *Manual*,
        5, 8, 63n61, 79, 104, 154–60, 168
ritual knowing, 8–10
ritual theory, 7, 10, 12, 44, 52–53, 63n61,
    66–67, 176, 202, 204–7, 209–10
ritualization, 12, 68n76, 204, 206, 210
Roman Catholic, ix, xxi, 6n25, 8n30,
    14–15, 42, 104n57, 114, 124, 133,
    152, 1/3
Rowell, Jeren, 112n85
Ruth, C. W., 59, 106, 196
Ruth, Lester, 30, 52–54, 74, 135, 137n172

sacramental revival, 39
sacraments, *See also* the Lord's supper
    and baptism,
    in Nazarene practice and thought,
        5, 8, 57–58, 61–64, 66, 68n76,
        73–74, 123, 142, 144–198
    in Wesley's Methodism. *See* Wesley,
        John.
Saliers, Don, 2–3, 131
sanctus, 156-57
Sanders, Paul, 26, 41
Scripture, ix, 6, 51–52, 74, 105n62,
        107–8, 116, 129, 162, 164, 166,
        185, 189, 202
    lectionary usage, 112, 123–24
    minimal use of, 66, 76, 83–86, 89,
        109–13, 204
    public reading of, 66, 69n78, 76, 78,
        84, 88, 90, 108–13, 208
Searle, Mark, 7
sermon and preaching, xiii–xiv, 1, 2, 4,
        6–8, 11, 62, 66–67, 69, 70, 73, 76,
        78–79, 83, 85, 90–91, 96, 110–11,
        116–24, 164, 168, 192, 196
    communion meditation, 122–23,
        161–62
    length of, 117–18
    preaching plan and themes, x, 112,
        122–28, 132, 161
    preaching that yields results, 75, 78–
        79, 84, 118, 120–22, 137, 141
    preparation of, 118–19
    problems with, 86–88, 122
shouting. *See* religious experience,
    shouting.
Smith, James K. A., 204–5
Smith, Timothy L., 58, 62n59, 147n13
soteriology, 23, 38
special music. *See* music.
special services of Methodism, 188
spontaneity, *See also* freedom in worship,
        46, 51, 55, 73, 85, 87–88, 104,
        107, 119, 124, 139, 155, 204
Staples, Rob L., xviii, 7n28, 57, 63n61,
        141–44, 152, 165n71, 177–79,
        182–83, 209
Suddarth, Fannie E., 151n26, 169n81

*Sunday Service of the Methodists in North
    America. See* Wesley, John.

Taves, Ann, 56, 134, 137–38
Test Act, 14, 16
Thanksgiving. *See* calendar.
Thirty-nine Articles, 14
Toler, Stan, 89
Toleration Act, 13–16,
transubstantiation, 14, 42
Trowbridge, L. B., 139n184
Trumbauer, Horace G., 58–60, 165n68
Tucker, Karen Westerfield, ix–xi, xviii,
        25, 27–28, 51–52, 54–56, 99–100,
        159, 188, 195

unity in essentials and liberty in
    nonessentials. *See* essentials and
    nonessentials.

via salutis, 23, 34–35, 37–38, 40, 60, 62,
        101, 178, 182, 203

Wainwright, Geoffrey, 2–3, 112, 115, 206
watch night service, xv, 43–44, 53, 188,
        195–7, 208
Watson, Richard, 17–18
Wesley, Charles, 7n28, 15–16, 38, 64,
        77n94, 93, 95–97, 101, 144, 177
Wesley, John,
    bands, 43
    The Circumcision of the Heart, 21
    Collection of Hymns, A, 36–38
    hymnody, 36–39, 43, 45n166, 53n19,
        77, 95–97, 204
    in Georgia, 43
    love feasts, 23, 43–44, 53–54
    loyal churchman, 15–16, 28, 73
    The Means of Grace, 21n45, 22–23,
        28, 40, 41n146
    prayer, 31–3, 43–45
    quadrilateral, 6, 27–29, 31, 33, 207
    real presence in the Lord's supper, 42
    sacramental practice and thought, ix,
        xiv, xv, 16, 21n45, 52, 53n20, 209
    Scripture, 16, 22–25, 27–28, 32–38,
        43–45, 55, 208

sermon and preaching, 19, 21–22, 27, 33–35, 40, 43, 45, 54, 108–9, 177–78, 208, 212

society meetings, 12, 20, 24n59, 27–28, 30, 32, 40–41, 43–44, 46, 50, 101, 134n158, 207–8

Sunday Service of the Methodists in North America, ix, 24–26, 32, 46–47, 50, 53n20, 56, 109, 156, 207–8, 211

Sunday Service of the Methodists in North America, abandoned, 46–47, 51–52, 54–55, 74, 178

tension with the American colonies, 48–50

tension with the Church of England, 15–16, 28, 31–32, 39

worship praxis and thought, xiv–xv, 1, 12, 23, 27, 39, 46, 48, 57, 64, 67, 144, 164, 167, 178, 197, 207, 211

Wesley, Susanna, 42

Wesleyanism, classical, 7, 12, 107, 144, 177–78, 202, 209

White, James F., xxi–xxii, 46

White, Stephen S., 172, 183

Wiley, H. Orton,
on the Christian year, 128–30
on the love feast, 194
on music, 97–98
on rebaptism, 179

Williams, R. T., 83

worship,
applause in, 77, 141–43
boredom and monotony in, 11
Christian identity, and, xiii, xv, 63, 133–34, 202, 210

formative potential of, xv, 1–12, 38, 63, 66–67, 108, 131, 134, 136, 198, 201–8, 211

liberty in. *See* essentials and nonessentials.

Nazarene liturgy, x, xiii, 1, 4, 6, 12, 47, 63–64, 73, 76–81, 84, 88–89, 107–8, 110, 123, 135, 140, 162–63, 167, 197, 204

order in and orders of, 4–5, 52, 65, 73–74, 76, 79, 83–90, 110, 137, 192, 204, 210, 211n45

practices nurturing the objective dimension of faith, 30, 51, 63, 98, 101, 204

prayer book, xvii, 70, 107, 112, 124, 130, 202, 208

response in, 22, 77, 85, 101, 107n71, 111, 115, 121–22, 136–43, 162, 202

revivalistic/camp meeting worship model, 55, 57, 67, 197–201

sermon dispatched in, 120

spontaneity in, xxi, 1, 5, 8, 48, 57, 63n61, 68–71, 79, 87, 113, 123, 154, 178

subjective experience in, 5, 38, 55, 95, 97–100, 102, 109, 131, 143n197, 163, 178, 180, 201, 203–4, 207, 210

success in, 54, 55n33, 65, 75–76, 117, 120–22, 120n120

vocal and bodily response in, 67, 77, 136–43, 202

worship and the philosophies alien to Christian faith, 4, 102, 113, 116, 133, 143, 205